NORA

NORA

✦

An Ordinary Girl from Inchicore

A Memoir

Nora Szechy

iUniverse, Inc.
New York Lincoln Shanghai

NORA
An Ordinary Girl from Inchicore

iUniverse books may be ordered through booksellers or by contacting:

iUniverse
2021 Pine Lake Road, Suite 100
Lincoln, NE 68512
www.iuniverse.com
1-800-Authors (1-800-288-4677)

ISBN-13: 978-0-595-39178-3 (pbk)
ISBN-13: 978-0-595-83568-3 (ebk)
ISBN-10: 0-595-39178-8 (pbk)
ISBN-10: 0-595-83568-6 (ebk)

Printed in the United States of America

To my dear family

and

To the memory of my beloved sister, Olga.

Contents

ACKNOWLEDGEMENTS

My sincere thanks to the following people who helped me along the way:

My family for their enthusiasm and support and especially my husband, Frank, for cheering me to the final page and for his forbearance while I deserted him to sit for hours at the computer.

My brother Billy for filling me in on his life in The British Army and for sending me an informative book called "Inchicore, Kilmainham and District" written by Seosamh O Bróin.

My brother Frank for providing me with the details of his early career in Dublin and his subsequent travels around the world aboard "The Irish Ash".

My brother Jack for taking the trouble to make me a CD of the favorite old songs of the 50's and for sending me a DVD of "The Magdalene Sisters".

My sister Ada for sending me early photographs of the family, a street map of Dublin and for sharing her memories of me.

My sisters Hilda, Joan and Doris for their enthusiastic response to early drafts and for sharing photographs and remembrances.

My sister Olga's daughter Aileen for searching her attic to send me forgotten photographs. Sadly, my sister Olga is no longer with us.

My brother-in-law Liam for a helpful book he sent me some time ago—"Dublin Stolen from Time" by Pat Liddy.

Our good friend Harry McGill for an informative book he sent me—"Lost Ireland" by Laurence O'Connor.

My cousins Mike in Michigan and Betty in Australia and my many nieces and nephews and my grandniece, Olga, for their complimentary letters, e-mails and telephone calls.

Frank's nephew, Csaba, for painstakingly translating my story so that our relatives in Hungary could read the first drafts.

My good friend, Marti Smith and her daughter Ginny Janczak, for their praise and encouragement.

You are all dear and special to me and I owe you a debt of gratitude.

Preface

My family always enjoyed the brief episodes of the good old days in Dublin and my adventures in The New World. I wrote these from time to time as they came to mind.

As a Christmas present in 1991 my daughter, Kathryn, designed and monogrammed a journal for me with the request to fill the blank pages with the stories of my life. This beautiful book remained untouched for thirteen years until the approach of Kathryn's 40th birthday and my 72nd year. Wracking my brains thinking of a meaningful gift for her I thought I would attempt to fulfill her request and write something in her book.

I was never told I could write. What was there to write about? I was a typical nobody—I had never done anything remarkable and never achieved anything (unless you would consider second place at The Gas Company cookery examination an achievement!) As far as I knew, nobody in my family had accomplished anything to brag about either. We were an ordinary Inchicore family like thousands of others. We had good parents who took responsibility for their own lives and accepted the challenges of daily living with humor and optimism.

Lying about our house for many years was a book entitled "How to Write the Story of Your Life" by Frank P. Thomas. My daughter, Ava, had given it to my husband in the hope that one day he would chronicle the interesting and tragic history of his native Hungary. I used this book as my main source of reference—it gave me hundreds of ideas on ways to recall past events of my life. Thank you Mr. Thomas!

During this time I was taking beginner computer classes for Senior Citizens at Downey High School. We were learning on Gateway computers and, since this was the only one I was familiar with, I invested in a Gateway. The computer opened a magical new world for me—it checked my spelling, my grammar and my punctuation. The internet provided me with much needed information.

When I had filled all the pages in my daughter's book in time for her birthday, I was totally unprepared for her reaction. She said it was more than she ever expected. She said she laughed and she cried and enjoyed every word. The other members of my family were equally complimentary and suggested I send copies to my sisters and brothers in Ireland and Canada. My husband said his family in

Hungary would enjoy a copy also. I was overwhelmed by the positive feedback especially from the younger generation, my nieces and nephews and even a grandniece. They wrote glowing letters, e-mails and many of them telephoned.

I wrote the stories I remembered and some that were told to me by others. Some may have been figments of my imagination. I rediscovered myself with new insights, understanding and forgiveness. I enjoyed my ramble down memory lane and said goodbye to an innocent era that has vanished for ever.

Some names in my story have been changed.

1

Humble Beginnings

"Life is a flame that is always burning
Itself out, but it catches fire again every
Time a child is born."

—George Bernard Shaw

Keogh Square, formerly Richmond Barracks, was located behind St.Michael's
Church in Inchicore, Dublin. It was a converted soldiers' barracks to give housing to the poor. It was a dark, dilapidated tenement, which smelt of poverty and
decay. This is where I entered the world at Number 66 on May 25th 1932—the
year of the 31st Eucharistic Congress held in Phoenix Park, Dublin. The Congress was to renew devotion to The Blessed Sacrament and it was considered a
great honor to have the Papal Nuncio and religious dignitaries from all over the
world visit Dublin.

There was no great rejoicing when I was born—the third girl! My mother
really wanted a boy. Not to worry—seventeen months later brother William
(Billy) arrived and all was forgiven. Six more brothers and sisters in rapid succes-
sion followed Billy. There were three boys and seven girls, ten in all—Olga,
Hilda, Nora, Billy, Betty, Frank, Joan, Doris, Jack, and Ada. Olga and Hilda
were born in the Rotunda Hospital, Dublin. Nurse Macauley, the local midwife
delivered me and the subsequent babies.

Nurse Macauley was a remarkable woman. She was competent, saintly and
cheerful. She bicycled her way in cold, wind and rain at any hour of the day or
night to deliver the local babies. If there was no money, her services were given
free. She was a single mother. Her husband absconded with another woman to
England when her son was an infant. There was no support and no communica-
tion from him and there was no welfare at that time. Years later, he returned,
broke and repentant. He admired the photo of a good-looking young priest on

1

the mantelpiece and was chagrined to learn that it was his own son. Nurse Macauley sent him on his way—she had no need for him at that stage.

I have no idea of my birth weight; there were no baby books or records and very few pictures. I was baptized at St.Michael's Church, Inchicore. My mother did not attend my baptism. Because of the high infant mortality rate at the time, it was the custom to baptize babies as soon as possible. The mothers were still in confinement. Some time later, the mother was churched. This was a special ceremony of thanksgiving for women after childbirth. Uncle Sam's wife, Kathleen, was my godmother. I don't think she knew it though because I never got a card or a present from her. I was christened Nora Bernadette—Nora after my mother's sister who died at age four and Bernadette after Saint Bernadette of Lourdes. My Dad always called me "Bernie"—I liked that.

◆

Large families were the norm. There was no birth control in Ireland. Contraceptives were illegal and anyway were considered a mortal sin by the Catholic Church. Some mothers overwhelmed by yet another pregnancy when they already had numerous children resorted to desperate measures. In the hopes of having a miscarriage, they went, usually by bus, to Tara Street public baths. There they consumed a bottle of gin and immersed themselves in scalding hot water to which a tin of mustard had been added. Sometimes this had the desired results.

Protestants generally had small families. We were taught not to be envious of them because they were all doomed to hell for not belonging to the one true Catholic Church.

◆

My mother and father were married in Coolock Parish Church, Coolock, Dublin on June 25th, 1928.

We were fortunate to have parents who were happily married. This was due in part to my dad's unconditional love for my mother and to his agreeable nature. Mammy was "the boss". She made all the decisions and my dad never questioned her judgment. He sided with her no matter what. If we ever complained to him about being badly treated, he would say

"Now your mammy wouldn't punish you if you didn't deserve it."

Parents' roles were clearly defined: the father was the provider and the child rearing was the mother's department. My dad never changed a diaper, never wheeled the baby out in the pram, never chastised us and never hammered a nail. In all fairness, my mother never asked his help, she could manage it all.

Dad was reserved, shy and intelligent. He never raised his voice and never used profanity. I thought he was the most handsome man in the world; he had regular features, strikingly blue eyes and a beautiful smile. He was an avid reader, his favorite author was A.J.Cronin. We often discussed his great books; "The Citadel", "The Keys of the Kingdom" and "The Green Years" among them. Dad had to leave school at age fourteen to get a job and support his widowed mother and his young brother, Sam. With his fine mind, he would have excelled in any field had he had a chance at higher education.

We were also fortunate in that Dad had steady employment with The Post Office. He took any overtime that was offered—very often working holidays and weekends which paid more. He traveled to work on his bicycle. To earn extra money, he attended auctions at the Custom House. He bought job lots of watches, fountain pens, jewelry etc. and then sold the individual articles at a profit. He also ran a "didley club". Neighbors could borrow from him if they had an unexpected expense such as an illness or a funeral. They would pay back weekly with a small amount of interest. When my mother ran short of funds, rather than tell my father that she couldn't manage on her household money, she would borrow from him under an assumed name and pay him back with interest. Surprisingly, we knew of this but my dad never did.

As a child, I remember my dad singing "The Big Turf Fire". It went something like this:

> Oh the big turf fire
> And the house swept clean
> Sure there's no one half as happy
> As meself and Paddy Neal
> With a baby in the cradle
> And another on me knee
> Wouldn't you go to sleep Alana?
> Till I wet your daddy's tea

I loved my dad.

My mother was his opposite in temperament. She was outgoing and quick witted. She had a wonderful sense of humor. She could see the funny side of almost any situation. A natural mimic, she could imitate any accent or mannerism. She was a great story teller and she had a unique way of putting words together. She was blessed with robust health. She didn't pay much attention to her diet but she did take a nap every afternoon. She had a wealth of common sense and she rarely complained. She had a positive outlook and in times of distress she would say,

"There are so many people worse off than we are."

My mother also had a quick temper. If we annoyed her, or if she was in a bad mood, she would let fly at us with what ever object was closest to her. It didn't end there; all past transgressions were brought up until we were reduced to tears and thought of ourselves as worthless. Who could blame her? She always had one or two babies in diapers and another one on the way. There were no "pampers" and no "tidy didy" service. The dirty nappies had to be soaked, washed, boiled, dried and used again and again. Money was tight. The weather was rainy, cold and dreary. We had no heat in the house except for a fireplace in the living room and coal, if available at all, was expensive. I was always blue with cold and I dreamed of living in India or some desert place where the heat was overbearing; I thought I could never be too hot.

My mother and father were romantic. We watched them through the muffed glass in the door as they kissed affectionately in the hall before my dad left for work. He called her "Lily Mia" and he wrote her name in tiny kisses on her cards and letters. He was full of admiration for her. When she complained that she was getting too fat he would say,

"I never cared for skinny women; a woman looks much nicer with a bit of meat on her bones."

He never failed to compliment her on a new hat or on a new outfit. When it was necessary for him to travel around the country, he wrote her loving and romantic letters every day.

Thursday night was their movie night. They went either to "The Green" or to The Rialto. We looked forward to the next day when Mammy would relate the whole movie verbatim. No doubt she added her own bits to make it more interesting.

On Saturday nights they met with their friends at Muldowney's Pub. There they enjoyed their smokes and their drinks and they took turns going back to one another's homes for supper and a sing along around the piano. When the gathering was at our house we sneaked out from our beds to the top of the stairs to listen. Betty Parker was a gifted pianist. Her mother "Girlie" would sing

"Jerusalem" at the top of her voice with great feeling and gusto. Auntie Annie was coaxed into singing "Frankie and Johnnie" and all of them sang "I'll take you Home Again, Kathleen".

My mother and father enjoyed soccer and on Sunday afternoons they would go to Croagh Park, Richmond Park or wherever there was a match being played. Occasionally they went to the horse races at Leopardstown or to The Curragh.

2

A Minor Miracle

"There's a divinity that shapes our ends,
Rough hew them how we will."

—William Shakespeare

At about two years of age, I contacted Scarlet Fever and I was taken to Cork Street Children's Hospital. I have no memory of this only what my mother told me. After the Scarlet Fever, I seemed to be doing fine. My hair, which had been shaved off in the hospital, was growing back and my mother was delighted that I was growing chubbier and healthier. One day she was walking with me down Tyrconnell Rd. when she met a lady friend of hers, Mrs. Looney. Observing me, Mrs. Looney said,

"I don't like the look of her, Lily, her color is unhealthy and she's very puffy. I think you should take her to see a doctor."

Unless you were seriously ill, you didn't go to the doctor. Sometimes the chemist's advice was asked but usually the cures were home remedies; cold tea or boric acid for sore eyes, red flannel for sore throats, Reckitt's Blue for bee stings, bread soaked in hot water for poultices, Germolene for cuts, bread soda for indigestion, Kruschen salts for rheumatism and Vaseline for chapped lips or rough hands.

The next morning Mammy had me sitting on the kitchen table buckling my shoes when I keeled over, my eyes turned up in my head until only the whites were visible and I was as limp as a rag doll. Mammy ran next door to Mrs. Clare and Mrs. Clare advised her to put me into a hot mustard bath. This Mammy did and I came to after a few minutes. Mammy then took me in the pram to see Dr. Tyrell who lived close by on Tyrconnell Road. Dr.Tyrell was a wise old family doctor. He pressed his thumb into my leg, shook his head and said I needed to be hospitalized immediately. I was admitted to Harcourt Street Children's Hospital.

Both kidneys had failed and I was blown up like a balloon. I was put on a strict salt free and albumen free diet. My eyes were like slits in my swollen face and one of my legs burst, oozing out all of the retained fluids. I was given up for gone. I have a vague recollection of the spirit leaving my body and I was looking down from above on my own lifeless body in the hospital bed. This may have been hallucination brought on by a high fever or the medication. The police came to our house in the middle of one night to escort Mammy and Daddy to the hospital to say their last goodbyes. Screens were placed around my bed signifying the end. The next morning I woke up and asked for sardines on toast, something I was not supposed to have because of the salt content. The doctor gave the go ahead—I could have anything I wanted; at this stage it could do no harm. Miraculously my kidneys started functioning. The doctors were baffled—I had what they called a "spontaneous" recovery. When I was home and well my mother used to take me to Saggart to an old lady who administered a potion to me supposed to be "very good for the kidneys". It was a grayish powder mixed in a glass of water and tasted bitter. I also had to drink gallons of barley water. These trips were a great sacrifice on the part of my mother—Saggart was out in the country—a good distance from Dublin. The bus fare would have been expensive. Our kindly neighbor, Mrs. Clare, looked after the other children while we were gone.

I was a bit older when my mother took me to Baggot Street Hospital for a checkup. Dr.Synge examined me. This is when I fell in love for the first time, not only with Dr.Synge but with the medical profession as well. Dr.Synge had a shiny bald head and a warm smile. He spoke with an attractive Indian accent. I have always been sensitive to pleasant or unusual speaking voices.

◆

I was very young when I had my first experience with the dentist. A back tooth was hurting, or I said it was, and Mammy took me in the bottom of the baby's pram to Dr. Dillon on Tyrconnell Road. The doctor said the tooth had to come out and that it would cost half a crown. There was no Novocain or any type of anesthetic. I was terrified.

"This won't hurt a bit," he said as he held me down by planting his knee on my chest. He pulled and pulled until I could feel every nerve screaming. I could taste the salty blood going down my throat. Coming home, Mammy gave me a rag to hold to my mouth. I kept feeling the big soft gap with my tongue; it seemed to me there was more than one tooth missing. I was delighted with all the blood on the rag and the sympathy I got from the whole family. I'm sure that tooth didn't need to be pulled—it was an easy 2/6d for "the butcher" Dr. Dillon. I never complained about a toothache again.

♦

Tuberculosis was rampant in Ireland and practically every family had someone with T.B or someone who had died from it. This was caused by the damp climate, poor nutrition, and air pollution from the coal and turf burning fires and the emissions from the buses. To try to combat this, The Health Dept. distributed free cod liver oil and Parishes Food. We were given a teaspoonful of this every morning. It tasted awful but Mammy said it was good for us—pure vitamin C & E. We also got free Extract of Malt. This had a lovely toffee taste and we didn't mind it at all.

3

Railway Avenue

"May the roof above us never fall in
And may friends gathered below
Never fall out."

—Old Irish Proverb

My mother said the only reason we lived in Keogh Square was that Dublin Corporation had promised tenants of "The Barracks" first preference on single family homes. True to their word, before Billy was born in 1933, we got our Corporation house at 20 Railway Avenue, Inchicore. There were rows and rows of these red-bricked houses. Every house looked alike, every road was the same, and there was not a tree in sight. The front door opened on to the stairs. There were two bedrooms upstairs and a small living room, kitchen and scullery downstairs. The WC was up the garden.

Our living room was made even smaller by the heavy antique furniture my mother bought secondhand from a Mrs. Kedney. The piano was beautiful; heavy mahogany with rose colored silk behind the scrollwork. It was my job to dust all the crevices and the decorated legs.

Olga and Hilda took piano from Madam Dawn on the South Circular Road at sixpence a lesson. They played some lovely duets—"Over the Waves", "The Blue Danube" and "The American Patrol". They had to practice for half an hour every morning before school. Mammy could play anything by ear.

"How does that new song go, Nora?"

I just had to hum it and she could sit down and play it. She learnt all the words to the popular songs. She also loved ballroom dancing but, unfortunately, my dad didn't dance. I took piano briefly but I wasn't much good. I loved to sing though. My mother would ask me to sing "I Wish I had Some One to Love Me" for her friends. It went like this:

9

I wish I had someone to love me
And someone to call me his own
I wish I had someone to live with
'cause I'm tired of living alone

I'm going to the new jail tomorrow
And leaving my darling alone
With cold prison bars all around me
And my head on a pillow of stone

If I had the wings of an angel
Over those prison bars I would fly
I would fly to the arms of my darling
And there I'd be willing to die

The friends all smiled, clapped, and said that I had a lovely voice and that it should be trained. It never was.

In Ireland, it would be difficult to find a man, woman, or child who was not a real lover of music. One of the greatest pleasures in my life was the music in our home. Olga had a pleasant voice and her favorite songs were "You Belong to my Heart" and "La Gonondrina". We had no TV, videos, DVD's, CDs or cassettes. The radio, the piano and singing were our entertainment. It was quite common for visitors to be asked to "sing a little song for us". I remember Granny Wright sitting by our fire and singing "My Sweet Little Alice Blue Gown" with great feeling. The radio programs were excellent. We could tune in to quality music all day long and old and young alike enjoyed the same music. Bart Bastable hosted The Irish Hospitals' Sweepstakes Hour from Radio Eireann. He had a charming personality and that rich agreeable speaking voice which seems to be the birthright of all Dublin people. He entertained us with selections from the operas as well as our own traditional faire. The BBC and Radio Luxembourg also provided us with delightful music. Most of the shows had a cheerful, upbeat quality; a saving grace for overworked housewives.

We looked forward to Sunday evenings when the whole family gathered around the fire. Daddy brought home a bag of sweets after his session with his friends in Muldowney's. All the lights were turned off and we listened to broadcasts from The Abbey Theater: Sean O'Casey's "The Shadow of a Gunman" and "The Plough and the Stars" and Synge's "Riders to the Sea" were among them.

"Twenty Questions" was a general knowledge quiz show. There was great excitement one time, when Dad's friend, Bill Tieth was a contestant. Bill was a highly educated man and we were all glued to the radio rooting for him. He was doing very well until it came to a musical question. He didn't recognize the tune "Kitty of Colerain", nobody else recognized it either; it was such an old out-moded song. We were disappointed that he lost the money prize to his opponent.

◆

Railway Avenue was a happy place. Although we were poor, we were not deprived. The pattern of our life was leisurely and made up of simple plea-sures—a whole bar of chocolate was a treat to be eaten in small pieces and savored. Everyone was in the same boat—large families, little money and plenty of time.

Apart from our own brothers and sisters, there were lots of other children to play with. We had freedom to play on the streets; there were few automobiles and kidnapping and child molestation were unheard of. The neighbors were kindly and religious. They knew everybody's children and looked out for them. Mammy was particular about the children we played with. We were not allowed to play with the O'Flaherty's across the street. Mammy considered them "common" because their mother sold vegetables from their house. We were not allowed to play with anyone who was dirty, who had bad manners, who used bad language or who was disrespectful to parents or adults.

◆

Our neighbor at Number 19 was Mrs. Clare. She was kind to all of us and she was a great help to my mother. She was always available to watch the children if my mother had to go out. She would make blancmange and invite us, one at a time, to her house. We would kneel in front of a chair and eat this delicious treat. She had only two children, May and Paddy. May saved her empty Pond's powder boxes for me to play with. I loved the smell and I treasured them. Tom, Mrs. Clare's husband was equally nice to us. He worked in The Great Southern and Western Railway also known as Inchicore Works. It was located at the back of our house and commonly referred to as "The Works".

Mrs. Clare had long gray hair tied in a bun. Every so often, we would see her brushing her hair in her back garden. Mammy said she would love to have gray hair like Mrs. Clare's because then she would be old and she would have no more babies. There was great excitement on the road when May Clare drew a horse in

The Irish Hospitals' Sweepstakes. The horse's name was "Jack Chaucer". May won 1,800 pounds—an absolute fortune then.

Our neighbor on the other side was Mrs. Gough. She was mean and cranky and she would barely say thanks if we ran an errand for her. The other neighbors would give us a penny or a sweet. The only good thing about Mrs. Gough was the visits from her granddaughter, May. May was a little older than I and she was an only child. She had a division in her front teeth and she had a stammer. Her parents were separated—this was considered shameful and spoken of secretively. There was no divorce in Ireland. May lived in Cabra and her house had a bathroom upstairs—she took me there one day when her mother wasn't home. She filled up the bathtub with cold water. We took off our shoes and socks and had a wonderful afternoon wading in her tub. May was a great reader and she read to us from the comic books "The Dandy" and "The Beano" at the same time popping the water blisters on her knees. She had great imagination for fun things to do.

"Let's play shop," she said.

Pretty soon all the little girls were gathering chainies. These were bits of broken glass and dishes which we used for money. The larger pieces were broken into smaller pieces to match three penny bits, sixpences and shillings. We then collected empty tins, boxes, bottles and anything of interest we could find. There were oohs and ahs as we inspected each other's treasures. We set up shop at the back of The Works—a plot of ground where the railway men entered. Our counters were pieces of cardboard set on two stones. Sheets of newspaper were torn into squares and wound around our fingers to make cones for bags. We bought and sold happily for hours.

◆

Our weekly bath was on Saturday mornings. The big galvanized tub (the same one Mammy used to do her washing) was set in front of the fire and filled with warm water from the stove. Each of us in turn had a bath and our hair washed with Lifebuoy Soap. My hair curled easily and Mammy wound it around her finger into ringlets. As I was sitting by the fire and my hair was drying Daddy looked at me and said,

"Nora's hair is really beautiful."

I was basking in his admiration until Mammy said,

"Don't tell her such things; you'll give her a swelled head."

Children were not paid compliments in case they would become vain or conceited.

"I love you" was never said to a child. You could say I loved a movie, I love God or I love a book but never "I love you" to your children. The fact that we were fed, clothed and not sent to an institution was proof enough. My greatest fear as a small child was that I would lose one or both of my parents. I prayed that "God would spare Mammy and Daddy till we're all big." I had a dread of being sent away to an orphanage where, it was said, the nuns were cruel and all of my brothers and sisters would be farmed out to different families.

Fine combing and inspection of hair was done on a regular basis. After the fine combing, my mother rubbed Harrison's Pomade into my scalp to prevent head lice.

◆

I remember one snowy Christmas when I was about four. I was eagerly awaiting Santa Claus. We dared not ask for anything but I would have loved a little doll with hair that I could comb and brush. Christmas morning arrived and Olga and Hilda were screaming with delight when they discovered a pair of roller skates for Olga (no doubt bought by Granny Wright) and a blackboard for Hilda. Billy was sleeping beside me—he would have been about two and a half. I searched around the bed for my present and finally found a rectangular tin box. Inside were two licorice pipes—one for Billy and one for me. I continued my search in the hopes of finding my real present but sadly no. I remember the feeling of emptiness and disappointment. Mammy said, "You must not have been good or else 'Santy' would have brought you something". My substitute dolly was an old one-eyed teddy bear. I unwound pieces of string and stitched them to his head for his hair. I spent hours brushing, braiding and curling Teddy's hair. I never got my dream dolly. I did get a new pair of gloves, which were a real luxury—no holes in them and no darns with mismatched yarn! People had little money to spend on gifts—a spinning top with a string, a lead soldier or a storybook were considered treats.

◆

All the children on the road played jump rope. One of the games was "double Dutch" where a girl stood on either end turning the rope. Through it we skipped, one after the other until one of us tangled, and then it was her turn at the rope's

end. We had other complicated skipping feats and different chants to the rhythm
of our skipping:

The rain, the rain, the rain blew high
The rain kept falling from the sky
Little Nora said she'd die
If she didn't get the fellow with the marble eye

He is handsome, she is pretty
She is the girl from Dublin City
She is courting, one, two, three
Oh please tell me who is he

◆

A dear little friend I had was Monica. We were almost twins—only two weeks difference in our ages, her birthday was June 6 and mine was May 25th. She lived in a
house similar to ours on Nash Street. She was vivacious and pretty with dark curly
hair and bright blue eyes. We played "piggy beds" together. This was a sort of hop-
scotch. We chalked long rectangles on the pavement and divided them into sections,
the top section being marked HOME. The "piggy" was an empty shoe polish tin
which we filled with dirt. We kicked it with one foot into the squares. The object of
the game was to get Home without foot or "piggy" landing on a chalk line. Our
mothers weren't too happy with "piggy beds"—it ruined the toes of our shoes. I loved
to go to Monica's house; her dad had made a wooden swing in the back yard and we
played there happily for hours. Monica had a pure soprano voice. She sang duets in
church with her father, Jack. They sang the "Ave Maria" and "Panis Angelicas". Jack
worked in the Railway and Monica often come to meet him after work. He would
hoist her on his shoulders and carry her home. He adored her.

I lost touch with Monica when we moved from Railway Avenue and I was deeply
grieved to learn that at age 16 she died from typhoid fever. There were no antibiotics
then. Her dad was inconsolable and he died of a broken heart shortly after her.

◆

There was nobody I loved to see coming to visit more than Granny Wright. I
adored her. She never came without a treat for us. We waited anxiously until she
opened her purse and gave us the little white paper bag. We were never allowed

to ask her if she had brought us anything. She usually brought "Bulls' Eyes". These were black and white striped peppermint candy balls. When they were doled out, we got little more than two apiece. In order to make them last longer, we wrapped them in paper and threw them up in the air. When they hit the pavement, they were broken up into little pieces and we savored them, one little piece at a time.

Granny was the sweetest, kindest person I ever knew. She had the same beautiful natural smile as my dad and my sister, Olga. She had plenty of time to talk to us and to listen to what we had to say. She was poorer than poor and she shared the little she had with those less fortunate. She gave my mother the only beautiful possession she owned; a royal blue bedspread elaborately embroidered with a colorful peacock. My mother only used it for very special occasions or if the doctor was coming.

Granny went to 10 o'clock Mass and Holy Communion every day. In those days, fasting from midnight the night before was mandatory before receiving Holy Communion. Her breakfast consisted of tea with bread and butter and that was probably her diet for other meals as well. She was tall and slim. Her beautiful clear blue eyes were full of love. I remember her black coat which was always well brushed and almost green from age.

Although we could hardly afford it, my dad gave his mother an allowance of five shillings every week. We took turns in taking it to her—all of us wanted to go. She had two rooms but she only occupied one. Her bed was in the right hand corner and her table in the middle of the room was covered with oilcloth. The linoleum floor was polished until it gleamed and there was always a welcoming fire in her grate. She had no electricity and I loved the smell and the warm glow of her paraffin lamps. She always gave us back a penny for ourselves and a treat of lemonade or bread and jam.

◆

Peggy arrived at my house with a bag full of wallpaper trimmings. These were the white margins on either side of the rolls of paper. When they were trimmed off, they fell in long curly streamers. We attached these to our hair and made believe we were princesses with long golden curls.

Peggy lived a few doors down from us on Railway Avenue. She was red haired, freckled and sassy. She was the eldest of a large family, which were mostly boys. The boys were wild and unruly. Their father tried his best to punish them and even threatened to send them to Artane. The Artane Industrial School in Marino was run by the Christian Brothers to discipline misbehaving young boys. If they mitched from school, broke a window, disobeyed their parents or talked back to their superiors, they could be sent to Artane. When the Artane boys came home on weekends many had black eyes, cuts and bruises inflicted on them by The Christian Brothers for the smallest infraction. The worst threat a mother could make to her sons was,

"I can't get any good of you, you're going to Artane."

Peggy's mother was thin, delicate, and incapable of handling all those children. She constantly yelled at them "bed or the street" which meant they were to go outside and play or go up to bed—just out of her sight. She would sit at the fire and send Peggy and me up to Moore's Public House at The Third Lock to get her a pint of stout. She lived on her pints and her smokes. Peggy and I were never in a hurry with our errand. We loved to stand at The Third Lock and watch the lock man open the gates to let the water level go down for the boats to pass through. We were warned never to stand close to the edge of the canal because that is what happened to the local hunchback. He fell over the edge and he had to be pulled out with a pitchfork.

Peggy and I helped as much as we could. We washed all the dad's dirty hankies and socks and the filthy nappies that her mother pushed under the sofa.

One day Peggy told me, her mother had had a new baby but it was dead. She asked me if I would like to see it. We went up to the bedroom—her mother lay in the bed, pale and wasted. Peggy opened a drawer and showed me the tiny lifeless baby—naked. I was overcome with sadness and I wanted to put a blanket around him and hold him.

Peggy's aunt owned a grocery shop across the street from our house. Since this was war time and chocolate was scarce, Peggy often stole a couple of bars of Cadbury's chocolate from the back of the shop and hid them in her underwear. We ate them at the back of The Works until our consciences bothered us and we decided it was better to put the chocolate back. Peggy's aunt caught her putting it back under the sewing machine and she was punished by not being allowed into the back of the shop any more.

4

Early School Years

"…Spare the rod and spoil the child."

—Samuel Butler

This was the belief of parents and the good nuns at Golden Bridge Convent School for Girls. I was four when I started school. The infant class was called "Low Babies", next came "High Babies" and then first Class. Nothing was said to me about starting school. My mother took me the first day. When we approached the big brown door, I became fearful and started to cry. My mother pinched me on the cheek, pushed me in the door and left. I was miserable and frightened. I sat with my head down on the desk and nobody paid any attention to me.

I was happy to see Olga's lovely smiling face when she came to walk me home for dinner. School was a good forty minutes from home and we walked back and forth four times a day.

◆

Our main meal was in the middle of the day. Everyone was home for dinner except Daddy. Daddy ate in the Post Office dining room. He said the meals were good—hearty and nutritious. Sara, the cook, was fond of him and served him extra large portions.

Since there were no refrigerators, mothers went shopping every morning carrying their shopping bags. In this way they socialized with their neighbors and got caught up on each others news. They wore hats, gloves and high heeled shoes.

The fresh vegetables were bought at the greengrocers. The cabbages were sold with their stalks and outside leaves on just the way they were pulled from the ground. All the vegetables were sold the same way with dirt and clay attached. Potatoes were bought by the stone (14 lbs.) and a meal wouldn't be complete without them. A visit to the butcher was next for whatever meat was needed for that day. Then on to Pay 'n Take, the general store for bread, tea, etc. The Monument Creamery sold butter, milk, eggs, and delicious fresh cream buns. They also made cream sponges and "gurcake" a type of moist, spicy fruit square. Once in a while, we were treated to these.

Mammy was a genius when it came to making nourishing and tasty meals for little money. From half a pound of meat, plenty of carrots, potatoes and turnips, and her secret ingredient, Bisto, she made a delicious and satisfying Irish stew.

Fridays were always fast days. No meat could be eaten. Mammy bought fresh herrings from an old woman who came down our street every Friday shouting,

"Get the last of the Howth herrings, caught fresh this morning, only tuppence each."

She sold her herrings from a baby's pram. The herrings were whole and Mammy had to take the heads and tails off and debone them herself. They were delicious—an inexpensive and healthy meal.

Monday was washday. There was a big vat boiling the "whites" on the gas stove, another big tub on the floor with soapy water and the washboard for scrubbing, another tub with the rinse water and a final tub with Reckitt's Blue added to whiten the clothes. Reckitt's Blue was also used for bee stings, scrapes, bites and anything else that ailed us. Mammy was so hot from the steam and the scrubbing she had every window in the house open. We were freezing and I hated the Monday dinner—the fried up leftovers from Sunday.

◆

Golden Bridge Convent was the original "no frills" all-girl school. Each classroom had an average of sixty children.

There were no report cards. At the end of the year, the nun decided if you passed or failed. If you failed, you were simply kept back for another year and nobody thought anything about it.

There were no assemblies—we didn't even have an auditorium.

There was no cafeteria—we walked home for lunch.

There was no picture day (hence, no school pictures of me).

There were no field trips and no bake sales.

There was no school nurse and no vice-principal.

There was no P.E. The walk back and forth four times a day and the running of errands before and after school gave us all the exercise we needed.

Mercifully, we had no PTA. If your mother was ever sent for to come to the school, you knew you were in deep trouble.

There were no school reunions.

The classroom equipment was a blackboard and chalk and the holder for the chalk so that it could be used down to the very last scrap. There were no projectors, overheads, slides, films or copy machines. There were no lockers, cubbies or coat hangers. The most essential piece of equipment was the bamboo cane. We got "six of the best" if we were late, if we talked, if we laughed, if we fidgeted or if we didn't know our lessons. We were ruled by fear. There was no use complaining to Mammy if we got slapped. Her stock answer was "The nun wouldn't slap you if you didn't deserve it."

The only source of heat in the classroom was a small turf-burning fireplace situated behind the nun's rostrum. Even if you were in the front row, you were too far away to benefit from the heat.

We didn't need air conditioning; the rooms were damp and cold even in summer.

While I had an intense desire to learn, I hated school. I learned to read at a young age and books became my refuge.

Children were required to attend school until age 14. Then most of them had to leave and find some sort of unskilled job to help support their brothers and sisters. The nuns and lay teachers were aware of this and genuinely concerned not only with their spiritual welfare but they tried to ensure that these children left school with at least a good foundation in the Three R's.

Some of the nuns were kind; others were mean to the point of cruelty. One such nun was my second grade teacher called Sr.Mary Jerome. She was a country nun, bad-tempered, red-faced and overweight. She was frightening in her long black habit with an oversized rosary and crucifix dangling from a belt at her waist. She favored the prissy little girls in their pastel sweaters. My clothes were always practical navy blue or dark brown.

One day Sister Jerome came into the classroom with her arms folded and her nose in the air, she said

> "I smell wet knickers. Would you girls please tell your mammies to wash your underwear."

She had no idea that laundry was such a challenge since there were no washing machines or dryers and it was always raining.

One of Sr.Jerome's little pets, Hilda, of the long shiny curls and pastel sweater, brought delicious fruitcake to school. She gave me a slice and told me to bring it up to the nun. I was happy to do this because my mother never sent anything for the nuns. Sister roared at me

"How dare you hand a holy nun food that is not wrapped."

I was embarrassed handing the cake back to Hilda.

Then there was the time Sister sat beside me at my desk to help me with a lesson. As usual, I had a runny nose from the cold. The nun said,

"Take out your handkerchief child and blow your nose."

I knew I did not have a hankie and if she hadn't been sitting beside me I would have used my sleeve. I bent down to my schoolbag and tore a page from my exercise book and tried to blow my nose with the hard paper, I prayed she would leave soon and never sit beside me again.

My mother dressed me in a secondhand brown dress that had a "B" embroidered on it. I begged her to take the "B" off but she said

"Your middle name is Bernadette and that's why you have the "B", in any case it's nobody's business."

My friend, Una, came to school with a dress that had a square cut neckline and it fell to just above her knees. Sister called her up to the front of the class and tacked a length of black paper on to her hemline and around the neckline. She then sent her home.

"Now children, tell your mammies, little girls should always be modest. Your dress should cover your knees. The same thing will happen to any of you who come to school immodestly dressed."

◆

After school, the girls on the road liked to swing on the lamppost; this was thrilling and dangerous. A rope was looped around the top of the standard and pulled down to make it taut. I was sitting in the fold and a big girl was swinging me around and around high in the air. She let go of the rope and I crashed into the iron lamppost. I saw stars for a while and got a huge bump on the back of my head. I got no sympathy from my mother.

"How many times did I tell you not to swing on that lamppost—that's what God gave you because you never listen."

I experience nausea anytime I think about that incident.

Spinning tops were a safer activity. We took little scraps of colored silver paper and stuck them by spit on the top's surface. This formed a dazzling kaleidoscope when the top was released from its lash and spun.

◆

At seven years of age and, having reached the age of reason, I was preparing to make my First Confession and Holy Communion. Preparations began well in advance. Sister instructed us daily on the examination of conscience. She said

> "If you take the Lord's name in vain, if you miss Mass or come late to Mass, if you disobey your parents or superiors, if you steal anything, even a teaspoon of sugar, if you tell lies, or if you are jealous or envious, these are all sins and must be told in confession."

We learned our prayers in Irish and English. We had to know our Catechism backwards and forwards. We had to know The Ten Commandments, The Seven Sacraments, The Seven Deadly Sins, The Seven Virtues, and The Seven Precepts of the Church.

The day before First Holy Communion, Sister led us to the church for our First Confession. We marched in pairs and if we so much as whispered, we got a thump on the back or on the head. The Sisters were very big on manners and eating on a public street was strictly forbidden. One girl was chewing a candy on her way to confession. When we got back to school, she was ridiculed in front of the class. Sister imitated her with her mouth open chewing. For that, she got six slaps with the bamboo cane.

My First Holy Communion Day was supposed to be the happiest day of my life. It wasn't. I hated my dress, it was a hand me down—dingy and limp. All the other little girls had fresh white dresses and new shoes. I had red and white sandals and the straps were broken. I had gloves that belonged to Mammy—they were huge on me. I had a little beaded purse for "the collection". The custom was that you went to visit neighbors and friends and they put money in your purse. The best part of the day was going into town with my Granny Wright. Mammy couldn't take me because she had just given birth to Joan. We went upstairs on the double-decker bus into Woolworth's in Henry Street. I forgot all about the dress when Granny treated me to a whippy ice cream cone and my favorite Cleaves' toffee.

◆

Once we made our First Holy Communion, we could walk in the May Processions. These were held every Sunday in May in the beautiful grounds of the Church of Mary Immaculate, generally known as the Oblate Church, in Inchicore. The priests carried a huge statue of The Blessed Mother on a flower decorated stand and the children, dressed in their communion clothes, walked behind singing hymns to Mary, "Immaculate Mary", "Hail Queen of Heaven", and "I'll Sing a Hymn to Mary."

We were thrilled to see Olga's picture in The Irish Press taken at the May Processions. She was carrying our little sister Betty who got too tired to walk and the caption read "A sister to assist her."

The Oblate Church is a local landmark in Dublin. It is a magnificent structure and, in the grounds, it has an exact replica of the Lourdes Grotto in France. Every year on February 11th, my mother attended the all-night novena and the Torchlight Procession. My grandfather, Pappy Mooney, is said to have built the confessionals in the church.

◆

World War 11 started in September of 1939. Ireland was neutral and we were not affected in the beginning. As time went by our cost of living rose dramatically. Food was rationed and each child was issued a ration book. Even the babies were allowed their ration of tea, sugar and butter. In this way we didn't suffer a shortage in our house because the babies were fed only "goody" which was bread cubes soaked in warm milk with a little sugar and butter.

Rabbits were cheap and plentiful and Mammy could make a delicious rabbit stew and sometimes fried rabbit thighs. Then the rabbits developed myxomatosis and it was dangerous to eat them.

There was no coal and turf was rationed. We had to take turns standing in line to get our ration of turf. The venders soaked the sods in water so that they would weigh heavier. It was impossible to light a fire with wet turf, with the result we were without heat. Most of us developed unsightly and painful chilblains on our fingers and toes.

Men who had been out of work for years joined the British Army and sent the money orders back to their families each week. Mammy joined the Air Raid

Patrol to help with the distribution of gas masks. We never had to use them. The Germans did drop one bomb on The North Strand. They said it was an accident, they meant to drop it on Belfast. I remember that night well. Our house shook and we were very frightened. Daddy was on night duty and we all got into bed with Mammy and prayed the rosary.

◆

At school, we were delighted to have a lay teacher for elocution and drawing. Her name was Miss Wallace. She was pretty and pleasant and she dressed beautifully. Every once in a while she would take out her little perfume bottle and dab some on her teeth—this fascinated me. She had a cultured British accent. She went over all the vowel sounds with us and she tried to replace the Dublin children's "dese" and "dose" with "these" and "those". These were the speech practice exercises we were required to learn by heart:

The Watchmaker's Shop

A Street in our town has a queer little shop
With tumbled down walls and a thatch on the top
And all the wee windows, with crookedy panes
Are shining and winking with watches and chains

All sorts and all sizes in silver and gold
And brass ones and tin ones and new ones and old
And clocks for the kitchen and clocks for the hall
High ones and low ones that wag at the wall

The watchmaker sits on a long-legged seat
And bids you the time of the day when you meet
And round and about him goes tickety tock
From the tiniest watch to the grandfather clock

I wonder he doesn't get tired of the time
And all the clocks ticking and some of them chime
But there he goes winding lest any should stop
This queer little man in the watchmaker's shop

The next poem was a practice in our "a's" which had to be pronounced "aw"!

Aunts

I have an aunt who lends me books to read
And one who sings to me when I go there to tea
I like them all very, very much indeed

I have an aunt who lives outside the town
She has a garden with a high red wall
And strawberries and bees and plum and cherry trees
And she is the one that I like best of all

Miss Wallace was pleased with my recitation. I tried to mimic her accent. I had an advantage over the other children in that Mammy had a good education at Eccles Street Convent. She was constantly correcting our grammar and pronunciation. Eccles Street was a posh private school. The girls had to remove their outdoor shoes and wear slippers in the classroom. Pappy Mooney sent the money home from West Africa to ensure that his children got a good education.

The only things I learned to draw were a tree, an owl, and a mouse. I was enjoying my introduction to art but Miss Wallace left abruptly and our elocution and drawing classes came to an end.

♦

We had to take turns going for the messages before and after school—after school wasn't too bad but the mornings were dreadful. O'Neill's shop, where Mammy had a running tab, was quite a distance in the opposite direction from our school. The store didn't open until 9:00 a.m. and we had to be in school at 9:30. No matter how I hurried, I knew I would be late.

"Mammy, please give me a note for Sister, so I won't get into trouble." She couldn't find any paper

"If you run, you'll make it." she said.

I knew I was already late and it was difficult to run in shoes that didn't fit properly. They were either too big or the soles were hanging off. Without a note from my mother, I got "six of the best", three on each raw chilblained hand. I got another thump when I put my hands under my arms to ease the pain.

One of my after school errands was to go to Boland's Bakery to pick up the discounted bread. We bought four loaves at a time. My brothers could eat a whole loaf at one sitting. The outside loaves were the cheapest, they cost five pence halfpenny each. The stores didn't give shopping bags with your purchase; you had to bring your own. Granny Wright loaned us a sturdy navy blue shopping bag with handles, just the right size to fit the four loaves. My friend, Maureen, came with me to the bakery. We were walking along, laughing, talking, picking at the bread and swinging the bag between us when disaster struck. One of the handles broke and Granny's bag ripped down the middle. I knew I was in serious trouble.

"I'll be killed" I said to Maureen "this bag is not even ours. My mother will have to buy a new one for Granny Wright."

The only thing I could think of doing was to destroy the evidence by throwing the bag over the Bob mill wall.

The next day, Mammy was frantically looking for Granny's bag.

"Have any of you seen Granny's blue bag? I know it's in this house somewhere, who had it last?"

This went on for days. I was eaten up with guilt but I couldn't bring myself to tell the truth. On Friday I went to confession and told the priest the whole story. I was amazed that he didn't scold me. He gave me absolution and he didn't even tell me to make restitution. It was ages before the matter of the missing bag was forgotten.

◆

I enjoyed my handwriting class. We had headline copybooks, nib pens and inkwells that were built into our desks. The nibs were old and rusted and the ink was usually dried up. Nevertheless, I envisioned myself doing beautiful copperplate writing just like my dad's. My hands were always so cold; it was difficult doing the "up light and down heavy" strokes. A blot would mysteriously appear on the page and I would get a rap across the knuckles from Sister.

Some of the headlines were:

Beauty is as beauty does
Practice makes perfect
The pen is mightier than the sword

We had to copy a whole page of each headline.

◆

My friend, Deirdre, was well off. She lived in a great big house on the Naas Road. She had lovely white even teeth and she took singing lessons. She had a short leg due to polio and she had to wear a big platform boot. Deirdre always had plenty of money and she was generous with it. After school, she would treat all of us to delicious fresh cream buns from The Monument Creamery. One day when we were walking home from school along Tyrconnell Road, we stopped at a little confectioners and Deirdre bought a bag of Macintosh's "Quality Street". These were luxurious assorted chocolates. We had our mouths full when a big car pulled up beside us. Out jumped Deirdre's father. He was a big, fat, red-faced man and he was very angry.

"What are you doing here? What are you eating?"

Poor Deirdre was dumbfounded. He examined the bag of expensive sweets.

"Who bought these? Where did you get the money?"

We had no idea Deirdre had been stealing the money from her parents. We assumed, because she was rich, she would naturally have money. After that, her dad picked her up from school every day and there were no more treats.

◆

Mammy gave me a half crown (two shillings and sixpence) to go to the butcher and get a pound of stew meat. As I was skipping along and flipping the precious coin up in the air, lo and behold, it rolled down the gutter and into the drain. I looked after it in disbelief—there was nothing for it but to go back and face Mammy. After a good belt on the head and a tirade

"You stupid little bitch, you'll be the death of me yet. Why don't you mind what you're doing? Your head is always up in the clouds. Show me exactly where you lost the money?"

She brought out a pot and a serving spoon from the kitchen. She got down on her knees and lifted the grating from the drain and proceeded to scoop out the debris until she found the half crown. I breathed a sigh of relief—had she not found it I might not be here now telling my story.

As luck would have it, some time later on my way home from school, I found a ten shilling note outside a shop. I was delighted running home with it to Mammy (ten shillings in those days would buy twenty loaves of bread!) Although Mammy could have used the money, she was not about to lose this opportunity to teach me a lesson in honesty. She asked me where I found it and marched me back to the shop. She said to the assistant

"My daughter found something valuable outside your shop. If anyone enquires about it and can describe what it is, I will be glad to give it back."

She left our name and address. Weeks passed and nobody claimed the ten shillings. I got sixpence for myself.

◆

The ten o'clock mass on Sundays was a special mass for children. The mass was said in Latin but we had our prayer books in English to follow along. We walked to church and the nuns were always there to poke us in the back if we weren't paying attention. Any adult in the pews behind was free to chastise us for inappropriate behavior. They often threatened to tell our mothers. The choir was beautiful. I knew all the words of the hymns and I loved to join in the singing. Canon Boyle was the pastor. He was a crusty old priest and God help anyone who came in late. He would stop the mass and berate them from the pulpit. The homilies were geared to the children in language they could understand. The Fourth Commandment to "Honor Thy Father and Thy Mother" was heavily stressed and we were told that this commandment encompassed our teachers and any other grown up in authority. The Seventh Commandment "Thou Shalt Not Steal" was also popular. Canon Boyle told us not only did this mean actually stealing things but if we put scratch marks on our desks or if we wrote on walls, that was defacing another person's property and was considered stealing.

Mammy generally went to early mass. It was years before I realized that Daddy didn't go to mass at all. He got dressed up and left the house. Mammy said he liked the mass in Marlborough Street Church downtown. In actual fact he met his pals, Teddy Stewart and Star Farrell, for a pint in Muldowney's pub. Daddy didn't like organized religion but he was a good Christian. He was a kind and caring man. He said it was the religion and the Irish language that were ruining the country.

When we came home Mammy had the big Irish breakfast ready: back rashers, fried eggs, black and white pudding and pork sausages from Hafner's, brown bread and strong tea.

Weather permitting, on Sunday afternoons we would walk to the Phoenix Park. Phoenix Park is the largest enclosed park in Western Europe. It has everything: cricket and polo grounds, picnic areas, jogging trails, lakes and birds, trees and a zoo but not a single swing or piece of playground equipment for children. We could either walk around the gardens, or run up and down the steps of The Wellington Monument to amuse ourselves. Wellington was born in Dublin and he was famous for having defeated Napoleon at the Battle of Waterloo, hence his beautiful monument. If we had money, we could go to the zoo. I never cared to go, it was so smelly and the antics of the animals disgusted me.

Aras an Uachtarain, the home of the Irish President, or Ireland's White House is also located in Phoenix Park. I never saw it—it is situated behind huge trees and shrubbery and heavily guarded, unlike our own White House, which is always being shown on the news and is open for the entire world to see.

The American Ambassador's residence, a magnificent building, is also located in the Phoenix Park. I have not seen that either for the same reasons that I have not seen Ireland's White House.

On Sundays, we always had a roast for dinner; delicious pork, beef, or leg of lamb. With this we had roast potatoes, Marrowfat peas, Brussels sprouts and mint sauce with the lamb.

For dessert, we had jelly and ice cream or jelly and custard. Sometimes we had hot apple tart dotted with cloves—Mammy could whip up the best apple tart in next to no time.

◆

On rainy Sunday afternoons, we went to the Inchicore Cinema or "The Core" on Tyrconnell Road. We got on the queue with what appeared to be every other child from Inchicore and we looked out for Jack Dwyer. Jack was an attendant and a friend of the family. He would let us in for free if he saw us. When Jack wasn't around and Billy had no money, he and his pal Austie Reed would stand outside begging

"Hey, mister, would you ball us a clod" which meant give us a coin. All hell would have broken loose if my mother ever found out.

We were transported to a fantasy world as we watched Shirley Temple, Jane Withers, and the golden-voiced Deanna Durbin singing "Who's that Pretty Girl

Milking her Cow". My brothers, Billy and Frank loved The Westerns: cowboys and Indians fighting and killing each other. These were "follyan uppers".

For the rest of the week the picture was told and retold. The boys played Cowboys and Indians with cap guns or guns made from pieces of wood. The girls sang the Deanna Durbin songs and tried to tap like Shirley Temple.

◆

On other Sunday afternoons we played "put and take". I loved this little game, especially when my dad played with us. We each put some pennies into the kitty. We would take turns spinning the hexagonal top and following the instructions; "take two" "put three" etc. When it landed on "take all" the player took everything in the kitty and we started all over again.

In fine weather Billy, Frank and the other boys on the road played soccer on "the green". This was a patch of vacant grassy land at the top of Railway Avenue. If they didn't have a ball, they made one from wadded up newspapers, twine and rubber bands.

◆

I adored my little sister Betty. She was a beauty—soft and cuddly with a personality to match. Her light brown hair was cut in a bob and her bangs accentuated her large blue eyes. She loved school. She thought the holy pictures and the lamp lighting under the Sacred Heart were lovely. Mammy always put a big taffeta bow of ribbon in Betty's hair. One day Mrs.Pack, the woman who cleaned the toilets, said to Betty

"That ribbon is so big; it would make a pair of knickers."

We thought this was very funny and we repeated Mrs. Pack's remark every time Mammy sent us to school wearing a big bow of ribbon.

One night Olga had the bright idea of putting tiny braids all over Betty's hair. The next morning when Mammy was trying to get Betty ready for school she couldn't undo the braids. Olga and Hilda were sitting at the piano practicing a duet. Mammy was getting more frustrated by the minute and screaming at Olga

"You feather-headed eejit—how could you do such a stupid thing? Look at the state of this child going to school?"

Next she let the hairbrush fly in the direction of Olga and the handle broke off as it hit the piano. Poor Betty was crying and she had to go to school with her hair half braided and half crinkly.

Easter time was approaching and Mammy ordered Easter eggs for all of us from Joan Kerrigan. Joan lived across the street and she worked in Jacobs chocolate factory—she could get the "seconds" at a cut price. Betty chose the egg decorated with lilac flowers.

Betty had had her fifth birthday on April 10th. A couple of days later she developed a high fever and my mother told her to stay in bed. I went upstairs to the bedroom to sit with her and I brought up her chocolate egg. Betty was very flushed but she smiled at me and put her hot little hand in mine. I coaxed her to taste her egg and she tried to please me. She only managed to put her teeth marks into it. The next morning the doctor came and he ordered an ambulance to take Betty to Cork Street Fever Hospital. That was the last time I saw my little angel sister. The Health Department came out and sprayed our house with some unpleasant-smelling insecticide. Betty died in the hospital on April 17, 1941, a week after her fifth birthday. I was eight. Mammy was crying all the time and she was very sad.

As was the custom in Ireland, the hearse carrying Betty's tiny white coffin and drawn by two white horses, stopped outside our house on Railway Avenue for two minutes on the way to Bluebell Cemetery. None of the children was allowed to attend her funeral. That was also the custom of the time

The doctors were not sure if Betty died from typhoid fever or from meningitis. Both were prevalent and since there were no antibiotics, these diseases were usually fatal. The following was printed on her memorial card:

> "As Angels hovered o'er the earth
> This blossom met their eyes
> So wondrous fair, they marked it out
> As fit for Paradise."

♦

Since we didn't have a telephone, on the rare occasions when my maternal grandparents, Pappy and Granny Mooney, came to visit, they sent a postcard with the date and time of their arrival. While Mammy loved to see them, this was a great hardship on her. The whole house had to be cleaned and all the children had to help. Mammy gave me two wads of newspaper, one wet and one dry. My job was to clean all the windows, inside and out. Hilda scrubbed the kitchen floor and waxed it with Mansion floor polish. Olga did the hall door brasses with Brasso and a soft cloth. Billy and Frank had to tidy up the garden and fill the coal bucket. Mammy sprinkled the rugs with tea leaves, then hung them across the clothesline and beat them with the back of a brush until they were clean. Then she got on her knees and black leaded the fire grate.

I was sent down to The Monument Creamery to get a fresh sponge cake for their tea. We were well warned to watch our manners and to be on our best behavior.

Pappy Mooney was one of the few people to have a car and when they arrived the neighborhood children crowded around and stood up on the running board to have a good look. He didn't mind, he was patient with children.

Pappy spent many years in Baro, Nigeria, West Africa. He was a coachbuilder and supervisor of rail construction. My mother said he built a church for the natives and taught them Catholicism. He was a devout Catholic himself. I inherited his little prayer book "The Key of Heaven" which was given to him as a Christmas present by his then girlfriend, Alice, in 1898. In this little prayer book he documented where he and Alice attended Mass on the First Fridays in 1899, where they attended Christmas Masses, Sodalities, etc. He also documented births, weddings and deaths of his ten children. Throughout the book he has written ILAMAWFE—I love Alice Moffett and Will For Ever—there was no doubt that he loved Alice.

Granny and Pappy Mooney had a lovely house (or so I thought as a child) in Killester. It was a treat to go there for a visit. There were only about six houses on a quiet country lane. Their hall door was fitted with amber colored glass, which gave a golden glow to their entry hall. To the left as you walked in was the parlor. In the parlor were all the treasures that Pappy Mooney had brought home from West Africa: a gorgeous silver tea service, fine china, and rare pieces of ebony furniture. At the end of the hall was the dining room. I remember two plaques on the mantelpiece, one was:

"A wise old owl lived in an oak
The more he saw, the less he spoke
The less he spoke, the more he heard
Why can't we be like that wise old bird?"

The other one read:

> "If you have a job to do, do it now
> If you're sure the job's your own
> Then tackle it alone
> Don't hem and haw and groan
> Do it now."

The windows of the dining room looked out over Pappy's garden. He grew lettuce, scallions and radishes and he would make me a lovely fresh salad for my tea. He also grew blackcurrants and gooseberries and Granny Mooney's larder was stocked with jams and jellies she made from the garden. Pappy took great pains to answer my never-ending questions and often had me look up articles in his encyclopedia.

There was a graveyard at the back of their house and Pappy Mooney liked to sit there smoking his pipe—his devoted little dog "Gyp" contentedly sitting beside him.

Granny Mooney, Alice Moffett, was short, buxom, and pampered. She was said to have been a beauty in her younger days. She had dainty hands and feet. Her hands were used in the advertisements for Pear's soap. She wore a fur coat and lots of fine gold jewelry. She had no patience with us whatsoever and after our initial greeting, she told my mother to send us outside to play. The fact that it was raining didn't matter. Unlike Granny Wright, she neither brought us a treat nor gave us any money.

On occasions when I went to Killester, I remember Granny Mooney packing a pile of ham sandwiches for herself and walking me with her to the local pub, "The Beachcomber". There she ordered a pint of Guinness ate her sandwiches and smoked her cigarettes while I played alone outside until she was ready to go home. She didn't even offer me a mineral. She did one nice thing for me though—she knit me a lovely mauve cardigan. I bought myself hair ribbons to match and I felt like a princess as I admired myself in the shop windows.

Pappy died November 4th, 1946. He is buried in Clontarf Cemetery. After his death Granny Mooney sold the house in Killester and went to live with my mother's sister, Auntie Greta, in England. The house was sold with contents—all the priceless treasures that Pappy had brought home from Africa. The only treasures remaining are a pair of hand carved ebony oars now in my sister, Ada's, possession and an inlaid lamp table which is in Olga's family.

◆

My mother's brother, Uncle Gary emigrated from Ireland to the United States in 1922. He settled in Michigan and he was successful in real estate and as the owner of a tavern. His wife, Virginia, sent us parcels of clothing from time to time. There was great excitement when these arrived—everything was packed beautifully and looked brand new. Gary also paid my mother's fare to visit him on several occasions.

♦

I was disadvantaged in school because most of my subjects were taught through the medium of Irish. I still say my multiplication tables by heart in Irish. I never did learn them in English. History and geography were the worst. How could I ever know where countries and cities were on the map if I only knew their names in Gaelic? I had to do a lot of relearning later in life. The nuns probably had difficulty teaching us because, much the same as our parents, English was the only language used when they went to school. Dad, being pro British, according to him, we were better off under British Rule.

♦

Rosaleen came over from England to escape the bombing in London. She stayed with her auntie, who lived a few doors down from us on Railway Avenue. Rosaleen was plump and pasty. She had an English accent and I was in awe of her because she was an only child. One day on our way to school, I was telling Rosaleen that Sister had asked us to bring flowers for the May altar. We had no flowers in our little patch of garden. Rosaleen said if I brought an empty can the next day she would show me where I could get beautiful flowers. Equipped with my empty can, we walked down Tyrconnel Park and stopped in front of a house that had a beautiful garden. In we went—Rosaleen said,

> "You take one side and I'll take the other. Take as many as you like and be quick."

In no time I filled the can with gorgeous blooms—tulips, daffodils, daisies, and sweet pea—surely Sister would be pleased. But what if she asked me where I got them. I began to have misgivings and decided to dump the stolen flowers, can and all over a fence. That afternoon, when I came home from school, Mammy was waiting for me at the door. She was in a terrible temper. She said the police had been looking for me and I was surely going to jail for stealing flowers. She gave me a few good thumps and sent me to bed without my tea. Feeling sad and ashamed, I was looking out the bedroom window and couldn't believe my eyes when I saw Miss Rosaleen skipping along O'Donoghue Street. She was off to her tennis lesson wearing her short pleated skirt and carrying her tennis racquet. Obviously, stealing flowers was no big crime in her house. It was in ours. To instill in us the seriousness of breaking the Seventh Commandment, Mammy told us the story of Goldie Roberts.

"Goldie was a hungry young lad and the temptation of an orchard full of delicious ripe apples was too much for him. He scaled the wall and took three apples that had fallen to the ground. The parish priest was watching him and he promptly turned him over to the authorities. Goldie's punishment was banishment to the dreaded Artane. The same priest came to see him off at the train station. As the train was pulling out, he handed Goldie an apple."

I heard later that the police never came to our house. A girl from my class had spied on us and came and told my mother.

◆

The good nuns realized that knitting and sewing were useful subjects since most of the clothes we wore were hand-me-downs and would need repairs and alterations. The sewing machine terrified me and I was forever being rapped across the knuckles because my material would bunch up and the nun would have to stand over me to sort me out. However, I did learn to make buttonholes and to let down or take up a hem by hand. I also learnt to do neat darning. I often darned the family's socks. I would stretch the holey part of the sock over a glass tumbler and do expert weaving. It would have been nice if I had matching yarns but I had to make do with what was available.

Knitting was a different story. I thought there was something creative about knitting and I enjoyed it. I started out doing scarves and mittens and then making my own sweaters and sweaters for my younger sisters, Joan and Doris. It was more economical to knit than to buy at the store. I wanted to progress to knitting dresses. A family of attractive girls lived on our road. Their auntie made for them the most exquisite lacy dresses in soft pastels. I envied their long dark curls and those gorgeous bouncy dresses. I just had to learn how to make them. I found out that the lacy look was achieved by crocheting and it would have been difficult to get the same effect by knitting.

◆

A strange thing happened to me when I was about nine years old. At school, we were transferring to an upstairs classroom. The sister walked ahead of us and she kept up a tirade telling us how badly behaved and ill mannered we were. My friend and I were giggling and imitating her and, for good measure, I stuck out my tongue behind her back. I was unaware that the principal was at the bottom of the stairs and she caught me in the act. She pulled me out of the line and said,

"Miss Wright, how dare you show such disrespect to a holy nun—a Bride of Christ? I want to speak to your mother in my office after lunch."

At this, my knees buckled from under me. Not alone was I in trouble with the nuns but I knew my mother would kill me if she had to leave her work and get herself ready to go to the school. Six slaps with the cane or even twelve would have been welcome punishment. I was devastated. When the bell rang for lunch, I didn't talk to anyone but ran home as fast as I could until my side ached and I was breathless. My mother said,

"You're all flushed. What's the matter with you?"
"I don't know, Mammy," I lied "I have a terrible pain in my side."

She felt my head, which was hot after the fast run, and mercifully, she sent me off to bed. Next thing I knew, Dr. Tyrell was examining me. He took my temperature, and then he told me to stick out my tongue and say "Ah". He put his stethoscope on my back and told me to say "Ninety Nine" and then "Again". He told my mother I had a fever and he didn't like the sound of my chest and he gave her a note to take me to Baggot Street Hospital. I couldn't believe my luck; this meant Mammy was not going to visit the nuns that afternoon.

At the hospital, the doctor examined me and sent me for X-Rays. He told my mother I had fluid on my left lung and I had to be kept in for treatment. The treatment was plenty of bed rest and plenty of nourishment. Mammy said good-bye to me and a nurse took me upstairs in the lift. The nurse was a buxom rosy cheeked country girl. She was cheerful and kind. She gave me a warm bath in a real bathtub and she put a fresh nightie on me. She then took me to the ward. I was delighted to have a bed all to myself. It had clean white sheets and a snow-white counterpane. The sheets were changed every day. She then gave me a tablet and a glass of water. The tablet tasted like chalk and I threw it up. I got to know all the people in the ward. In the bed next to me was a six-year-old boy named Zoltan Zinn. He was from Czechoslovakia. I don't know what was wrong with him but his case must have been interesting because he was visited every day by the chief surgeon and an entourage of medical students. He was a handsome little boy with huge dark eyes. He loved bananas and he always had a supply of them. On the other side of me was a little girl from England. Her name was Robina Baird and she must have been very well off because she had plenty of toys. She was always crying for her "Mummy". Across the ward, there was a beautiful young girl with dark shoulder length hair, which she put up in curlers every night. She put curlers in my hair too.

The staff sister was mean to the young nurses. She was constantly berating them "Lift up your feet", "Straighten your cap", "You're not on the farm now".

Visitors were allowed only twice a week. Mammy usually came by herself. Children were not allowed to visit so I did not see any of my brothers and sisters. Mammy often brought me a brown egg. She would write my name on it and the nurse would soft boil it for my breakfast. She brought my special salad; lettuce, scallions, sliced tomatoes, cucumbers, beetroot and hard-boiled eggs, all arranged beautifully on a plate and drizzled over with Chef's Salad Cream. The hospital food was good too. My favorite dinner was fried filet of sole with green peas and mashed potatoes. This was served on Fridays.

Mammy came in one day wearing a lovely gray suit she had had tailor made. When I admired it on her she said,

> "I'm not a bit happy with it. I'll never have anything made again. With all the pinning and measuring and fussing, to say nothing of the cost, they never turn out the way you expect. It's much better to go and try something on and if you don't like it, you don't have to buy it."

Although Daddy was uncomfortable in hospitals, he came regularly to visit me. I loved to see him come through the door. He brought me my favorite pink and white marshmallows and he was never in a rush to leave.

My friend, Maura O'Byrne's mother from Tyrconnell Park came to visit me and brought me cutout dolls with paste-on clothes. I never got tired of playing with them and wished I had some of those lovely outfits for myself.

I was never bored in hospital especially as I didn't have a pain or an ache. The book lady came around with her trolley and I read everything; it didn't matter if they were adult or children's books. It was here I formed the habit of reading, which has always provided me with great pleasure. There was no pastime more enjoyable than a good book or even a bad one. I loved "*Just William*", Richmal Compton's series about a bumbling schoolboy who got himself into the funniest of scrapes. I read Enid Blyton's "Noddy" books and Jonathan Swift's "Gulliver's Travels". I read the classics, detective stories, romances and everything offered on the book trolley. The book lady was my friend. She was ladylike with her bobbed hair and well-scrubbed look. She wore a sensible tweed suit and laced up Red Cross shoes.

After about two months, I was well enough to go home. I was delighted to be with my brothers and sisters again. They never tired of hearing the funny stories about the hospital.

I left with a pang though because I loved everything about the hospital; the cleanliness, the orderliness, the beautifully polished floors, the patients and the doctors and nurses. I knew I would be back, not as a patient but as a nurse. My mind was well made up. I could visualize myself in that snow white starched uniform and my nurse's cap on my head shaking down a thermometer or holding a wrist to take a patient's pulse. I had great empathy for those who were sick and suffering. Girls didn't dream then that they could become doctors.

◆

I was now ten years old and preparing to make my Confirmation. Confirmation was the Sacrament to make us "True and Perfect Christians". We had to know all about sanctifying grace. Sister rolled her eyes when she told us that with Confirmation we would have the seven gifts of the Holy Ghost: Wisdom, Understanding, Counsel, Fortitude, Knowledge, Piety and The Fear of the Lord. We learned selected parables from The Bible by heart: "The Wedding in Cana of Galilee", "The Ten Virgins", "The Sower went out to sow his Seed" and many more. Canon Boyle made surprise visits to our classroom. We stood up to greet him and then he asked us questions from our catechism. He was a gruff man and we were terrified of him. He reminded us that if we obeyed the laws of God that the gates of hell would not prevail against us. But, if we lived a life of sin then we faced an eternity of torment in hell. Hell was a place for lost souls, filled with fire and brimstone.

"Now my dear children" he said "Be sure to live a good Christian life and I pray that none of you will hear that awful sentence of rejection *'depart from me, ye cursed, into the everlasting fire which was prepared for the devil and his angels!'*"

The tailoress was making my coat for Confirmation. In fact, she was making three coats: one for Olga, one for Hilda, and one for me. Mammy must have gotten a good bargain on the material because it was horrible, a sort of mohair rusty brown color. I wanted a coat from Cassidy's like my other friends. Renee got a beautiful leopard skin coat with a hat and muff to match. At Cassidy's you could buy cheap up-to-the minute styles and pay by the week. My mother said,

> "I wouldn't let you be seen in anything that common. No wonder these people have nothing, the clothes are worn out before they're paid for."

Next came my dress, made by a dressmaker in Drimnagh. It was royal blue crepe de chine, high waisted with little shirt buttons. It was awful. I wanted a beautiful pink accordion pleated like Sylvia's. I wished I could have made my Confirmation in my slip—that was peach satin with coffee colored lace at the hem and at the top. The worst part of the whole outfit was the hat, a black velour schoolgirl hat. I was mortified. Everything was my mother's choice; she didn't consider what I might like. At least my clothes were new and I was grateful for that.

◆

I joined our church choir. My voice was in the alto range and I was assigned to the back row singing seconds. We were doing well with Thomas Moore's "Oft in the Stilly Night" when the girl next to me poked me,

"Suck on that and pass it along," she said as she handed me a lemon

Innocently enough, I did as she asked. Lemons were a rare commodity in Ireland. A delicious smell permeated the room and we became giddy. The choirmaster was not amused. His face red with anger, he approached the back row,

> "You, you, you, all of you out, out, out and don't ever come back here again. How dare you disrupt this choir? Your behavior is a disgrace."

That was it; no explanations, no excuses, no second chance.

◆

The recipe for stuffed heart had to be copied into our notebooks in preparation for our first cookery lesson.

My mother gathered the ingredients for the stuffing; breadcrumbs, onion, butter, thyme and parsley and salt and pepper. I was sent to the butcher shop on Bulfin Road to buy the heart. There was a big fat woman behind the counter shaking a metal canister over a tray of pork chops seasoning them. When I caught her attention, I said,

"Can I have a heart please?"
"What kind of a heart d'ye want?" she asked
"I need it for school, we're making stuffed heart for our cookery class." I said

She went into the back and came out holding a huge disgusting looking heart. It was dripping blood all over her white apron.

"This is a nice beef heart," she said as she put it on the scales
"There's tree pounds in that one."
"That's grand," I said, I was expecting something much smaller.

She wrapped it up in white butcher paper and I paid her.
The school kitchen was spotless. Everything gleamed. The long deal tables and the draining boards were snow white, not a speck of grime or grease anywhere. I had to put on an apron and cover all of my hair with a white mop cap.

"Now girls," began the nun "the first thing you do is to wash the heart thoroughly, trim the fat and remove the arteries and strings from the inside."

Most of us were awkward with this procedure but Sister was patient and she came around to help us out.

"Rub the inside with salt and fill with the stuffing. Sew up the opening and rub the outside with salt," she continued.

My heart was now ready to go into the roasting pan to which water had been added for basting.
While our hearts were baking, we had to copy the next week's recipe which was to be apple tart. I was really looking forward to that.
Next we had to clean the kitchen. Coarse sand was used to scrub the tables. I got rapped on the knuckles for not doing it correctly.
The smell of the roasting hearts filled the room. I took mine out of the oven and put it with the others. It looked and smelt delicious, nothing at all like the bloody red blob I had put in. I couldn't wait to get home to show it to my mother. She sliced it thinly and with the stuffing in the center, she said I had done a great job. Daddy had some for his tea and he said it was delicious. But you really couldn't go by Daddy's taste; he even liked tripe

and onions, (tripe was the white crinkly stuff found inside a cow's stomach).

♦

The Gas Company was having a competition and Sister encouraged all of her cookery class to participate. The prizes were one pound for the winner, ten shillings for second place and five shillings for third place. The competition involved writing an essay on making a meal for the family using staples usually found in the home plus some leftover cooked fish. Neatness, handwriting, ingenuity and composition would all be considered in the judging. It was rumored around school that the finished recipe would be for fish cakes.

I wrote my essay as neatly as I could incorporating what I thought would be a recipe for fish cakes. We never owned a cookery book, my mother learned to cook from her mother and nothing was ever measured, a pinch of this and a handful of that, she know the right amounts instinctively. I used the required ingredient, leftover cooked fish. I mixed it with mashed potatoes and seasoned it with salt and pepper. Next I shaped it into patties, dipped them in beaten egg, coated them with breadcrumbs and fried them in a little butter until they were golden.

We waited weeks for the results and much to my amazement; Sister came in one day and announced that Nora Wright had placed second in The Gas Company competition. This was the first time in my life I had ever won anything. Not only did I get a certificate and ten shillings but I was invited to afternoon tea at The Gas Company.

The awards day arrived and, dressed in a striped jumper belonging to Olga, Mammy said I looked grand and she gave me the bus fare to go into The Gas Company in D'Olier Street. When I arrived at the door, I was given my name tag and my table number.

I never saw such a beautiful spread in my life. The tables were set with linen tablecloths, elegant china teacups, flowered teapots and beautiful napkins. There were plates of dainty finger sandwiches of every variety. There were scones with clotted cream and jam, fresh cream éclairs, miniature tea cakes and tarts, petit fours and meringues. It was all intimidating and my stomach was in knots. All the other girls were beautifully dressed, full of confidence and chatting and laughing with each other. I was so shy, I hardly ate anything. I felt uncomfortable and my face was burning. The judge shook hands with me, presented me with my certificate and gave me my prize. I was glad it was all over.

My mother was delighted with the ten shillings and she gave me a shilling for myself.

5

Kickham Road

"Be it ever so humble, there's no place like home."

—Payne

There were ten of us in the family. The children were getting older, Olga was already 15, and our little two-bedroom house on Railway Avenue was just too cramped. My mother, being a creative business woman, heard of the possibility of getting a swap to a bigger house. Mrs. Rooney lived at 31 Kickham Road. Her husband was ill and she was behind in her rent to Dublin Corporation. The prospect of being turned out on the street frightened her. The rent on Railway Avenue was more affordable and the house was big enough for Mrs. Rooney and her husband. They were agreeable to the swap. My mother bargained for the price and in the end the sum of £400 was agreed upon. Dad wasn't much for change. He worried if we could afford the higher rent and he hated all the fuss and commotion of moving. However, he couldn't deny my mother anything and he trusted her judgment.

We were excited at the prospect of a bigger house. All of our conversations were about the move and what it would involve. Imagine three bedrooms! The boys would have their own room, the girls would have theirs and Mam and Dad would have one of their own. Like Railway Avenue, our house was in the middle of a row of houses all attached and all alike. It had a front garden and a big back garden with a gate at the end leading out to an alleyway. The gardens were much neglected except for a beautiful tall lilac tree by the back wall.

The hall door led into a small entry with the stairs leading up to the bedrooms. The living room was much larger than our old one. The piano fit nicely on the left side wall and the settee was placed in front of the fireplace. There was a perfect little corner for Pappy Mooney's inlaid table.

The kitchen and scullery were combined and there was a bathtub in the kitchen with a hinged lid on it..

The toilet was off the scullery.

We ran up and down the stairs checking out the bedrooms. It was decided that the girls would have the large front room, the boys the box room, and Mammy and Daddy the other back room.

Even though the whole house was in a state of disrepair with its peeling paint and drab old wallpaper, we were delighted with the extra room and we knew it wouldn't take too long for Mammy to have it all spruced up.

The trouble started when my mother went to The Corporation Office on Bulfin Road to pay the rent. The burly official behind the counter made out the receipt to Mrs. Rooney. Mammy explained that she was now the new owner, that she had swapped the house on Railway Avenue with the Rooney's,

> "Oh Missus, you can't do anything like that without the permission of the Corporation. You know we have long waiting lists for these houses; some of the people have been waiting for years."

Mammy used all of her wiles and wit to convince the official that she had actually done a good turn for Mrs. Rooney by swapping the smaller house with the lower rent.

> "Well Missus, I understand all that but we'll have to put your case before The Board. Be prepared to move out."

Mammy came home distraught.

"I want all of you to pray to St.Jude that we'll be able to keep the house."

The Corporation Officials went to visit the Rooney's and when they heard their plight and saw how ill the husband was, they allowed them to stay there and they let us keep 31. My mother was elated,

> "St.Jude, the patron of hopeless cases, can work miracles. I'll be sure to put something in the poor box in thanksgiving."

◆

The McLoughlin's lived next door to us. They had five children; a small family in those days. Patty was my age and we were in the same class in school. She was blond, petite and pretty. She was an accomplished Irish dancer. She encouraged me to take lessons with her at Harry McCartney's. Harry was small, slim and red haired and proud of the fact that he was a well-known champion. He danced regularly at The Mansion House in his little kilt and his chest full of medals. He started me off with the reel; one, two, three, and one, two, three, then across; one, two, three, four, five, six, seven and so on. Most of the students had been taking lessons for years and they were good. At twelve, I was a bit old to start. I learned the reel and the slip jig but I didn't get as far as the hornpipe.

The McLoughlin's had a friendly little dog named "Trixie". My mother saved the scraps for him and he made himself at home with our family. We adopted him as our own because we were never allowed to have a pet.

Patty had friends, Rita and Daisy Waters, who lived on Nash Street. They had a playroom built on to their house and, on rainy days, Patty and I would go there. They had a huge assortment of cutout paper dolls and dolls' clothes spread out on a long table. Mrs. Waters always welcomed us and once in a while, she treated us to lemonade and a biscuit. We brought our scrapbooks filled with our collection of silver paper and scraps. The silver papers were the wrappings on expensive chocolates. We smoothed them out with our nails until they gleamed. The scraps were lovely shiny pictures of angels, flowers and butterflies. We played for hours; laughing, talking, admiring the dolls' outfits and swapping silver papers and scraps.

At school we were required to learn, by heart, a patriotic poem called "The Wayfarer" written by Padraic Pearse on the night before his execution.

> "The beauty of the world had made me sad,
> This beauty that will pass,
> Sometimes my heart hath shaken with great joy
> To see a leaping squirrel in a tree,
> Or a red ladybird upon a stalk,
> Or little rabbits in a field at evening,
> Lit by a slanting sun,
> Or some green hill where shadows drifted by,
> Some quiet hill where mountainy man hath sown
> And soon would reap; near to the gate of Heaven;
> Or children with bare feet upon the sands
> Of some ebbed sea, or playing on the streets
> Of little towns in Connacht,
> Things young and happy.
> And then my heart hath told me:
> These will pass,

Will pass and change, will die and be no more,
Things bright and green, things young and happy:
And I have gone upon my way
Sorrowful."

I studied my lines night after night. Olga and Hilda coached me, making sure I knew every word. Walking to school with Patty on the day we were to give our recitation, I asked her if she had memorized the poem,

"I didn't have time, say a prayer she won't call on me," she said

I was feeling sorry for her because I knew Sister would let her have it if she didn't know her lines. We were called upon randomly. Luckily, Patty's name wasn't called.

Mrs. McLoughlin was a loving mother to her children. When she spoke of them she would say "My Patty did this" or "My Eileen did that". I wished my mother would talk about me like that. One day when we came home from school, there was great commotion in the neighborhood; Mrs.McLoughlin had collapsed and died of a heart attack. She was only in her forties. My mother and all of the neighbors rallied round by providing meals for the family and helping out any way they could.

◆

The Tierney's, Mick and Kathleen, lived on the other side of us. They were a middle-aged couple. They had no children of their own and they were fond of all of us. Mrs. Tierney's old mother lived with them. Their garden was a mass of flowers and their home was always neat and clean. Mrs. Tierney tried to befriend my mother by bring over an apple tart, a piece of fish or a cigarette. My mother didn't encourage her. She didn't like anyone dropping in.

"I have no time for that house hatching and I'm sick of her boasting about the lovely things her relatives send her from America."

Mrs. Tierney would hang out the brand new American sheets on her clothes-line without ever washing them just to show them off to the neighbors.

Mr. Tierney (we were never allowed to use adult's Christian names) worked in Aer Lingus. He was always helpful and friendly.

◆

My mother took great satisfaction out of making the outside of our house a show place. Every week, summer and winter, she got down on her hands and knees and whitened the garden path and the wall outside with a pumice stone. Nobody else on the street did that. The windows were cleaned and the door brasses polished every Friday. She was proud of her rose trees and the spectacular purple clematis which climbed on the trellis over the front door. She loved it when the people passing stopped to admire her handiwork,

"Isn't that Mrs. Wright a marvelous woman?"

◆

The war ended in May 1945. There were celebrations all over Ireland with the people singing "It's a Long Way to Tipperary" and "Pack up Your Troubles in Your old Kitbag."

On August 8th in the same year, my sister Ada was born. She was the last of the ten children. My mother was then 41.

◆

Annie lived in the corner house. She was the youngest in her family and she could do whatever she liked. Her parents were elderly and her mother was in bad health, suffering from erysipelas. Annie had pale skin, auburn hair and green eyes. I liked her because she was forward and cheeky—the very same reasons my mother didn't like her.

One day Annie and I were playing in our back garden. She was upset at having been chastised by her father,

"He's just an ignorant aul' country bugger." she said

My mother, with her unusually sharp hearing, heard this remark and ran out into the garden,

"Miss Annie, you will not talk so disrespectfully about your parents at my house. Go home now; I don't want to see you over here any more."

To me she said,

"If I ever catch you with that girl again, I'll wool the head off you. She's nothing but a common little switcher."

Of course I played with Annie again but she was never allowed near our house. My mother kept a very watchful eye on our companions,

"Show me your company, and I'll tell you what you are."

was another one of my mother's mottos.

♦

On an occasional Saturday, my mother let me come into town with her to do her shopping. We took the Number 24 bus from Bulfin Road into Abbey Street. Mammy invariable met someone she knew on the bus.

"Scootch over and give Mrs. So and So some room," she would say to me.

I would sit with my face glued to the window hardly daring to breathe. I would love to have asked her what the Dublin landmarks we were passing were, but I dared not interrupt her conversation. Children were never allowed to interrupt and they were not encouraged to ask questions. They were likely to get a reply,

"You're a nuisance, stop annoying me; I'll never let you come with me again."

Having arrived at Abbey Street, we turned on to O'Connell Street and walked up to Henry Street. We turned around by Boylan's into the secondhand market known as Cole's Lane. The dealers had their wares laid out, the better stuff on hangers and the rest piled on tables. Footwear of all sizes and description was lined in pairs; some badly worn and others nearly new. Gathered around each stall, crowds of women rummaged through the merchandise.

"Here y'are girls" the dealer called holding up a coat. "Who'll give me five shillings? Ah come on, won't one of youse give me hansel?"

We pushed through the crowds until we reached Peggy's stall. Peggy knew my mother well and she saved the better quality merchandise for her.

"I have something here for you Lily. Look at this, nearly new, not a brack on it. It's from Switzers and your size too. You can have it for two pounds."

She held up a nice looking black and white dress.

"You must be joking, Peggy, where would I wear something like that. I'll give you thirty shillings."

"I couldn't give it to you for less than I paid for it, thirty five shillings."

"Come on", my mother said to me, preparing to walk away, banking on Peggy calling her back.

"Listen Lily, c'mere, make it thirty three, that's the best I can do."

"All I have is a pound note and ten shillings—thirty shillings."

"God you're a terrible woman" she said as she wrapped the dress in a sheet of newspaper and handed it to my mother. She put the money into her enormous apron pocket.

As we were walking from Cole's Lane, my mother warned me,

"If you breathe a word of my business to any of your pals, I'll cut the tongue out of you."

From Cole's Lane, we walked to Moore Street where dealers in shawls were selling fruit and vegetables. They had aprons tied around their waists with huge money pockets in front.

"Lovely Jaff oranges Missus, you won't taste better anywhere, only thruppence."

"C'mere missus wit the woite gloves. Lovely red apples two pence each, I'll give you a bargain, four for seven pence."

My mother ignored them and walked on to a rosy-faced dealer who was selling tomatoes,

"I'll have two pounds please and mind you don't put any bad ones in the bottom of the bag."

My mother told me, if you didn't watch them, they would throw a few bad tomatoes in the bottom of the bag; they were clever in the way they held the bag open so that you wouldn't notice. Then they would let you pick the good ones yourself and put them on top. You wouldn't realize until you got home that the tomatoes in the bottom of the bag were rotten.

♦

Kickham Road was named after a fine Irish patriot named Charles J. Kickham. Despite the fact that he was sight and hearing impaired, he was a highly accomplished literary man. His "Knocknagown" was a phenomenally successful novel, making him the most popular Irish author of the 19th Century. He was loved and respected by the Irish people.

6

Secondary School

"I am not a teacher, but an awakener."

—Robert Frost

A brilliant nun named Sister Anne was in charge of the 6th, 7th and 8th Grades. I had the greatest respect and admiration for her. She was dedicated to her profession and she had a divine sense of humor. She was tall and slim and she smelled of fresh lavender. She had great empathy for her students and she encouraged us to make the most of our abilities. She stressed the importance of education.

> "Remember girls, your mind is your greatest asset. Fill it with learning. Don't clutter it with cheap novels and trash from the cinema. You can lose all your earthly possessions but no one can take away your knowledge."

Sr. Anne made it her business to know the family circumstances of her pupils. She knew whose father was out of work and when it was necessary to have a child leave school and start earning money. She worked hard to set the children on the right road and often begged parents to keep a bright child in school. She was so capable she could have run the whole country.

Olga never cared for school and when she finished her Primary at age fourteen she was anxious to leave. Sr. Anne had a chat with my mother,

> "Olga is a people person and she is not too fond of the books. She is a beautiful girl and she has an unusually charming personality. I would advise you, Mrs. Wright, to let her leave school. I have a very suitable little job for her in a drapery shop in Drimnagh."

Olga was ecstatic when she heard the news. She started right away and she rode her bicycle to and from work. Although her pay was small, she could buy everything at cost. She brought home new brown boots for Billy and lovely blankets for the baby. She loved the shop and Mammy was delighted with the extra few shillings. This was the beginning of Olga's career as a most successful salesperson.

Hilda was thirteen when the ninth baby, Jack, was born. Jack cried all the time. The doctor said he had colic and that he would grow out of it. Hilda stayed home from school for several months to help my mother. She was a fantastic little housekeeper. She could clean, do laundry, cook and look after Jack. She loved being home from school and Mammy was happy to have her. Once again Sister Anne became involved, she sent for my mother:

> "Mrs. Wright, I know how helpful it is for you to have Hilda give you a hand with all those children, but you are doing her a grave injustice by keeping her home from school. Hilda is a bright girl and she has great potential. She deserves a chance."

On Monday morning, Hilda reluctantly returned to school. Olga and I then had to take turns minding Jack. After school, I had to take him out in his pram. He bawled and bawled. One time a lady stopped me,

> "Poor little lamb, what's up with him?" she asked
> "I don't know, he's always crying, he has the colic."

She went into a shop nearby and she bought him an ice cream cone.

> "There now luv" she said petting him

With that, Jack grabbed the cone and dashed it to the ground.

I walked and walked pushing the pram all the way up Tyrconnell Road to The Oblates. I was cold, tired and hungry but I was told not to bring him home until six o'clock.

During the night Hilda would get up and pace the floor with him. Her bare feet were blue with cold as she rocked him in her arms. She tried everything: a warm bottle, sugar water—nothing seemed to help. Eventually he outgrew his colic and became quite a happy and amusing little toddler.

◆

Sister Anne introduced us to our first Shakespearean play, "As you Like It". We had to learn most of it by heart and we took turns playing the different roles. Sister usually played Rosalind herself because, like Rosalind, she was "more than common tall".

The "Seven Ages of Man" fascinated me—a whole life condensed to a few lines. I especially liked the last lines:

> "Last scene of all,
> That ends this strange eventful history,
> Is second childishness, and mere oblivion,
> Sans teeth, sans eyes, sans taste, sans everything."

I enjoyed "The Merchant of Venice" especially the part where the Jewish money lender, Shylock, asks for a pound of flesh if he his not paid back on the date and time agreed.

◆

We prayed at the beginning of each class and we had Religious Education every day. We were approaching the age when we would soon be women. The Sixth Commandment "Thou shalt not commit adultery" was heavily emphasized. Our catechism carried the warnings further:

> "The Sixth Commandment forbids all immodest actions, looks or words, all immodest songs, novels or plays, and anything dangerous to chastity."

The facts of life were never spoken about. Anything could be discussed; murders, hangings, alcoholism, but never sex or how babies were born. Sister said our bodies were temples of The Holy Ghost and we must keep them pure. She rolled her eyes and said,

> "There are parts of our bodies that should never be seen or touched."

We were completely ignorant about sexual matters and would have been embarrassed to ask our mothers.

In a conservative Catholic country, the very worst misfortune that could befall a girl was for her to become pregnant outside of marriage.

If the parents could afford it, they sent their daughter to a nursing home to have her baby. The neighbors were told she had gone to England to visit her auntie. The baby was given up for adoption and the girl returned home.

Poor girls who got pregnant were disowned for having shamed their families. They were taken in by The Sisters of Charity at the Magdalen Laundry in Sean Mac Dermott Street. The laundry did the washing for the local hotels, restaurants and hospitals. The girls worked there and were known as "Maggies". They got no pay only a roof over their heads and their meals. The nuns were cruel to them, considered them outcasts, and often beat them. Their babies were taken away from them as soon as they were born and sent for adoption, sometimes to America. These girls couldn't go back home. They had disgraced their families and they were not wanted. For a moment of human weakness or, in many cases, having been victims of rape they were now slaves to the laundry and to the nuns. Some remained there all of their lives. It was not unusual to hear of a young pregnant girl's body being dragged from The River Liffey. She would have committed suicide rather than face the consequences.

◆

My favorite subject was physiology. I was fascinated by the functioning of the human body. I loved the colored charts showing the location of the organs, nerves, bones and muscles. I learned about the digestive system, the names of the teeth and the division of the vertebrae in the spine. I knew medicine was in my future, I loved anything to do with hospitals and I had a natural inclination to help those who were suffering.

Sister Anne's sense of humor added zest to our studies. She didn't fly into a rage if we asked a question. When slaps were in order, she would say

"Come up here and get your *sweets.*"

She talked about the wonderful work The Medical Missionaries of Mary were doing in Drogheda and I imagined myself being there.

◆

Miss Clifford was my math teacher. She taught arithmetic, algebra and geometry. She came from County Kerry. She was tall and angular. She had black, lank, greasy hair and a pale intense face. Her dark eyes were like burning coals, nothing escaped her, she must have had another pair in the back of her head. She wore only one outfit; a black pleated skirt which was greenish and shiny from age and some sort of a nondescript jumper. When she reached to write on the blackboard her skirt slipped down over her skinny hips and she was constantly hoisting it up.

It seemed her only mission in life was to teach sixty unmotivated girls the fundamentals of mathematics. Arithmetic was taught through the medium of Irish. We recited our tables in a singsong fashion until we knew them by heart. Algebra and geometry were taught in English. She made charts showing proportions, ratios, equations, and relationships of points, lines and angles. None of it made any sense to me and I couldn't see what use these subjects would be to me later in life.

Miss Clifford had a unique way of caning. She put her left hand under her right arm, raised the cane high in the air and, with anger spitting from her eyes, brought it down with full force on the palm of the hand. We were caned for not knowing our lessons, for not paying attention, for coming to class late or for not doing our homework. She would often kneel down in front of the big picture of The Sacred Heart, make an elaborate sign of the cross and say in her strong brogue,

"Oh Sacred Heart of Jesus, grant me patience with this class."

She had no favorites. She never smiled and she never complimented any of us.

♦

At around this time, my dad went into partnership with an acquaintance of his named Ronnie Moore. They opened a bicycle shop in the heart of the business district at 20 South Anne Street just off Grafton Street. This was also a bicycle park. People couldn't afford bus fare and very few owned cars, they rode their bicycles to and from work. For sixpence a day, they could park their bikes. From the main floor, the shop had a ramp which led to a huge basement. Overhead were big hooks, like meat hooks, on which to hang the bikes.

When Hilda turned fourteen, despite the opposition of Sr. Anne, she left school and went to work in the shop. My dad still had his job at The Post Office and he came to the shop after work to let Hilda go home. Although it was a big cold draughty old place with no heating except for a little oil-burning stove, Hilda loved working there and she was indispensable to my dad. The shop stayed open until past midnight to facilitate the dancing crowd at the Crystal Ballroom which was next door. Hilda very often rode her bicycle back in the evening to help Dad or just to keep him company.

Mr. Moore turned out to be an uncooperative partner. He was seldom there except for Fridays when he came to collect his share of the profits. My dad tried to buy him out or to have him buy my dad's share but Mr. Moore wouldn't agree.

♦

Hilda was an enthusiastic member of the Girl Guides. She took great pride in keeping her uniform pressed and her belt and shoes polished. She won numerous prizes in the form of colorful patches which she sewed on to her sleeves. She won a Brownie camera for neatness. It was a great little camera—the first one our family ever owned. I was delighted when she let me go hiking with her to The Sugarloaf Mountains on Saint Patrick's Day. I helped collect twigs to light the fire and I joined in singing the campfire song:

> "Tramp, tramp, tramp along the highways
> Picking flowers where ere we go
> We haven't got a care
> Our joys we always share
> For we're happy, healthy Guides."

In Ireland Saint Patrick's Day was a national holiday as well as a holy day of obligation. At the children's mass they sang "Hail Glorious Saint Patrick". The girls wore green ribbons in their hair and the boys wore sprigs of shamrock in their lapels. The shamrock was used by Saint Patrick to explain The Trinity.

Although corned beef and cabbage is a common dish in Ireland, it is associated more with Saint Patrick's Day in the United States than it is in Ireland.

7

The "Inter"

"There is unspeakable pleasure
attending the life of a voluntary student."

—Goldsmith

Upstairs in the small back bedroom is where I did my studying for The Interme-diate Examination. I sat on the edge of the bed and used Pappy Mooney's inlaid table as my desk. It was peaceful up there and I was happy to be relieved from my household chores and the child minding. I enjoyed looking out the window at the neighbors' gardens, the rustling trees, the children playing and the miles and miles of washing drying in the breeze.

It was June and exam time was drawing near. The weather was beautiful. Fine weather was a rarity in Ireland and sunshine put everyone in a good mood. My mother was in such a mood when she decided she would take me into town to buy me a new dress for the occasion. We went into several stores but Mammy could find nothing that she liked. There were plenty that I liked but I was afraid to say anything because I might end up getting nothing at all. Finally, in Win-ston's of George's Street she spotted a sale rack. She rummaged through all the clothes, rubbing the material between her thumb and forefinger and checking the price tags. Then she held up this god awful green and yellow checked gingham.

"Now this is lovely, go and try it on."

I know I frustrated my mother. She admired tall, well-built preferably tanned people. Here was I, petite, delicately structured and fair skinned. I didn't suit at all. My one redeeming feature was my hair. I took the dress into the fitting room. The fit was OK but it was like a child's dress; a little peter pan collar, short sleeves, a flared skirt and a belt. I hated it. When I came out, my mother said,

"Now that's only gorgeous on you. A perfect fit. We'll take it."

There were no cash registers at the counter. The assistant wrote out the sales slip and reached over her and undid a little box suspended from wires running across the ceiling to the cashier's office. Into the box she placed the money and the sales slip. She joined the box to the other half and sent it zooming across to the cashier. It zoomed back the same way with the change and the receipt.

♦

Examination time came. Sister Anne gave us words of encouragement,

"You've worked hard and I expect all of you to do well."

I was nervous and I was freezing in the silly checked dress, little ankle socks and sandals. The exams were held in a big classroom in our school. The atmosphere was subdued as we got our instructions. Papers were handed out for the first subject, Religious Knowledge. I felt comfortable with most of the questions and had time to recheck my answers before the bell rang. The exams continued for the week. I felt I did better in Physiology than in any of the other subjects.

Weeks later the results came out. Sister Anne was beaming as she read off our names,

"Nora Wright passed with honors and placed sixth in the school!"

Only two of her students failed.

I ran home breathlessly with the good news. Mammy was proud of me and said,

"I knew you'd do well with all of that studying upstairs day and night."

Daddy was full of praise and he said I had the brains of the family and that I would be successful in anything I attempted. He gave me a present of my first watch; a silver secondhand one from his auction collection.

It was now Sister Anne's duty to see to the future of her school leavers.

"Now Nora, you are a bright girl. Have you thought about your future? Have you ever thought about entering the convent; you would make a lovely little nun."

"Oh no Sister, I have wanted to become a nurse since I was a little girl. I have my heart set on it. I want to go to nursing school."

"Tell your mammy to come up and see me."

The next day, Mammy dressed herself in her good black suit and went for her conference.

"Nora tells me she wants to become a nurse. What do you think of that Mrs. Wright?

"She'll never make a nurse Sister. She's too fragile—she would never be able to lift a sixteen stone patient, never mind the long hours on her feet all day."

Sister Anne agreed with her completely.

"What about her becoming a nun?"

"Ah no Sister, I wouldn't want any of them entering the convent. I think it's a very hard life."

"Well, Mrs. Wright, she has great potential and she should further her education. She is certainly not shop girl material. How about enrolling her in secretarial school? It is clean easy work and she would always be assured of a position."

So my future was decided. I had no voice in the matter. I didn't dare question the authority of a holy nun and my mother. Daddy agreed with them and he enrolled me in Skerry's College.

◆

There were regular talent shows at The Father Matthew Hall in Church Street. These were great fun and since we knew many of the contestants, we looked forward to attending. There was no shortage of talent or personality. There was everything from Irish dancing to comic routines. One very funny fellow made up his own songs:

> "All of you have plots I'm sure In Inchicore and Terenure
> If you want a load of fine manure,
> Take a shovel and follow me donkey
> Hey Ho Jerusalem, Jerusalem, Jerusalem
> Hey Ho Jerusalem, take a shovel and follow me donkey."

We sang his songs on the way home and for a long time afterwards. There was great excitement when Hilda's friend, Gabriel, won first prize for her rendition of "Cruising down the River."

◆

That summer, my mother rented a beach cottage in Laytown. It was really more of a shack than a cottage but it was located right on the beach. We were all excited because nobody we knew had ever gone on a month's holiday. It was also something to brag to the neighbors about; The Wrights were off to the seaside for their holidays. By this time, Daddy had acquired a used car, it was a Hillman Minx. He took good care of it, only used it for special occasions and he housed it in a garage on Tyrconnell Road. We took turns going to pay the rent. The old lady who owned the garage always gave us a treat—an orange, a few biscuits, or a few sweets.

The weather was sunny and warm on the day of departure. Mammy was in great humor, she loved the beach and the sunshine. We piled all our gear into and on top of the car; pots and pans, dishes, bed linens, bathing togs, towels, buckets and spades and the baby's pram. Daddy said we were like a bunch of gypsies.

The tide was going out when we arrived. Joan and Doris played in the damp sand with their buckets and spades filling the pails, turning them upside down, beating the bottoms and chanting

"Pie, pie, come out, I'll give you half a clout."

Billy and Frank went for a swim. There was loads of seaweed and the children liked to squish the pods. Billy was nearly successful at teaching me how to swim.

In the meantime, Mammy lit the Primus stove and put the kettle on to boil for our tea. Everyone helped to unload the car and to make up the beds. Some slept in bunks and others on the floor. Daddy, Olga and Hilda had to leave to go back to work. I went home to run the house. We came down with many of our friends on the weekends and everyone had a good time.

Mammy was happy. She got into the ocean for a dip every day. The sea and the sun rejuvenated her and she got a lovely healthy tan.

Stafford's was a general store and pub a few yards from our cottage. Anything we needed, we could buy at Stafford's. Mammy bargained there just the same as she did at home. With a few slices of their cooked ham and a pot of boiled new potatoes, we had a delicious meal. They also sold whippy ice cream cones decorated with Cadbury's chocolate flaky bars. These were to die for.

Butlin's Holiday Camp was located about half a mile along the beach at Mosney. This was an all-inclusive expensive camp. Mostly visitors from England vacationed there. The back entrance was on the beach side and we often walked along the strand to look through the fences at the guests enjoying themselves on the tennis courts and in the swimming pool. It was easy to sneak into the ball-room at night to enjoy the dancing and the music.

Julianstown and Bettystown were interesting little towns within easy walking distance.

Everyone enjoyed the holiday so much that Mammy booked the cottage again for many more years to come.

8

Skerry's College

"'Tis education forms the common mind;
just as the twig is bent the tree is inclined."

—Pope

Skerry's College was located in the heart of the city at 76, Saint Stephen's Green. The building was once a private home. The hall door, the fanlight, the steps and the placement of the windows were typical Georgian.

My subjects were Shorthand, Typing, Bookkeeping, Business English and Math; all completely dry and boring as far as I was concerned. It was strange to be attending a coed school without nuns as teachers.

My math teacher was a good humored roly-poly bald headed gentleman.

"Round it out, round it out in your head before you begin; that way, your answer won't be in the millions instead of the thousands." He said.

This was good advice and it stayed with me.

Bus fares were expensive and it was decided that since Daddy was going into town at the same time as I was that he would take me on the crossbar of his bicycle. He suffered from asthma or, as they said, "a bad chest". Even though I was no heavyweight, he huffed and he puffed against the biting wind and rain as he cycled with me through the short cuts into town. I always felt sad kissing him goodbye. He was ill and it wasn't fair that he should be burdened taking me to school. He never complained.

Mr. McNamara was my English teacher. He had long hair and an unkempt appearance but he was quick witted and charming and I looked forward to his classes.

There was no caning at Skerry's College. Parents paid the tuition and it was the students' responsibility to learn or not.

Mammy gave me sixpence every day to go to Woolworth's in Grafton Street on my lunch hour and buy myself a cup of hot Bovril. The slogan in the advertisements was

"Bovril Puts Beef into You"

I never got the Bovril. I headed straight for Noblett's chocolate shop and bought myself sixpence worth of sweets. I ate these as I strolled down fashionable Grafton Street. I gazed longingly at the elegant clothes displayed in the windows of Richard Alan and Brown Thomas and at the cakes in Bewley's Coffee Shop. I often slipped into the Ladies' Room in the Grafton Cinema which was nice and warm and I listened to the stylishly dressed women as they chatted about their social events whilst repairing their makeup.

Sometimes I would go into Daddy's shop in South Anne Street and visit with Hilda. She was always cheerful despite the fact that she was blue with cold. She would share a cup of tea with me from the flask she brought from home.

My best friend in Skerry's College was Agnes Concannon. Agnes was heavy and happy. On fine days, we would stroll around Saint Stephen's Green. There were beautifully laid out walkways banked on each side by masses of brilliantly colored flowers. We talked and laughed and threw bits of bread to the swans. The aromas of delicious food coming from the gratings of the nearby Shelbourne Hotel were tantalizing.

Despite the fact that I had little interest in my subjects, I was progressing quite well. The shorthand I was learning was Isaac Pitman. It was considered more difficult than Gregg Shorthand but more accurate and easier to translate even from stale notes. My teacher was Miss Piggott, an elderly spinster lady, who wore her pince-nez down on her nose and her gray hair in a tight bun at the nape of her neck. She had infinite patience and from her I learned my strokes, loops, prefixes, suffixes, diphthongs and grammalogues. She was always encouraging.

I have fond memories of coming home from Skerry's on cold and rainy afternoons at about 2:30. Nobody was home at that hour except Mammy. She had the fire lighting, a cup of tea ready for me and a plate of Jacob's Cream Crackers and Galtee cheese. We would sit by the fire, enjoying our tea and talk. Normally she didn't have much time to listen, but, on these occasions, she was interested in hearing about my day. Had I met anybody in town? How did they look? What were they wearing? It would have been unusual in the City of Dublin not to run into someone you knew. I loved these fireside chats and having my mother all to myself.

One evening a friend of mine from school, Maura Moore, came to our house and asked me if I would be interested in taking over her job. She was leaving to enter the convent. She said it was a very good company to work for and that she had been happy there. They were a firm of electrical engineers located in Abbey Street. The pay was thirty five shillings a week. The thought of leaving school and earning my own money filled me with excitement. Maura said if I was interested she would arrange an interview for me. Mammy and Daddy thought I should give it a try.

The next Monday morning I went for the interview. I had a bowl of porridge and a cup of strong tea for my breakfast and I wore a lovely gray suit and black patent shoes that Uncle Gary had sent from America. Mammy insisted that I wear a hat and gloves.

"No outfit is finished without a hat and gloves," she said

As I was leaving, Daddy kissed me and said,

"Good luck Bernie, I know you'll get the job, anyone can see that you are an intelligent and well brought up girl."

I took the bus from Bulfin Road into Abbey Street and looked for the address. The offices were on the third floor.

I liked the manager, Miss Herron, right away. She was plump, pleasant and motherly. She was crippled from polio and she used a crutch. She asked me a few questions and then proceeded to give me a test. She dictated a letter slowly, and then asked me to type it for her. I had no trouble transcribing my notes and when I handed the letter back to her she seemed pleased.

"You did very well," she said "would it be possible for you to start next Monday?"

I was on cloud nine going home with the good news. I had not graduated from Skerry's College, but that didn't matter. I was now sixteen, grown up and ready to earn my own money.

◆

Around this time, Olga had started working in the offices of The Irish Hospital Sweepstakes in Ballsbridge. My mother, with her usual ingenuity, had gone to visit her cousin, Frank Saurin. Frank was one of the directors in The Sweep. He agreed to interview Olga and told my mother she would have to take a test. One of the requirements for the test was that she should have legible handwriting. That was no trouble for Olga, she had beautiful handwriting. The other requirement was that she should know the abbreviations of all the states in the United States. We drilled her and drilled her night after night until she knew them perfectly. She got the job as a receipt writer which paid seven pounds ten shillings a week—a princely sum in those days.

◆

Uncle Gary wrote to my mother offering to pay the fare and sponsor one of us to have a chance at a better life in The United States. My mother needed no encouragement. She had visited her brother in the past and she loved everything about America; the cleanliness and the efficiency; the automatic washers and dryers, the refrigerators to keep your food fresh and the electric Hoovers. She often said

> "If I was a young girl, I'd never live in this godforsaken country, I'd be off to The States if I got the chance. A woman's work is so easy over there."

It was decided that the opportunity should go to Hilda. There was a mixture of happiness and sadness at the prospect of her leaving. Daddy would certainly miss her in the shop and Mammy would be lost without her help in the house. But the opportunity was too good to miss and preparations began for Hilda's departure. We gave her small gifts of a rosary, a prayer book, a diary and a crioss. Mammy and Daddy went to Cobh to see her off.

Things were looking up at last. Olga and I were working. Hilda was in America. All the children, except Ada, were in school. The girls attended Golden Bridge. Billy attended The Christian Brothers in James' Street and Frank and Jack were in Saint Michaels. There were no more new babies.

◆

Halloween was my favorite holiday of the year. Mammy bought apples and grapes and a big bag of mixed nuts. These were rare luxuries. We didn't have a nutcracker so we cracked the shells with a rock or with the heels of our shoes.

For dinner, Mammy made a huge pot of colcannon into which she put a sixpence wrapped in a piece of paper. Whoever found it could keep it and look forward to a prosperous year. It is delicious and simple to make:

Colcannon

    1 ½ lbs potatoes
    1 ½ cups milk

6 scallions
1 ½ cups cooked kale or cabbage
1 tablespoon butter
Salt and pepper

Boil and mash the potatoes. Add the boiling milk and scalded chopped scallions, beat until fluffy. Add the butter, cooked kale finely chopped and fold well. Season generously with salt and pepper.

The boys blackened their faces with soot from the chimney and they dressed up in any old clothes they could find. They went house to house calling "any apples or nuts". If the people didn't give them anything, they played tricks on them. When they came home the games began. Mammy suspended an apple from a string and tied our hands behind our backs. Whoever took the biggest bite got to keep the apple. She then put a sixpence in a basin of water and again tied our hands behind our backs. Whoever could pick up the sixpence in their teeth could keep it. We didn't carve pumpkins although it is said that the practice started in Ireland in the eighteenth century.

9

Earning My Bread

"Work is the refuge of people who have nothing better to do."

—Oscar Wilde

The weekend went by quickly. I was excited and apprehensive about my new job. Daddy brought home an unredeemed bicycle from the shop and he and Billy were in the backyard fixing it up for me. They checked for punctures, pumped up the tires, oiled the chain and lowered the saddle. I was happy to see there was a nearly-new basket attached to the handlebars.

Mammy was in great form deciding what I should wear. She went upstairs to the wall wardrobe and brought down a glen check suit that Auntie Gin had sent from America.

"Try this on and see how it fits."

The suit was a bit big but I liked it. Mammy said,

"It's only gorgeous on you. I'll run the iron over it and sponge out those few spots. Put a bit of Vaseline on your good black patent shoes and do something with your hair. You know you never get a second chance to make a first impression."

On Sunday night, I dampened my hair with sugar water and curled it up in rags.

I was awake early on Monday morning. The weather was cold and drizzling. Mammy made a fresh pot of good strong tea. I had two cups with buttered toast for my breakfast. Then I washed, got dressed and brushed my hair into a pageboy. Everyone said I looked lovely. Mammy dusted my face with her powder puff. She shook out an old raincoat from under the nook. The nook was the space under the stairs for the gas meter. It was also a catchall for everything else; Daddy's stock from the auctions, shopping bags, brooms, Russian boots, overcoats, umbrellas, newspapers, dusting rags and any old junk you didn't know what to do with. Mammy said,

> "Put this around you and pull the hood up so your hair doesn't get wet. I made a few sambos for you and if it is raining at dinnertime, don't cycle home."

I put the banana sandwiches wrapped in newspaper into my bag.

Daddy kissed me, wished me good luck and told me to be careful on the bike.

"Bless yourself with the holy water," Mammy shouted from the kitchen.

Off I went down The South Circular to join dozens of other cyclists on their way to work. At Kilmainham Jail I turned into The John's Road and sped along until the Heuston Station came into view. The smells of Guinness' Brewery were replaced by the smell of the sea coming from The Liffey as I cycled along The Quays; Wolfe Tone Quay, Arran Quay, past The Four Courts, auctioneers' offices, solicitors' offices, ramshackle houses, Ormond Quay, The Ha'penny Bridge, pawn brokers, B&B's, and Bachelor's Walk. At O'Connell Street I turned left to Middle Abbey Street.

I arrived in good time, parked my bike in the hallway and climbed the creaky wooden stairs to the third floor. The offices were shabby and gloomy. Miss Herron showed me where to hang my coat and told me I would be sitting at the desk beside her. There was a pile of manila folders on my desk which Miss Herron asked me to file in the big metal filing cabinets. After that I was to type the billing envelopes—requests for payment going out to all parts of the city; Phibsborough, Ballymun, Finglas, Clondalkin and to places I had never even heard of.

The chief accountant was a huge man from County Mayo. Despite the fact that his hands were like two big hams, his ledger entries were extremely neat and tidy. Every morning he placed a pint bottle of milk in front of the fire. By break time at eleven o'clock the milk was nice and warm. He poured out a mug for me and one for himself.

> "Drink that up now, it'll do you good," he said in his thick country accent.

I hated hot milk but I couldn't hurt his feelings so I drank it. Miss Verby was the other secretary. She was a relative of one of the owners. She was short, fat and Jewish and she looked rich. She had on a pale pink Dorothy Pinnock twin set—a status symbol in those days. She had pretty little hands and beautifully manicured nails. I was self conscious about my own hands; they were blue from the cold and scarred from chilblains. My nails were ripped to bits from pounding on an Underwood Manual with old-fashioned indented keys.

At one o'clock Miss Herron said,

"Miss Wright, we're going to Bewley's for our lunch, would you like to come with us"?

Since I had no money, I said

"Ah no, thank you, I brought some sandwiches."

Everyone left and I opened my lunch. The bananas were black and the bread had the imprint of the newspaper on it. I wasn't hungry, so I tossed the lot into the bin and went out to explore the city. The rain had stopped and the air smelt fresh and clean.

Looking in Lemon's at the luscious confections reminded me that I had a couple of Fox's Glacier Mints in the bottom of my bag. I sucked on these as I browsed around Eason's Stationery Store. I looked at the beautiful cards, fancy notepapers, Parker and Conway Stewart fountain pens, diaries, calendars and blotting paper in all colors. I then passed the General Post Office and turned into Henry Street. Henry Street was crowded with lunchtime shoppers and the music was blaring from the record store

"Put another nickel in, in the nickelodeon
All I want is loving you and
Music, music, music."

I went into Arnott's, one of Dublin's most exclusive Department Stores. I took note of the latest fashions with an eye to updating some of my own clothes. I marveled at the displays of elegant shoes and I sampled the expensive perfumes and hand lotions until it was time to walk back to the office.

In the afternoon, Miss Herron gave me some invoices to type and she dictated a couple of letters which demanded payment of overdue bills. At around three o'clock, my stomach began to growl and, as if by magic, a young lad came in carrying a tray of steaming mugs of tea. Miss Verby passed around a packet of Mikado Biscuits—what a treat! I ate and drank hungrily.

At five o'clock it was time to put the cover on the typewriter. Miss Herron complimented me on my work and said she hoped I'd be happy there.

When I got home, Mammy had my favorite tea ready for me; beans on toast, a fried egg and fried tomatoes. I was starving.

The whole family was full of questions about my first day. I felt important as I told them everything. I described the office and the type of work I was doing. I told them about Miss Herron and Miss Verby. They laughed when I told them about the old fellow warming the milk.

I was getting used to the routine. Although the work wasn't difficult, I found it boring. On Friday Miss Herron handed me a little brown envelope—my first pay packet. I was excited bringing it home to Mammy.

"The blessings of God on you," she said as she counted the money; a one pound note, a ten shilling note and five shillings in silver. She gave me the ten shillings for myself.

"Now you can take the bus or treat yourself to your lunch in town."

The pay wasn't much but at that time a pound bought forty loaves of bread.

Another big parcel arrived from Auntie Gin. There was a suit in it for Daddy, an assortment of dresses and some beautiful towels. I put my eye on a navy shot silk dress with a white lacy collar.

"I'd love that one Mammy." I said

"Well you can have it, but now that you're working, you're going to have to pay me for the American clothes. You can pay me a little every week. The duty I have to pay on those parcels is very dear and, as you well know, I send a lot of stuff to Auntie Gin."

This was true. Mammy sent Auntie Gin Waterford Crystal, Irish Linens and Belleek China for herself and for her friends.

I bought the dress and Mammy wrote down the payments and the balance every week in my notebook—I didn't have much left for my lunches in town.

◆

One day as I was walking up our street, a crowd of unemployed young lads were playing pitch and toss at the corner of the cul-de-sac. As I passed, they shouted,

"Skinnymalink malogin legs," and they all started laughing at me.

When I got home I was delighted to see that my mother's sister, Auntie Molly had come to visit. They were sitting by the fire having a cup of tea and a cigarette.

I loved Auntie Molly. She was pretty and witty. When I had emptied my tea cup I asked her to read my tea leaves.

> "I see a tall dark man here Nora and the letter "F". You will be taking a speedy journey by night. There's money in your cup—somebody is going to leave it to you or you are going to win it."

She read Mammy's cup

> "I see lots of children here Lily. You will cross water many times and you will have a long, happy life."

Reading the tea cups was a common and fun past time.

When Molly was a child, Granny Mooney favored her and took her every-where to show her off. She now lived in Monkstown and she was very posh. Every day of her life she took a brisk walk along The Dunlaoghaire Pier to keep herself trim and healthy. My mother didn't appreciate it when she said,

> "Lily, I don't know how you can stand living in Inchicore, it's such a dread-fully common place."

What Molly didn't realize was that my mother was well known and respected in Inchicore. People talked about "that marvelous woman, Mrs. Wright, and all her lovely children". She enjoyed being well thought of and admired.

During the course of the conversation, I told them what the young bowsies at the corner had called me. Molly said

> "She is a bit on the dawny side Lily; I'll tell you what you'll do. Give her a glass of half Guinness and half milk every day and that will buck her up in no time."

When Molly was at our gate saying goodbye, in her humorous way, she turned to my mother and said,

> "Now Lily, be sure to share the money I gave you with all the children."
> I said, "What money?"
> Mammy said, "Don't mind that feckin eejit; she didn't give me any money at all."

Poor Mammy stood over me as I gulped down the horrible Guinness concoc-tion. She tried making extra tasty meals for me but the minute her back was turned, I pushed the food on to someone else's plate or hid it in my pocket. I dared not throw it in the bin because she would notice it. The fact is I never felt hungry. I lived on sweets and chocolate. Didn't the Cadbury's ads say?

"One and a half glasses of milk in every bar" and didn't the toffee ads say "Keep fit by eating our toffees. They're delicious and very wholesome."

Other people were remarking on my thinness and offering suggestions,

"Give her an egg flip Lily. A raw egg whipped up in a glass of milk with a little sugar, that'll do the trick."

I knew I was an embarrassment to my mother. She had always struggled with her weight and she didn't want anyone thinking she was eating all the food and giving me none. She had reached the end of her patience with me and she said,

"That's it. There has to be something wrong with you. You must have worms or something. I'm taking you to see the doctor."

Young Dr. Roche examined me. He checked my heart with his stethoscope and tapped on my lungs with his fingers. He pulled down my lower eyelids and had a look in there; he poked an instrument in my ears, shone a light down my throat, and took my temperature and my pulse. Then he asked me some very impertinent questions:
"Are your bowel movements regular?"
"Do you notice any blood in your stools?"
"Are your periods regular?"
"And how old were you, when you got your first period?"
I remembered that day well. Olga had told me what to expect. I was in school when it happened. I was afraid that the blood would come rushing out of me and form a pool on the floor. It didn't happen like that and when I told Olga that I had gotten the cramps and something strange was happening, she told me not to be afraid. All girls get them, she had hers and so did Hilda. The Blessed Mother had them and even all the nuns. It meant that I was a woman and not a girl anymore. It would now come every month. It was strange that my mother, having had all those children, never talked to us about the facts of life. Granny Wright explained everything to Olga in her kind, gentle way and Olga did the same for me.
The examination over, the doctor said to my mother,

"Well, Mrs. Wright, the good news is I can find nothing physically wrong with your daughter. Of course you must realize she has a slight build and she will never be a big buxom girl. However, she is run down at the moment. This is quite a common complaint among young women. What she needs is fresh air, rest, and plenty of good nutrition. I am admitting her to a Sanatorium for a few weeks; you won't know her when she comes home."

Mammy was relieved to know there was nothing wrong with me and all I needed was a bit of building up. Between The National Health and The Civil Service all expenses were covered.

I told Miss Herron I would be leaving at the weekend. She wished me well. She said she was sorry to lose me and my job would be waiting for me when I got back.

The Sanatorium was a pleasant place. It reminded me of a convent. The rooms were bright and airy. There were fresh flowers everywhere and soft music played in the background. There were no wards. I had my own little cubicle, furnished with a narrow white bed over which hung the inevitable crucifix. The atmosphere was of peace and tranquility. Nobody was sick or moaning. They were there to build up their strength following tuberculosis, surgeries, nervous breakdowns, illnesses or injuries. They got dressed every day and went about chatting and laughing. Some were knitting or crocheting baby blankets and matinee coats, others read newspapers or books from the well-stocked library. Some played bridge or the piano. Everyone attended the daily 11:15 Mass in the quiet little chapel.

The food was plentiful and nourishing; homemade brown bread and jam, newly laid eggs and plump pork sausages for breakfast. There was beef tea and calves foot jelly available at all times. There were expertly prepared meals for lunch and dinner and fresh fruits and vegetables in abundance. The dining room tables were beautifully set and the food was placed in bowls or on large platters in the center of the table. I could have as much or as little as I wanted and there was no pressure to eat more.

A girl came over to talk to me. Her name was Jenny. She was the thinnest girl I had ever seen in my life. She was in her mid-twenties. Her cheekbones and jawbones stuck out and her face was all sunken in. She had spindly legs and gangly arms—a walking skeleton. To make matters worse her hair was cut short like a man's—it was black and spiked on the top. I was lucky that my face never got thin and I had a good head of hair. My legs were the giveaway. If slacks had been fashionable, I would have looked normal.

"What's up wit chew?" Jenny said

"Nothing, the doctor says I'm too thin."

"Indeed an your not, you're gorgeous." Beside Jenny, I looked positively blooming. "What's your name?"

"Nora"

She thought about this for a minute

"Nora. That name doesn't suit you. You look more like a Maxine to me."

"What's the matter with you? I said

"I had a lung removed but I'm grand now—just trying to give up the smokes."

I still never felt hungry, but I was determined to eat as much as possible. I was afraid of ending up like poor Jenny. I opted for Ovaltine instead of tea and snacked on cheese and crackers or strawberries and cream instead of sweets. I put lashings of butter on my potatoes and vegetables.

Mammy always came on visiting days. Sometimes she would bring me a siphon of Lucozade, Ribena or a bunch of grapes. One time Joan wanted to come with her. Joan would have been about eight at the time.

> "OK you can come but don't you dare eat any of Nora's grapes. Put these shoes on you and hurry up."
>
> "But Mammy," Joan said "They're Nora's shoes and she'll be upset if she sees them on me."
>
> "You do what you're told or you're not coming at all. Keep your feet under the chair and she won't notice them. I'll be buying Nora a new pair anyway."

Of course I noticed the shoes but I knew it wouldn't have been Joan's idea to wear them. Mammy had a bad habit of telling the children to wear each other's clothes. This caused many a row between us.

After a few weeks, I was discharged. I felt refreshed and healthy and everyone said I looked marvelous. I had to be careful though to eat proper meals and not fall back into my old habit of skipping meals and ruining my appetite with sweets.

◆

Daddy was sitting by the fire reading the Irish Independent. He looked at me over his glasses,

> "I don't think you should go back to your old job, Bernie, the paper is full of ads looking for secretaries. Listen to this,

'Secretary required for busy
Import/Export office. Must have
Good shorthand and typing skills.
Knowledge of basic bookkeeping
And invoice processing desirable.
Must have a good telephone manner
And ability to work on own initiative.
Salary five pounds weekly.
Apply in writing in strictest confidence
Box 2914 Dublin.'

That's just the ticket for you. Why don't you answer it and see what happens."
Sister Anne was right again; there was never a shortage of positions for secretaries.
I made several attempts at writing out my resume. When I was satisfied that it
was neat enough and that I had boasted enough about myself, I enclosed a self-
stamped-addressed envelope and mailed it off.

A few days later I received a reply setting up an appointment for an interview.
The company was a spice merchant called Drysdale & Dennis on Anglesea Row.
I was interviewed by the owner Mr. Keats. He was a crusty shriveled up old fellow with a purply complexion. He asked me a few questions, and then gave me a
test. He seemed to be satisfied and asked me if I could start the following Monday. I was breathless coming home with the good news.

I went down to the kiosk on The South Circular and phoned Miss Herron to
tell her I wouldn't be coming back as I was starting a new job with better pay. She
said she didn't blame me and she was solicitous about my health. She said she
would be happy to give me a good reference if I needed one.

♦

On Saturday Olga and her best friend, Lynn Kearns, were in front of the little
mirror in our kitchen getting ready to go to The Dublin Skating Rink. I was
going with them as a spectator. They had put the brown makeup on their legs
and Olga was sponging Miner's on her face when she turned to me

"Let me try a bit of this on you."

She smoothed it over my face

"Let me look," I said
"No, I'm not finished."

Lynn said

"Try a bit of this on her eyes."
"Look up," Olga said as she brushed my eyelashes with mascara
"Now you can look."

The transformation was magical. My face was smooth and tan, not a freckle in sight, my eyes never looked bluer or my teeth whiter. Who would believe that that little sixpenny box of Miner's makeup could make such a difference? Olga let me borrow all of her cosmetics until I could buy my own. I never went back to a naked face again. Olga and Lynn were fantastic skaters. I loved to watch them. They wore little short flared skirts. Olga had her costumes made by Clodagh in South Anne Street. This particular day she was stunning in her royal blue with white fur trim—she reminded me of the life sized cardboard ad for Nivea Cream that stood outside Boles' Chemist.

When the music started for The Skater's Waltz, Olga was the first to be invited to dance.

◆

I started my new job with confidence. I had been eating well and I was filling out. Mammy gave me my bus fare and money for my lunch.

"Now be sure and get yourself something nourishing and don't go filling yourself up with aul' sweets."

I was hoping I wouldn't be seeing too much of old Keats but as it happened we were the only two in the office. There were salesmen in and out but they spent most of their time in the field collecting orders. There was a warehouse in the back where the crates of spices were packaged and shipped. The company imported spices from all over the world and supplied the hotels and restaurants in Ireland and abroad. I knew nothing about spices except the ones Mammy used at home; nutmeg, cloves, mustard and ordinary pepper. I was fascinated by the strange exotic names: Turmeric—a golden musky spice related to ginger, cardamom—an aromatic spice from the tropical rain forests and, one of the world's most ancient spices, ginger from Southeast Asia—required in Chinese cooking and indispensable for gingersnaps and ginger ale.

The office was in a shambles and there was nobody to show me anything. My predecessor, Miss Harnett, had been with the company since its inception; she obviously ran the place and knew where everything was but she left abruptly to become a nun. All I heard from old Keats was,

"Miss Harnett used to do it this way or Miss Harnett used to do it that way."

"Well she's not here, is she?" I said to myself and "God forgive you, Miss Harnett, for not staying long enough to train the new girl."

I muddled through the best I could. The days flew by. I was busy all the time typing letters, invoices, filing and answering the phone. Old Keats was cantankerous but I didn't care, I was happy and the pay was good. On the days I didn't go home for dinner, I had my lunch in nearby cafes; chips and egg, soup with brown bread, or salmon sandwiches. On Friday I got my pay envelope—five one pound notes all in cash. Mammy was delighted and she gave me back a pound for myself.

◆

One Friday, Olga handed up her pay and the flap of the envelope was torn. Mammy was annoyed,

"What's this" she said "did you open it?"
"Well, yes, Mammy, we had a collection in the Sweep for a girl who was getting married and I gave half a crown."
"What? What girl? Do you know her?"
"No Mammy, I don't know her. It's a general collection and everyone is expected to give. You can deduct it from my allowance if you want."
"No I won't deduct it this time but in future me lady don't be so flaithiulacht with my money. I wouldn't mind a worthy cause but for a girl you don't even know."

That's the way it was. Our pay was never considered ours; it had to be handed up unopened.

◆

Hilda was only a few months in America when she wrote to Mammy and Daddy saying she was desperately homesick. She hated her job as a filing clerk and she said she could never fit in with the American way of life. She felt out of place in Uncle Gary's house. For one thing, there wasn't enough room; there were only two bedrooms and one bathroom upstairs. Auntie Gin and Uncle Gary had their bedroom downstairs. Cousin Tommy had to give Hilda his bedroom and he had to sleep on a bed in a makeshift hallway.

Hilda was too young and ill prepared for such a drastic change. The farthest she had ever been from home was to Laytown. She was self conscious about her rosy schoolgirl complexion and the fact that she was a bit overweight. To add to her misery she had open sores on her legs from the chilblains and she had to keep them bandaged all the time. The Americans, being fastidious, looked upon this as something disgusting and maybe even contagious. To add to her unhappiness, she told us of the time she desperately tried to hide her underwear in the bathroom. The young cousins discovered her big blue interlock knickers with the elastic in the legs. This was uproariously funny to them and they ran downstairs to where the company was assembled, holding up the drawers and laughing

"Everyone look! This is what girls wear for panties in Ireland."

Auntie Gin was kind and did her best to make Hilda feel welcome. Soon after she arrived, she took her to Wurzburg's Department Store and bought her a whole new wardrobe.

Uncle Gary tried everything to encourage Hilda to stay but she could not be persuaded, she wanted to go home. She missed her old way of life, Daddy's shop and the family.

"Nil aon tintean mar do thintean fein."

This is an old Irish proverb which, roughly translated, means

"There's no fireside like your own fireside."

Gary wasn't happy. He had no choice but to buy a return ticket. Auntie Gin and her friend, Mrs. Jones, accompanied Hilda to New York from where she sailed for Cobh. Much to the annoyance of Uncle Gary, Auntie Gin and her friend stayed in New York for a week to do some shopping.

When Hilda arrived in Cobh, she was overjoyed to see Olga there waiting for her. They missed each other terribly and had a great time on the way home by train exchanging news of the family and news of life in Michigan.

We were all delighted to have Hilda home. She had lost weight, her chilblains had healed up and we thought she looked lovely in her new American clothes. My mother, however, was disappointed

"Throwing away a beautiful chance like that, you're a very foolish girl. You know opportunity only knocks once. You'll be sorry when you're back in that freezing shop on Monday."

While Hilda was away, Olga, Billy, and Marie Murphy helped Daddy in the shop. Billy and Marie were married a few years later.

One day while Olga was working in the shop a customer said to her

"You're a very lovely girl. Your eyes are like two drops of the Pacific Ocean!"

We often teased her with that remark—it was so true—she did have the most beautiful blue eyes.

Hilda was happy to be home helping Mammy in the house and back working for Daddy in the shop.

♦

Preparations for Christmas started in October when Mammy made the traditional Christmas pudding and Christmas cake. She bought the ingredients a little at a time—the glace fruits, nuts and raisins. She put chopped suet and Guinness' stout in the plum pudding. It was wrapped in a muslin cloth and steamed for hours. The recipe used for her Christmas cake was handed down by her mother and it was long and complicated. When it was baked she stored it in an airtight tin. Every so often she poked holes with a knitting needle in the cake and the pudding and poured brandy into them to keep them moist and fresh.

10

An Old Man's Darling

"Crabbed Age and Youth
Cannot live together:
Youth is full of pleasance,
Age is full of care."

—William Shakespeare

The 1940's and 50's were the "Golden years" of ballroom dancing in Dublin. Everyone danced. The ballrooms echoed to the beat of life and provided romantic opportunity and interaction. Many a young Cinderella met her Prince Charming on the dance floor. We learnt to dance at the parish halls and the local clubs—Bective Tennis Club and The Garda Siochana. Arus Mhuire in Inchicore held well-supervised dances where the priests stood around making sure the boys were not holding the girls too closely. If they were, they got a tap on the shoulder and the priest would say,

"Let's leave a little room for The Holy Ghost."

One Saturday afternoon I walked over to O'Leary Road to visit my friend, Polly. She was getting ready to go to a dance at The Four Provinces Ballroom.

"Why don't you come with me? It'll be a bit of a laugh." she said
"Oh, I don't think so. I'm not a good dancer, the hops at the clubs are OK but I'd be a bit nervous in a big ballroom."
"Don't be silly, come on, I'll show you a few steps. It's dead easy."

Polly was a beautiful and graceful dancer.

"The waltz is only one, two, three, one, two, three and that's all there is to it."

Next she hummed a tango and dipped me up and down and sideways.

"That one is a bit harder but you'll catch on in no time," she said.
"Come down with me to the chemist, I want to dye my hair black. Why don't you dye your hair?"
"Black?" I said
"No, black wouldn't suit you—you have lovely reddish highlights, we'll ask the chemist for something to bring out your color."

Down we went to Hayes, Conyngham and Robinson. I loved looking around the chemist breathing in all the lovely smells and admiring the exotic faces of the models in the cosmetic ads. There were jars of Ponds Vanishing Cream, tins of Nivea, Andrews Liver Salts, Ce-mul Cough Medicine, Beechams Powders, Rennies Tablets, bundles of orange and black licorice sugar barleys, a baby weighing scales, Evening in Paris perfume and, Olga's favorite, Tweed soap and talcum powder. Behind the counter were stacks of tiny drawers with brass knobs and labels on them.

"Well girls, can I help you?" smiled the good looking young chemist in a starched white coat.
Polly knew what she wanted for her own hair.

"Do you have anything for my friend here? If you take her outside to the sunlight you will see she has very nice reddish highlights in her hair. She just wants something to bring out her color."
"I have the very thing" said the young man "It's called Henna. It's only a temporary rinse and it will wash right out. It's three pence a packet."
"That sounds nice" said Polly" We'll give it a try."

We paid the man and on the way home, Polly said to me

"Now you go home, wash your hair and follow the instructions on the rinse packet. I'll be over for you at half seven. What are you going to wear?"

"I don't know, Hilda brought home lovely things from America and she might lend me something."
When I got home, my mother was at the kitchen counter pouring the boiling water over the jelly for Sunday's dessert. I told her I was going to a dance with Polly and she said it was OK so long as I was home by 11:00 p.m.
"No decent respectable girl is out after eleven o'clock," she said.

I dissolved the packet of rinse in a bowl of warm water according to the instructions. It was a rich orange color. I then washed my hair at the kitchen sink and I was pouring the rinse through it when I got an unmerciful thump on the back of my head.

"What on earth are you doing? You've poured the jelly over your hair. You stupid little bitch, you've ruined the Sunday dinner."

"I'm sorry Mammy; I thought I was pouring the rinse."

"You thought. When do you ever think? I've a good mind not to let you go to the dance."

My little brother Frank was looking at a comic at the kitchen table. He was the peace maker and always obliging

"It's OK Mammy; I'll go down and get another orange jelly."

I gave him sixpence; four pence for the jelly and two pence for himself.

Thankfully Mammy left the kitchen while I rewashed my hair and poured the proper rinse over it.

Hilda let me borrow her white fuzzy sweater and I wore my black skirt and my black court shoes. When I was ready, Mammy said

"Let me have a look at you. You need something on your neck."

Thankfully, she had forgotten all about the jelly. She was like that; she could flare up in a temper and then get over it just as quickly. She went to her strong-box under the nook and took out a lovely silvery necklace and matching earrings.

"I'm lending you these against my better judgment because everyone knows how careless you are. If you lose them, I'm finished with you; I'll never lend you anything again."

Polly arrived at half past seven. I hardly recognized her with her shiny black straight hair.

"I thought I'd try The Cleopatra Look for a change. What do you think?"

"It's only gorgeous" I said

And it was.

Polly wasn't what you'd consider good looking but she was attractive. She had a nice slim figure and she was creative when it came to style. She could take a plain old black dress and make it look chic and modern by adding a new scarf or some other accessory. She was the head of her household. Her father was in England and her mother was bed ridden suffering from tuberculosis. She had two younger sisters and a ten year old brother, Bernard. Bernard was freckle faced and good natured. He would say

"If you ever go to New York and you see a place called 'Bernie's Burgers'—that will be my place. When I'm old enough, I'll be off to New York to make my fortune."
"What happened to your hair? Did you not do the rinse?" Polly said
"Oh yes I did and I'll tell you all about that later. You don't notice the color at first but under certain lights and outside in the sun, it is quite nice."

Off we went on the bus to Harcourt Street. Polly thought the story about the orange jelly was hilarious.

"I can just imagine your mother" she said "She was probably ready to kill you."
"She was nearly not letting me go to the dance. But she got over it and she loaned me her jewelry."

We got off the bus at The Four Provinces. The admission was three shillings and sixpence. There was a big burly fellow standing by the entrance. Polly told me he was the bouncer and an ex boxer. If anyone misbehaved or caused any trouble, he was the one to throw them out. We left our coats in the cloakroom and entered the ballroom. I was mesmerized at the size and the beauty of it, the shiny maple dance floor and the soft pink lighting. There were seven musicians sitting behind music stands and a fat girl wearing a black evening gown standing out in front of the band singing in a beautiful clear voice the "Unchained Melody"—

"Oh, my love, my darling I hunger for your touch A long lonely time"

There was seating all around the perimeter mostly occupied by girls. I said to Polly

"Where are the men?" She said
"Oh, they'll be along. They go to the pub for a few jars before they come in. It gives them courage."

There was no alcohol served in the ballrooms.

We were barely sitting down when this red faced awkward looking fellow nodded at Polly—his way of asking her to dance. I watched them disappear into the crowds. When Polly came back; she was all hot and bothered

"If that galute comes near you, don't dance with him. There is a terrible smell of booze off him and he has two left feet, he trampled all over my good shoes."

The next tune was "Always" and Polly was asked up again. I was beginning to feel like a wallflower. The men were slowly straggling in from the pubs. A young fellow with a pimply face and big ears nodded in my direction. He wasn't a bad dancer but he had awful sweaty hands. He said he came from County Cavan and he was living in digs in Harold's Cross. At the interval between the dances he looked down at me and said

"You know, you have a funny little squezzed up face."

If this hadn't been so funny, I would have been insulted. I couldn't wait to tell Polly and indeed the whole family when I got home.

For the next dance, Polly's boozy partner came back to her. She grabbed my hand quickly and said to him

"I'm sorry we were just heading to The Ladies."

In the bathroom there were crowds of girls pushing to get near the mirrors. A sweet mixture of perfume and perspiration filled the air. My cheeks were on fire and I held them against the cool tiles on the wall to tone them down. This only succeeded in making them hotter.

As we returned to the ballroom, the band was playing "Some Enchanted Evening" and Polly was off again.

I was sitting demurely on the bench when an elderly gentleman approached me. He smiled, bowed and said in a posh accent

"May I have the pleasure of this dance?"

He moved beautifully to the music and he complimented me on my dancing which was only because I was able to follow his expert lead.

He was of medium height, with graying hair, soft brown eyes and a moustache. He was immaculately groomed and dressed in a well-cut dark suit. He thanked me for the dance and as intermission was being announced he asked me if I would join him in some refreshment. Upstairs he found me a seat while he went on the queue to get us cold drinks and fairy cakes. We chatted easily. He told me his name was John Lucan Hillwood. He was of Irish ancestry and he was educated in public schools in England. He was an only child and seemed fascinated by the fact that I came from such a large family.

"Ladies Choice" was announced and I invited John to dance with me. He said he was flattered to be asked "by the loveliest girl in the ballroom". This may have been a mistake on my part as I think I led him to believe I had a romantic interest in him. He was far from the tall, dark and handsome knight of my dreams.

I was watching the clock and I told Polly we had to leave as I had to be home by eleven. I knew very well the consequences if I was late.

I said goodnight to John and thanked him. He wanted to leave me home but I told him I had to go with my girl friend. He said he would like to see me again and would it be alright if he met me at my office after work on Monday. I couldn't go on Monday because, like all young girls at the time, I had to go to The Miraculous Medal. I said he could meet me on Tuesday.

Going home on the bus, Polly said

"Who was that auld fella you were dancing with?"
"Oh he is really nice and he's a beautiful dancer. He wants to take me out on Tuesday."
"How old is he? I'm sure your mother won't let you go with him."
"I didn't ask him his age but I told you he is very nice, unlike the other gurriers I was dancing with."

Lucky for me I was home on time. Mammy was in bed but she was awake. I sat on the side of her bed and told her all about the evening including the remark the fellow made "you have a funny little squezzed up face". I was teased about this for a long time afterwards.

◆

A few weeks earlier Olga had been locked out of the house because she was a few minutes late. She was dating a tall, dark and handsome fellow who looked like Clark Gable. His name was Sean. They were very much in love and they made a handsome couple. My mother didn't approve of Sean and she let Olga know it

"You'll live in poverty your whole life with a ne'er do well like that—a bread delivery man with no prospects and no education."

The night she came home late it was pelting rain and Mammy had locked her out. We heard her knocking but we weren't allowed to open the door. Not knowing what to do, Olga cycled out to Killester to Granny Mooney's house. She stayed with Granny for about a month and had to cycle in to Ballsbridge to work every day. She also had to hand up her pay packet to Granny Mooney just the same as she did at home.

I missed Olga and I felt so sorry for her. Finally she came home looking as glamorous as ever. She had cut and permed her hair and she had on in a new navy costume, a matching beret and oxblood platform shoes. I adored her—I felt loved when she was around.

◆

On Tuesday evening John was waiting for me outside my office. He was immaculately dressed and he had on a soft brown hat. He was so pleased to see me and asked me about my day. He was attentive as I did my best to make the mundane happenings in my boring office sound interesting. We went to The Adelphi Cinema where "Quartet" was playing. These were four beautifully presented stories by one of my favorite authors, W.Somerset Maugham—"The Colonel's Lady", "The Kite", "The Alien Corn" and "The Facts of Life". Each had its own charm and all were enjoyable. As was the custom, he bought me a pound box of Cadbury's Milk Tray chocolates.

After the film, we went to The Bailey in Duke Street for dinner. I never felt so pampered in my life. The Bailey had a delightful ambiance; tables set with snowy white damask, fresh flowers and soft candlelight. Romantic piano music played in the background and delicious aromas emanated from the kitchen. Judging by the attention paid us by the staff; it was obvious they were well acquainted with John. He asked me if I would care for a cocktail. I declined and explained that I had taken the pioneer pledge to abstain from alcohol until I was twenty one. He ordered a gin and tonic for himself and a glass of orange juice for me. As we were looking at the menu, John took out a silver cigarette case and offered me a cigarette. He seemed surprised that I neither smoked nor drank. After all I was only seventeen. He asked me if I minded if he smoked. I didn't mind at all. All adults smoked in those days; my mother, my father, their neighbors and friends, aunts, uncles and Granny and Pappy Mooney. The priests lit up after Mass and even doctors puffed away while doing their rounds in the hospital. The waiter came to take our orders and, upon his recommendation, we both decided on the roast spring lamb.

John was an interesting conversationalist. He was well educated, and he had traveled extensively. He had spent years in Hong Kong as Secretary to the British Colonial Governor. He told me he was 45; I would have guessed he was older.

He said people living in the tropics tended to age earlier due to the hot and humid climate. Although he had a home in London, he planned on settling in Dublin. He liked everything about Dublin—its location at the foot of The Wicklow Mountains, the fine Georgian architecture and most of all the aliveness of Dublin people.

The waiter brought our first course; a delicious light amber clear soup served with little crusty rolls and sweet butter. Next came the roast lamb, I had never tasted anything like it; it was tender and succulent and served with mint sauce, tiny green peas and new potatoes. For dessert, we had raspberries and cream.

I enjoyed the whole experience immensely. John had beautiful manners and he treated me like a china doll. I was looking forward to our next date.

When I got home, Mammy shouted down the stairs

"Is that you Nora? Did you bring any sweets?"

I went upstairs with the box of Cadbury's and we ate them as I sat on the bed relating the details of the evening.

"He's a decent fellow anyway and he sounds nice. When are you seeing him again?
"He's meeting me at my office on Thursday."

I asked her if there was any news and she told she had had another letter from Daddy and she handed it to me to read. Daddy was working down the country with the wireless detection program for the Post Office. He traveled around Cork, Kerry and Limerick. At that time owners of radios were required to pay an annual fee for a license. He didn't like the work. If the poor people didn't have a license it was because they couldn't afford it and he had to threaten them with the confiscation of their only source of news and entertainment. The pay was good and he got plenty of overtime but that didn't compensate for the loneliness he felt at being away from home and his one and only Lily Mia.

◆

When John met me on Thursday he had tickets to see "Carmen" which was playing at the Gaiety Theater off Grafton Street. Since it didn't start until 8:00 o'clock, we had plenty of time to walk to St.Stephen's Green for high tea at The Shelbourne. We went into the Lord Mayor's Lounge where John ordered an orange for me and a Guinness for himself. He lit his pipe and told me the story of "Carmen". I had never been to an opera before. It sounded so interesting I was anxious to see it. He then took a silver locket from his pocket and showed me the picture of his mother. It was the loveliest face I had ever seen; delicate porcelain features, gentle blue eyes and a halo of rich auburn hair.

"She is very beautiful," I said.

"Sadly, she's gone now" he answered "I loved her very much. You look just like her."

Now I knew I looked nothing like her but if that's what he thought why would I disagree?

Our tea arrived—an elegant silver teapot filled with aromatic strong tea, piping hot scones with clotted cream and strawberry jam, dainty cucumber and cress sandwiches and an assortment of delightful little cakes.

I loved everything about "Carmen". The production company came from Madrid and captured all the excitement of old Spain in the tragic love story laced with gypsies, murder and passion. John squeezed my hand; it gave him great pleasure to see how much I was enjoying my first opera. When we came out of the theater he bent down to kiss me. I turned my face and the kiss landed somewhere near my ear. He appeared to be disappointed but the truth was I was not physically attracted to him in the least.

Mammy and Daddy were fond of John and they had no objection to him taking me out. He loved coming to our house and Mammy was always at her charming best when he came—she made a great fuss of him altogether. She would make a fresh pot of tea, use her best china and always had on a nice clean blouse. For his part, he enjoyed the hustle and bustle of our big family which was in direct contrast to his own solitary life in his flat in Merrion Square.

We were having tea at the elegant Hibernian Hotel in Ballsbridge when John shyly handed me a beautifully wrapped little package. He said

"I thought you would enjoy this, darling."

It was a small beautifully bound volume called "Palgrave's Golden Treasury"; a book of the best lyrical poems in the English language. I glanced through it and we discussed some of his favorites: "Past and Present"

"I remember, I remember
The house where I was born"

"Sally in our Alley"

"Of all the girls that are so smart
There's none like pretty Sally;

She is the darling of my heart,
>   And she lives in our alley."

I was touched by his thoughtfulness and thanked him sincerely. To this day, this small volume continues to give me much pleasure.

After tea, we went to a theater in Dun Laoghaire where The International Ballet Company was performing Tchaikovsky's "Swan Lake". This was to be my first ballet. On the way, John told me the love story of Odette and Prince Siegfried.

From the moment the curtain went up, I was enchanted by the drama, the romance, the music, the exquisite dances of the swans and the magnificence of the production. I didn't object to John holding my hand throughout the performance.

◆

Dublin was a treasure trove of good theater. We had ballets from Moscow and London; operas, musicals and dramatic plays from Europe and around the world.

The National Theaters, The Abbey and The Gate, presented plays by Irish writers; Sean O'Casey, James Joyce, J.M.Synge, W.B.Yates, Oscar Wilde, George Bernard Shaw and many more.

At Christmastime, we were treated to the uproariously funny pantomimes. Dublin's famous comedians, Jimmy O'Dea, Maureen Potter, Cecil Sheridan and Harry O'Donovan were the stars.

◆

John was interested in opening a business in Dublin. He discussed several possibilities with my dad. There was a couture type fashion house called Helene's for sale. He wanted my opinion on their work so he took me there and had me fitted for two new frocks. It was obvious the lady Helene herself had designs on John. She was a dark haired attractive woman and much closer to his age than I was. However, he was oblivious to her overtures and continued discussing my fittings. When I brought home the dresses my mother thought they were absolutely beautiful—one was a cocktail dress in white and gold with an unusual zigzag hemline and the other was a pretty summer print pique with a sweetheart neckline. John was pleased and he continued the negotiations to buy the business.

◆

One Saturday afternoon as I was doing my household chores, there was great commotion going on outside. I looked out the window and, parked in front of our door, was a spanking new sand colored Studebaker. Every kid on the road had gathered round to examine this streamlined marvel with its chrome fixtures gleaming in the sunlight. Out stepped John complete with driving gloves and soft hat. I walked out to greet him and he proudly showed me the soft leather interior, the adjustable seats and all the modern gadgets. I congratulated him and said how beautiful I thought it was. He looked at me with great tenderness and said "I bought it for you, darling." I tidied myself up and John took me and as many of the family as would fit in the car for a spin to The Phoenix Park. It was all very exciting and my mother was beside herself

"You'd better hang on to him, it's obvious he's madly in love with you," she said.

"As a matter of fact I was thinking of giving him up" I said, "I love all his lovely ways but he's far too serious about me."

"You'd be a very foolish girl to do that. You've always been delicate and you need someone like him to take care of you. He has pots of money and you'd have a lovely life with him."

"That's all very well, Mammy, but he is just too old for me and I'm not in the least attracted to him."

"It's better to be an old man's darling than a young man's slave, give him a chance, you can grow to love somebody who is that good to you." she said.

◆

John was excited planning on taking me on a picnic to Glendalough. He went to Findlater's in O'Connell Street and bought the finest of foods for our picnic basket. I didn't care for the idea of being out in the country alone with him so I made up an excuse that I had to mind Ada, she was about four at the time. John wasn't too pleased but I felt safer having her along.

Off we sped in the new Studebaker along The Merrion Road to The Vico Road with the magnificent views of Killiney Bay and Dalkey Island, then on to Glendalough—the valley with the two lakes. It was a rare spring day and the journey was delightful. John unfolded a blanket on the fresh green grass. He lit his pipe while we sat enjoying the magnificence of the scenery; the clear blue sky, the still waters of the lake and the Wicklow Mountains in the background. Ada was happily picking daisies and buttercups while John spread out the table cloth. It was a feast for the Gods; cold roast chicken, thin slices of ham, assorted cheeses, crusty French bread, tomatoes, rich fruit cake with thick marzipan on the top, assorted fancy biscuits, luscious black grapes and huge juicy pears. He had a flask of piping hot tea, cups, saucers, napkins and cutlery—he thought of everything. I made a daisy chain for Ada and put it around her neck.

We tidied up after our meal and went on to see the historic church with the round tower oddly named Saint Kevin's Kitchen. Everyone knew the story of Saint Kevin. He was a young hermit monk who, when tempted by a young girl, stripped himself naked and rolled in a bed of stinging nettles to cure his lust. It was said he used to stand in the shallows of the lake and pray all day.

It was a perfectly serene and romantic day except for the fact that I had no romantic inclinations toward John.

◆

The 7th of April was approaching and Mammy was going all out to give Olga a big party for her 21st Birthday and giving her the key of the door—symbolic of becoming an adult. This was the very first birthday party in our house. Mammy and Daddy had plenty of Saturday night parties with their friends but there was never a birthday party for any of the children. We were lucky if anyone remembered it was our birthday at all

"Oh today is the 25th, its Nora's birthday—'Happy Birthday Nora'."

That was about the extent of it.

The house was cleaned and polished from top to bottom. The cake was ordered from a girl in The Sweep and the invitations were issued. Olga was popular and she had a wide circle of friends but only selected ones were invited—Jimmy Maclehose, Irene O'Shea, Terry Shannon and Harry McGill. Harry was like a member of our family—he had dated Olga for a while then he dated Hilda. He was helpful if my mother asked him to do odd jobs around the house. He could make anything and fix anything. He carved the big wooden key for Olga's party. The rest of the guests were Mammy and Daddy's friends. Granny Wright and John were invited.

On the day of the party Mammy was a bit flustered in the kitchen making the sandwiches. Joan came over to the sink to wash her hands and before she knew it Mammy let the knife fly at her and caught her on the wrist

"You careless little bitch, look what you're doing, putting the soap all over the lettuce."

Poor Joan got a great bleeding cut—now there wasn't only soap on the lettuce, there was a river of blood on it as well. Mammy quickly tied a rag around it and shouted at my brother Frank to take her on the crossbar of his bike to Stephens' Hospital. She had to have a few stitches and Mammy told her if anyone asked what happened she was to say she gashed it on a nail in the backyard.

The dining room table with the extra leaves was moved into the center of the lounge and set with Mammy's best ironed and starched linen table cloth and her good blue china which had been one of her wedding presents. In the center of the table was placed the birthday cake on a silver stand. It looked like the top tier of a wedding cake; rich fruit and thick marzipan and elaborately decorated with royal icing. On either side were platters of assorted sandwiches, bowls of raisins and almonds, a huge luscious trifle with tiny silver balls sinking into the heavy whipped cream. There were bowls of jelly and jugs of cream, clusters of purple grapes and a big glass bowl full of chocolates and sweets. On top of the sideboard and in crates on the floor were bottles of minerals and lemonade for the girls and bottles of stout and ale for the men. There was also a bottle of whiskey and a bottle of Sandeman's Sherry. Empty milk bottles covered with crepe paper and filled with tulips were placed on the table and around the house. Long before the guests arrived we were all dressed and ready as the photographer from Ross Studios was coming to take pictures of Olga, the family, and the elaborately set table. Olga was beautiful in a pale turquoise dress with a cape collar. She had her photo taken beside her cake and holding up Harry's key which had been covered with tinfoil paper.

There was great laughter and confusion as the guests started to arrive. Some brought presents and some brought champagne. John gave her a modest little gift of embroidered hankies.

Mammy sat at the piano and asked everyone to join in singing "Happy Birthday" to Olga. Then they all sang the traditional 21st song

> "Twenty-one today!
> Now she's got the key of the door
> She'll never be twenty-one any more
> Her father says she can do what she likes
> So shout Hip-hip-hooray!"

The food was enjoyed by all and the young children were packed off to bed.

Betty Parker, a gifted pianist, entertained us with a sing-a-long of popular songs. We played "Spin the Bottle" and "Postman's Knock"

We coaxed Olga's good friend, Terry Shannon, to sing something for us. He abandoned his crutches and leaned against the piano as he sang in his beautiful tenor voice "che gelida manina" from Puccini's La Boheme,

"Your tiny hand is frozen
Let me warm it into life."

With more pleading, he encored with another one of our favorites—Core n'Grato or "Catharie" as we knew it by. He sang this with great passion. Terry was a frequent visitor to our house and my mother always welcomed him. Like many at the time, he was crippled due to infantile paralysis. This never seemed to bother him, he was always good company and he loved to sing.

Olga sang "Let the Rest of the World go by" and everyone joined in.

Next, Uncle Star was called upon to do his party piece "Feeding the Ducks in the Pond". As usual, he wouldn't start until my mother scattered pieces of bread about the floor. By this time, he was well oiled and the song was hilarious. Not to be outdone, Auntie Annie sang "Hold Your Hand out, You Naughty Boy" which was also very funny.

John left the party early and gradually the young people left. The birthday party evolved into the usual Saturday night get-together with Mammy and Daddy's friends.

◆

"Old John" as I had begun to call him was becoming more and more attentive. One day as we were sitting in the lobby of The Russell we were admiring a little girl who was standing beside her mother. She was a charming child with fair curls to her waist and dressed in a perfectly tailored little coat. John took my hand and said,

"Perhaps one day we shall have a little girl like that."

This upset me. Obviously we were not thinking along the same lines. There was no way I was having any little girl with John. I told him that while I enjoyed his company I could never marry him—there was too great a difference in our ages. He said he would like to continue to see me because his only happiness was when he was in my company.

He took me to his service club in Stephen's Green to introduce me to his friends.

This was an exclusive club. The members were wealthy retired gentlemen who went there to pick up their mail and relax in the comfortably furnished rooms. He introduced me around and said to me afterwards "I knew they would all love you."

I was becoming uncomfortable with the relationship and had to think of a way of ending it without hurting this gentle man's feelings. He wasn't happy when Hilda and I signed up for evening classes at Rathmines Tech. That meant I couldn't see him on Tuesdays and Thursdays or on Mondays which was my Miraculous Medal night. He mentioned that it would be necessary for him to go to London in the near future to settle his estate. I thought this would be a good opportunity, I would not see him when he came back.

He bought tickets for us to hear Yehudi Menuhin at the Gaiety. I had never heard of this violinist before and as was his practice, he told me all about him during dinner at Jammet's restaurant. Menuhin was American born and the foremost virtuoso of our time. He appeared as solo violinist with the San Francisco Symphony at the age of seven. He toured widely and later conducted the Bath Festival Orchestra. He moved to London where he was knighted. The music was classical and very much over my head—John was positively enraptured.

On the weekends we went in the Studebaker to picnic in the most scenic spots; Killiney with its magnificent views of The Wicklow Mountains or to Howth Castle where we were surrounded by a magnificent display of rhododendrons. I always took Joan or Doris or Ada along with us. This didn't please John—he wanted to be alone with me.

We often strolled around town looking in the shop windows. This particular day I was admiring a beautiful coat in The French Shop in Wicklow Street. John turned to me and said

"Would you like it, darling?"
"Oh no thank you," I said.

I knew it would be expensive. The French Shop was an exclusive little boutique and I didn't want him buying me presents when I planned on leaving him.

On my 18th Birthday, John arrived at our house carrying a huge box elegantly wrapped. He was as excited as a child.

"Happy birthday, darling" he said handing me the box.

I was nervous opening it, my fingers were shaking. Under the mounds of tissue paper was the magnificent coat I had admired in The French Shop. It was a fitted beige coat with tiny buttons and mink trim. Mammy was speechless

"Try it on," she said.

It was a perfect fit

"My God, you look like a film star."

She ran Frank out the back door to buy a sponge cake in The Monument and she put the kettle on for John's tea.
I thanked John and said

"You shouldn't have done that. I know it must have been very expensive."
"It was a pleasure buying it for you, darling."

We continued to go out to dinners, shows and ballroom dancing until it was time for John to go to London. We were having our "farewell" dinner in the Shelbourne and John was talking of his plans for us when he returned.

"I'm sorry John; I won't be seeing you when you come back."

He was silent for a moment, his face ashen. He kissed my hand

"I was afraid of that. You must know by now how dearly I love you. I thought eventually you might grow to love me too."
"I do love you as the most kind and considerate person I've ever met but the difference in our ages is too great and there could be nothing more than a beautiful friendship."

When I came home Mammy and Daddy were sitting at the fire smoking and listening to the news on the radio. I handed Mammy the box of "Black Magic"

"Oh lovely" she said "Where did you go?"

She loved hearing all the details.

"Well" I said "I finally did it, I broke up with him and I won't be seeing him when he comes back from London"
"Oh my God, you'll be sorry me lady. Mark my words, you'll never find anyone like him again."
"I think she did the right thing Lily" said Daddy "After all he is my age and

she could be left a very young widow."

"Yes, and a very rich one too!"

John wrote to me from London but I never answered his letters. He didn't die of a broken heart though—Daddy saw him around town a few times with a certain attractive dark haired lady much nearer his own age. I missed him; he was so good to me. In the few months I had known him, he introduced me to fine literature, the ballet, the opera and classical music. Most of all, he awakened in me an appreciation of the beauty of the city of Dublin. He was a gentle man and a perfect gentleman.

11

Dismissed

"There is nothing permanent except change."

—Heraclitus

One morning old Keats was in an unusually good mood.

"I've great news" he said "Miss Hartnett has left the convent and she wants her old job back."
"Oh" I said "Do you think there is enough work here for both of us?"
"No, there isn't, but in fairness to you, you can stay until you find another job. You have done your best and I will give you a good reference."

I wasn't a bit upset. I couldn't have stayed there much longer. I didn't like old Keats, the office was depressing and the work was boring. Besides, John used to meet me there and I was just as happy to be gone before his return from his trip.

Miss Harnett came in that afternoon. She was a typical ex nun. She had salt and pepper tightly-permed hair, a sensible tweed skirt and laced up Red Cross shoes. She had buck teeth and nice eyes. It was evident that she and the old man got along well together.

◆

There were plenty of jobs in the Situations Vacant for stenographers and secretaries. Daddy marked off the ones he thought were suitable for me and I sent in my applications. Some I never heard from and others gave me an interview. One interview I went on was an architect's office in Dawson Street. A snobby looking fellow interviewed me and asked me all kinds of ridiculous questions that had nothing to do with shorthand and typing

"Now tell me, Miss Wright, do you have any hobbies?"

Trying to think of the right thing to say, I said

"Oh yes, I like to read and I like to travel (I had only been as far as Wicklow) I am also fond of stamp collecting"

Then he said with a smirk

"So you're a bit of a 'philanthropist' are you?
"Oh yes" I replied pretending I knew what he meant.

I was embarrassed afterwards when I was telling Daddy about the interview and he said

"Bernie I'm surprised at you, you should know that a stamp collector is known as a 'philatelist'. A 'philanthropist' is someone who gives away loads of money to the needy. I think he was trying to trip you up."

I didn't get the job.

◆

My next interview was with The International Chemical Company in Island-bridge. This was a British Company and I was interviewed by a Mr. R.H. Boyd who was the Irish representative. He was a kindly man and he asked me normal questions

"Why are you leaving your present job?"

I told him the truth about the return of the nun. I didn't say I hated old frosty face and that I was glad to be leaving.

"How are your bookkeeping skills?"

My skills were OK. I didn't say I detested bookkeeping.

"Do you think you could work on your own initiative?"

Now what could that mean? Was I supposed to make responsible decisions for the Company?

"Oh yes, I believe so" I answered with all the confidence I didn't have.

He called in the office manager

"Mrs.Granby, this is Miss Wright. Would you please set up the usual tests for her?"

The tests were more difficult than I expected but since they were paying very well, seven pounds ten shillings a week, they were looking for someone efficient. When I had finished Mrs. Granby thanked me and said I would hear one way or the other within a few days.

I told Mammy I didn't have much hope of getting the job.

"It would be beautiful if you did, and the place only down the road, you could walk to work. The money is terrific; I'll make a novena that you'll get it."

Sure enough, within a few days I got a letter saying I had been hired.

The International Chemical Company offices and factory were located on The South Circular Road at Islandbridge. Islandbridge got its name from its position at the junction of the Camac and the River Liffey. It was formerly known as Sarah Bridge and it linked Kilmainham to The Phoenix Park. There was a large working mill wheel on the property which may have been used to power the factory.

The company manufactured packaged and distributed pharmaceuticals for Wyeth Company. They also manufactured Anadin, MacLeans Toothpaste, Anne French cosmetics and Lucozade.

From my very first day I loved working there. The offices were modern, bright and airy. There were fresh green plants all around and an ashtray on every desk. Anyone could smoke any time they liked. I had a brand new electric typewriter fitted with a wide platen; this was to accommodate the large pages I used in typing up the monthly cumulative figures.

There were ten girls and two men in the office; most of them cheerful and helpful. The company provided us with office coats. Some of the girls complained but I didn't mind them. For one thing I liked the color, hunter green, I thought it suited me. I also liked the style, buttoned down the middle, a belt and two handy patch pockets. I was relieved not to have to think about wearing different dresses every day.

One of the perks was the delicious hot lunches which were provided every day at nominal cost for the factory workers and the office staff. Tuesdays were the best—they served my favorite—steaming hot bread pudding loaded with plump raisins, cinnamon and nutmeg. Another perk was that we got to take home all the dinged tubes of toothpaste, the cosmetics that were slightly damaged and an end-less supply of Anadin.

I loved the morning and afternoon tea breaks when we sat around in a friendly circle by the window discussing everything; operas, plays, pictures they had been to, romances or new clothes. They often brought in their purchases for us to admire. Invariably, someone passed around the latest copy of "Modern Screen" "Photoplay" or "Woman's Own". We were interested in the film stars and the latest trends in fashions and hair styles. Dublin girls took great pride in their appearance.

I enjoyed the walk to work every day. It would have been healthy exercise had I worn sensible walking shoes but I wouldn't be caught dead wearing "Mary Hick" shoes—besides I had to pass The Orchard every day. The Orchard was a fruit shop on the corner of Emmet Road and The South Circular and a well known Dublin meeting place. There was always a group of good looking young men hanging about inside. They would smile and wave at me as I teetered by in my high heels. The discomfort of my feet was well worth the price of looking glamorous.

◆

Olga said to me,

"You need to do something with your hair, Nody. There's a great place in Nassau Street—'Jimmis'—all the girls in The Sweep go there. I'll make an appointment for you. I'm sure you would look lovely in a poodle cut."

I agreed. The poodle was a short curly style and popular at the time.

Off we went on Saturday morning. Olga had to go somewhere so she left me at "Jimmis" but she said she would come back for me in an hour. This was my first time ever in a hairdressing salon. It was crowded, noisy and intimidating. There were mirrors everywhere. Mr. Scissorhands came over to me

"I understand we are to cut all this hair off today" he said in a high—pitched girlie voice
"Yes" I said, assuming that Olga had told him what I wanted.
"Follow me to the shampoo bowls" he said mincing along to the back.

He sat me in a high chair then hiked it up some more. He put a black cape around my shoulders and started cutting; snip, snip, my crowning glory was falling to the floor. I couldn't bear to watch. I closed my eyes, the tears were stinging them and I was hot and uncomfortable. He was taking the cape off me

"Now my dear, what do you think?" he said holding up yet another mirror to my face. I was speechless, it was a disaster. He had cut my hair straight around in a bob with a fringe over my eyes. Only school children wore their hair like that.
"You'll find it is so much easier to care for now" he said patronizingly.

I was in a daze as I paid the cashier the fifteen shillings. I had a headache and I wanted to vomit. I had a headscarf in my pocket and I put it on. In misery I waited outside for Olga. I was glad of the cold and the rain.

"What's the matter with you? Were you crying?"
"Oh Olga he ruined me, my hair is dreadful, I'm like a plucked chicken."
"Well let me have a look at it."

I took off the scarf

"You're being silly. It's lovely and healthy looking. You just have to get used to it, that's all. Let's go and have a nice cup of tea at Mitchell's."

On Sunday afternoon when everyone was out, I took the kitchen scissors to my own hair. I layered it two inches all over and set it in pin curls. When it was dry I brushed it out and I was pleased with the results. I now had a poodle cut.
The girls in the office said it was lovely and that I looked like the film star, Jean Simmons. I didn't, but my new hair cut was similar to hers and I had brought my eyebrows up to date by thickening them with an eyebrow pencil.

◆

At that time the most important things in life for girls were beauty of person, a pleasant manner and good style. Their destiny was marriage; their lives depended on the quality of husband they got. Higher education was not encouraged as women did not work outside the home after marriage.

12

An Bhfuil Gaelic Agat?

✦

(Do you speak Irish?)

"…….I am always sorry when any language is lost, for languages are
the pedigree of nations."

—Johnson

Uncle Gary was President of The Friendly Sons of Saint Patrick. This was an
Irish organization in Michigan and Uncle Gary was proud of the fact that he was
born in Ireland. He wrote to my mother asking if she would come over and bring
clay pipes, shillelaghs and Irish Flags. He wanted to distribute these to his board
members. Mammy didn't have to be persuaded; she loved America and Uncle
Gary was paying all expenses.

She was getting ready and trying out the latest hair style for the trip—this was
called "the roll". She cut a length of nylon stocking and knotted it to make a hair
band. She combed all of her hair forward over her face, put the hair band on top
of her head, and then tucked her hair piece by piece into the band to form the
roll. The family said it was lovely and would it be easy for her to manage.

Daddy went to the airport with her and told her not to worry about anything;
Hilda was capable of running the household.

Gary and my mother were fond of each other. At a big celebration he introduced her as his sister who had come all the way from Ireland. After a huge round
of applause, the people started asking Mammy questions

"You speak very good English, where did you learn it?"
"Thank you. We speak English in Ireland but I also speak Irish fluently"
"Oh Lily we'd love to hear it, could you say something for us in Irish?"

Now she was in trouble. The only Gaelic she knew was The Hail Mary. Undaunted, she cleared her throat, took a swallow of her drink, and began

"Se do bheatha, Mhuire
ta lan de ghrasta
ta an Tiarna leat
Is beannaithe thu idir mna"

and all the way to the end. When she was finished she smiled and sat down. Everyone clapped.

"Lily, that was wonderful, could you translate it for us?

Never at a loss for words and having the gift of being able to think on her feet, she took a deep breath, glanced around the room and began

"I said it is a real pleasure for me to be your guest here tonight. Everyone has been so kind to me. Americans are the most generous and hospitable people in the world. I can't wait to get home and tell everyone in Ireland of the marvelous time I've had here. You have made me feel most welcome. God bless all of you and God Bless America."

More applause and congratulations. Gary was thrilled—he couldn't have picked a better representative from Ireland.

The Americans loved Mammy. She was invited to dinner parties by everyone who was anyone in Grand Rapids. She was full of *plamas* (flattery) and never lost an opportunity to compliment them on their appearance, their homes, or their lovely children. The ladies were intrigued by her hair style and she demonstrated to them how it was done.

◆

We were having a great time at home while Mammy was away. Hilda was economical with the budget and she always managed to save a few shillings for us to go dancing. It was lovely not to have an 11:00 o'clock curfew. We could stay for the "Goodnight Sweetheart" at the end of the dance at midnight. Hilda and I were talking about moving out on our own. We hadn't been too happy—Mammy couldn't forgive Hilda for leaving America or me for giving up old John. We decided to look at the ads for flats to rent. After looking at a few, we found one we liked in Rathmines. We told the landlady, Mrs. O'Neill, we wouldn't need it for about a month. She was understanding and she said, with a pound deposit, she would hold it for us as we seemed to be nice respectable girls. We gave her the pound and although we were a bit nervous taking such a bold step we convinced ourselves we were doing the right thing.

Mammy came home delighted with herself. She had had a wonderful time and she related everything that happened including the funny story of her speech in Irish. She brought toys and sweets for the younger children and silk scarves and nylons for us. Nylons were scarce and expensive. If we got a run, we took them to the Lyknu shop and paid to have them repaired. A little man sat in the window of the shop and painstakingly picked up all the dropped stitches.

We waited a couple of days before breaking the news. Hilda, being the eldest, had the pleasure

> "Mammy, we want to talk to you. Nora and I are thinking of moving out."
> "What do you mean moving out? Moving out where?
> "We found a flat in Rathmines and we're going at the end of the month."
> "Mother of God is this what happens the minute my back is turned. No decent girl would leave her good home to live in a flat, it's only the ones who are up to no good would do a thing like that. I hope the two of you have plenty of money. You know, as well as your food and bus fares, you will have to buy sheets, pillows and bedclothes. You will also need pots and pans and delph. Don't think for a minute you are taking any of those things from here.
> And, me ladies, I hope you know that on top of your rent you will have to pay for gas, electricity and water. No doubt, the two of you are so smart, you have already thought about these things."

No, we hadn't thought about those things. Mammy was very clever. She knew if she frightened us enough we wouldn't leave. If we left, she would lose my good pay and she would have been lost without Hilda's help in the house and with the younger children. Also it would have been necessary for Hilda to leave Daddy's shop and find a job that paid enough to meet our expenses.

We decided to postpone our plans. We rang Mrs. O'Neill to tell her we wouldn't be taking the flat after all. We lost our pound deposit.

◆

With a sense of relief and to prove to Hilda how foolish she would have been to move out, my mother began elaborate preparations for Hilda's 21st birthday.

She did as much, if not more, than she had done for Olga. The house was cleaned and polished from top to bottom. This was done mostly by Hilda herself. Hilda was a regular little "Martha". She was fast and efficient and she took great pride in seeing a spotless, orderly house.

The cake was ordered and some of Hilda's selected friends invited. Mammy and Daddy's friends were naturally invited too. The dining room table was magnificently set with an array of tempting foods and fresh flowers for decoration. There were cases of minerals and plenty of assorted drinks.

Hilda looked lovely in a black and cerise dress and she had her photograph taken beside her cake and holding the same key that Harry had made for Olga. Mammy sat at the piano and everyone joined in singing the traditional 21st birthday song. Betty Parker then led us in a sing-a-long of all the popular tunes. We ate, we drank and we played party games. A good time was had by all. After the young people left the party continued with Mammy and Daddy's friends into the wee hours of the morning.

13

The King's Shilling

'The army is a school where obedience is taught,
and discipline is enforced; where bravery becomes
a habit and morals too often are neglected..."

—Ladd

Daddy enrolled my brother, Billy, in McNally's Commercial College. He thought Billy had more brains than brawn and that clerical work would suit him. It didn't. He worked for a while as a solicitor's clerk in Middle Abbey Street and then as a clerk in Roadstone on the Naas Road. He detested clerical work and made up his mind to do what many of the local lads were doing—join The British Army. Daddy was noncommittal about his decision and Mammy wasn't happy at all. Nevertheless she gave him his train fare to Belfast. Off he went at age seventeen to sign up for five years. Many of the Irish lads were criticized for taking the king's shilling. They had no alternative, their families needed the money. Jobs were still scarce and the army offered good pay, an education and a chance to see the world. Billy was assigned to the R.E.M.E unit—Royal Electrical and Mechanical Engineers—the same unit as Her Majesty, Queen Elizabeth, served in during World War 11. He worked mainly as a vehicle mechanic and his salary was four pounds per week. He made arrangements that his pay be signed over to Mammy except for a few shillings for himself for the occasional packet of cigarettes or a beer. As he said, he didn't need much money; his uniforms, meals and housing were all provided by Her Majesty.

Billy wrote home regularly and sent pictures of himself in his uniform. I can still see Mammy standing in the kitchen looking at his picture and wiping her tears with the end of her apron

"I'm sure those boots are too tight on him."

Billy advanced from Private to Craftsman, to Lance Corporal and Corporal. He came home on short leaves before being shipped on "The Empress Pride" to Korea. It took five weeks to reach Korea. He had a stopover in Hiroshima, Japan. He said little evidence remained of the devastation caused by the atomic bombs dropped by the U.S in 1945. 130,000 people were killed in those blasts. Next Billy was stationed in Cyprus where he continued to recover and repair attacked and damaged equipment. When his time was served, he was happy to be home and alive. He didn't talk too much of where he had been or what he had done and seen.

◆

Although my brother Frank was the middle child, he displayed none of the negativity associated with a middle child. When he was a toddler just learning to talk his first words were "working—Mammy all the money". He was a hard worker, an independent thinker, a peacemaker and unspoiled He never asked for help for himself but he would oblige anyone else. In the summer of his 13th year he lined up outside Guinness' Brewery before 5:00 a.m. in the hopes of getting a day laborer's job. He usually did get hired and he spent his days from 5:00 a.m. until 8:00 p.m. in the racking shed filling barrels with Guinness' porter.

When Frank was 14, my mother's brother offered him a job at Blackwood Hodge on The Naas Road. He was hired as an apprentice machinist in the engineering department. At the time, Blackwood Hodge was rebuilding marine engines for The Liffey Dockyards. Frank worked there for four years and the training he got was invaluable. Like all of us, his pay packet was handed up to my mother every week unopened. Uncle Frank was to be a great influence on his future success.

◆

The older members of the family were now nicely settled and contributing money to the household. The younger children; Joan, Doris, Jack and Ada were enjoying a charmed life. The schools were now distributing free milk and sandwiches. There were new radiators to heat the classrooms and there were cloakrooms where the children could hang up their coats and change their wet shoes.

There was no doubt that my mother was now "ar mhuin na muice"—on the pig's back. There was money for everything. All the children had new Holy Communion and Confirmation outfits. Mammy's good friend, Gwen, who lived on The Inchicore Road, was kept busy sewing matching outfits for Joan and Doris.

Ada was even allowed to have a cat. In winter there was plenty of coal for the fire and the children had warm woolen socks, clean underwear and new shoes that fit. At Christmastime "Santy" brought dolls' prams and dolls with massive hair for the girls and toy guns and trains for Jack; it didn't matter if they were good children or not. They still went to Laytown every summer for their holidays.

Plans were being drawn to build an extension on to the house; a new kitchen and a proper bathroom. Mammy was now in her forties and the years and the good life had mellowed her. She was not nearly as strict with the younger children as she had been with us. In a way, the second half was like a different family.

14

A Circle of Friends

"He alone has lost the art to live who cannot win new friends."

—S.Weir Mitchell

The staff at R.H.Boyd readily accepted me into their office family. They were full of life and great fun. They did wonders for my morale. They were generous with compliments and included me in their social activities. They were all in or about my own age except for the manager, Mrs. Granby and Eileen Carney. Mrs. Granby was middle aged. She had a nice face, big square hands and thick piano legs and ankles. She was separated from her no-good alcoholic husband and she lived in Bluebell with her daughter, Grainne. She ran a tight ship but for the most part she was even tempered and fair. She was like a mother hen; every Saturday morning she marched us into the factory and weighed each one of us on the big industrial scale. She recorded our weight in a notebook and if anyone had gained weight they weren't allowed any biscuits with their tea the following week.

Eileen had worked there for many years. She had never married and she lived alone. She was hunched over from arthritis in her spine and her fingers were knotted and gnarled from the same complaint. Although she was not blessed with good looks, her face was made beautiful by the beauty of her mind and soul shining through it. The girls came to her with their problems, especially stories of romances that had gone wrong. She listened sympathetically and always had something wise and comforting to say

"Don't worry pet, if he's in a bandbox you'll get him if it's meant to be."

I had some wonderful times with the girls from the office. We spent many an enjoyable evening at The Theatre Royal. The Royal was the largest cinema in Dublin. It combined movies with variety stage shows. Dublin's famous comedian, Jimmy O'Dea often topped the bill. They had a dancing troop called The Royalettes mod-

eled after The Rockettes at Radio City Music Hall. We loved the sing along before
the movie with Tommy Dando playing popular songs on the Compton organ.

In fine weather we cycled out to Tallaght to pick blackberries. With the addi-
tion of sugar and a few sliced apples, Mammy made huge pots of the most delicious blackberry jam. My brothers could demolish a whole loaf of bread slathered
with butter and blackberry jam at one sitting.

We went to each other's homes and gave each other Toni's (permanents) and
we swapped clothes for special occasions.

Ivor Braydon worked in the executive office as an assistant to Mr. Boyd. He
was a great big fat fellow with a red moon face and fingers like plump little sausages. He was full of himself because he attended University College Dublin and
he lived on Mespil Road in Ranelagh. He came into our office to dictate the letters. I was sending out letters to places in Ireland with the strangest names; Borris
On Ossory, Belgooly and Mullinahone.

Peter O'Brien lived on The South Circular Road and he walked me home from
work every day. He was a tall good looking fellow, younger than I and still in school.
He told me I was very witty and I had lovely slanty eyes. I refused to go out with him
because he was too young. He still came every day, rain or shine, and walked me to
our front gate where he kissed me goodbye in broad daylight. The office girls thought
he was lovely and said I was mean not to go out with him.

◆

Two girls from the office, Peg and Anne, were accomplished Irish dancers and
they often went to the ceilis at The Mansion House. I went with them occasionally—the ceili band was wonderful. There were always more girls than fellows
there but that didn't matter because most of the dances were set dances. The
dance master went over the routines to The Walls of Limerick and The Bridge of
Athlone—everybody knew the eight handed reel.

I was dancing to the waltz "Come Back to Erin" with a fresh faced young
fellow. He told me his name was Dennis, he pronounced it "Dinnis", and that he
worked as a chemist in O'Connell Street. He said I was a beautiful dancer and
asked me if I would go to the pictures with him on the following Wednesday. We
agreed to meet at eight under Clery's clock (a well known meeting spot in
Dublin). On Wednesday I got all dressed up but I didn't have the bus fare to go
into town. I asked my mother for a loan of sixpence. She wouldn't give it to me

"If you weren't so extravagant spending all your money on foolishness you would have your fare. Anyway it's a freezing cold night and you would be better off staying at home."

I was sitting there moping all dressed up and nowhere to go when my brother, Frank, came to my rescue. He loaned me the sixpence and off I went. I arrived at Clery's in plenty of time at ten minutes to eight. Eight o'clock came and no sign of "Dinnis". There was a biting east wind cutting the face off me. I huddled in a doorway. Twenty after and still no sign of him. At half past eight I gave up. It only dawned on me then that I had no money to take the bus home. There was nothing for it but to walk the long way in high heel shoes and in the bitter cold. As I turned into the John's Road, the heel of my shoe snapped and I had to hobble up and down the rest of the way chilled to the bone and exhausted. I was cursing "Dinnis" for being such an ignoramus and cursing myself for being so stupid and not listening to Mammy.

When I recounted my story to the girls, Eileen said

"Never mind love, that's happened to all of us. If he was so ignorant, it is just as well you didn't go out with him, you're too good for the likes of him."

◆

I signed up for dramatic arts at Grafton Productions in Gardiner Place with a girl from the office named Grace Mary. Grace Mary looked like Ingrid Bergman. She had bobbed hair and a fringe. She wore lovely clothes and she was blessed with talent. We had a great time and the classes were interesting. We did breathing exercises and learned the art of speaking clearly and distinctly. We learned how to sit without looking at the chair and about weight distribution and proper balance. I loved the tongue twisters we did for vocal exercises

"A shot silk sash shop full of Surah silk sashes"

"The Duke paid money due to the Jew before the dew was off the grass on Tuesday and the Jew having duly acknowledged it said adieu to the Duke for ever."

◆

Mammy shopped around and interviewed several contractors before she gave the job to Mr.O'Reilly. He offered her the best price and he seemed to be honest and to know what he was doing. After months of hammering, banging and the floor being torn up to lay the new plumbing pipes, the new extension was ready. The original kitchen, minus the bathtub with the lid, now became the dining room. Mammy bought the kitchen windows second hand and Mr.O'Reilly had to build the walls to fit the windows. He didn't mind. He was an easy going skinny little man and he was anxious to please. He wore overalls and glasses and he whistled and smoked as he worked. Mammy gave him his lunch every day so that he wouldn't waste time going home. The new kitchen had plenty of cupboards and even a portable washing machine. We had a chair rail installed and Mammy painted the top half of the walls glossy white and the bottom half red. She decided to go to Cavendish's and buy a brand new tubular kitchen set on the hire purchase—something she had never done in her life before. The problem was the kitchen set she liked only came in green and that didn't match up with her red walls. She repainted her red walls green.

A door from the kitchen led into the new bathroom. Such luxury—the bathtub, sink and toilet were the latest; apple green enamel with shiny chrome faucets. Mr. O'Reilly had a problem with his measuring—the walls of the bathroom didn't quite reach the ceiling. There was a gap of about four inches of fresh air coming in at all times. In a way it was good because we didn't have a problem with condensation and the mirror never fogged up. Another inconvenience was the glass panel in the ceiling. It didn't afford much privacy and once we caught Gickey McGuire up on the roof ogling down at Olga as she took her bath.

15

Some Enchanted Evening

"You may see a stranger
Across a crowded room
And somehow you know...."

—Rodgers and Hammerstein

Hilda and I took the whole afternoon to get ready for the dance at The Crystal. We washed and pin curled our hair. Hilda starched and ironed her white broidery anglaise blouse and ironed her navy polka dotted skirt. I decided to wear a Chinese style flame colored silk dress that had come from America.

The Crystal was magical. As we entered the vocalist, Jon Clarke, was singing the hauntingly beautiful "Mona Lisa". The glittering crystal ball was rotating and casting enchantment around the ballroom. Jon Clarke was very popular with the ladies. He was tall, dark and handsome and known as Ireland's Nat King Cole. He had a deep brown velvet voice and he sang all the romantic songs of the day. The female vocalist was a redheaded colleen named Carmel Quinlan. Although we weren't impressed with her in Ireland, she won fame and fortune in the U.S. She appeared regularly on The Arthur Godfrey Show and played up her stage Irishness by talking about "me Mammy's brown bread" and about the pigs sleeping in the kitchen.

I had several dances with easily forgotten partners and then when the band was playing "Some Enchanted Evening", this tall, thin, fair haired fellow asked me politely if I would care to dance with him. He was a good leader and, in a refined accent, told me his name was David and he was a medical student at Trinity College. At the end of the dance he didn't return me to my seat but continued talking to me. He told me he was a twin and that his brother was in the British Navy. He also had a young sister. He asked me about my life and he was genuinely interested. He said his favorite aunt was named Norah (with the aitch) and that she lived in Clontarf. The next number was the romantic "Tennessee

Waltz" and we danced together again. He thanked me for the dance and took me over to meet his roommate Ken. I introduced him to Hilda. The "Ladies' Choice" was next and he was pleased that I asked him. He danced with me exclusively for the rest of the evening. He was from New Hampshire in England and he was 22. I was 20. At the end of the dance when the band was playing "Auf wiederseh'n Sweetheart" he asked if he could see me home. I told him I was going home with Hilda and he asked if he could see me again. We agreed to meet on Sunday at 3:00 p.m. at the bus stop in College Green.

I told Hilda on the way home I thought I had met my soul mate. I liked everything about David; his kind gentle face and slightly absent-minded charm. He had a beautiful smile and humorous, intelligent blue eyes. The fact that he was studying to be a doctor appealed to me since, for as long as I could remember, I was interested in the field of medicine.

I took extra care getting myself ready on Sunday. Hilda loaned me her new blue cardigan and I wore it buttoned down the back. I felt good if a little nervous. David met me at the bus stop. He was smiling and happy to see me. He said I looked lovely in blue and that was his favorite color. He took my hand as we walked over to Trinity College. I had never been inside the gates before. Catholics were not allowed to attend Trinity until 1970 when the hierarchy lifted the ban. At that time the college drastically reduced its intake of British students and Irish Catholics were allowed to attend. As we entered the front gate, he talked to me about the statues of the two famous Irishmen, Edmund Burke and Oliver Goldsmith. We crossed the cobbled way and into the library's long room where I saw the 8th Century Book of Kells for the first time. He told me the history of the great buildings of the college. I hung on to his every word.

It was getting chilly and he suggested we go to his rooms for a cup of tea. We climbed the rickety old staircase to Number 13. We were greeted by his roommate, Ken, who had a big fire blazing and the kettle on for our tea. David fried some eggs which we had with bread and butter and then we had chocolate biscuits. The rooms were shabby. The furniture was comfortable but well worn and there were books everywhere. He proudly showed me a carving he was doing of his family crest.

After tea, we queued up for over an hour in the rain at The Grafton to see Charlie Chaplin and Claire Bloom in "Limelight". The music alone was well worth the wait in the rain. Charlie Chaplin wrote the theme, known to us as "Eternally", and he won an Oscar for best original score.

I'll be loving you
Eternally
With a love that's true
Eternally
From the start within my heart it seems I've always known
The sun would shine when you were mine and mine alone....

David held my hand throughout the movie and told me I had lovely soft little hands. He left me home just in time to catch his last bus back to town. We made arrangements to meet on the following Wednesday. It was a perfect day and I had never been happier.

David didn't have much money. He had an allowance from a family trust to pay his tuition and living expenses. He was from a privileged upper class but his family had lost most of their wealth because of high taxation. I had no money to contribute; I still had to hand up my pay packet unopened and I got back barely enough to clothe myself. I still had to pay for the American clothes. Nevertheless, although we were not dining at The Shelbourne or Jammet's, we enjoyed simple outings together.

Some Sunday afternoons we took the bus out to Powerscourt in County Wicklow. There we spent the day enjoying the beautifully laid out gardens, the lakes, the waterfall and the spectacular view of The Sugar Loaf. David had a great appreciation of nature and he could identify every tree and shrub. He also knew the history of the fine statuary on the estate. We enjoyed reading the inscriptions on the headstones in the pet cemetery. Back in town in the evenings we had a simple meal in one of the cozy inexpensive coffee shops.

Other Sundays I spent the afternoons typing up his medical notes. This I loved. I found the medical terminology fascinating and he patiently explained to me what words like postural hypotension and macular degeneration were. He was appreciative of my help and while I typed he often kissed the back of my neck or lovingly massaged my shoulders. He made our tea—fried eggs or beans on toast. We then went to the pictures.

David was not in good physical health, he was very thin. He suffered from asthma and eczema and he was prone to bouts of depression. He was on various medications. He was a chain smoker and often lit two cigarettes and handed me one. I didn't care for them but I thought smoking made me look sophisticated. His health didn't worry me; in fact I had great sympathy for him. I felt I could take care of him and give him my own strength and vitality.

My mother made no secret of the fact that she didn't like him. She never invited him in to have a meal and when she knew he was coming to collect me, she didn't bother to tidy the house as she normally did when company was expected. She said to me

"Are you out of your mind going out with a fellow like that? Just look at him. He's a delicate man; so pale and thin. Did you see the way he scratches at his arms and legs? I'm telling you there's something wrong with him and he's stupid as well—he forgot his gloves when he was here the last time and before that he walked off without his umbrella. You're wasting your time with him and he's not even a Catholic."

"Mammy, he suffers from eczema and it flares up especially if he is nervous. He knows you don't like him and that makes him uncomfortable. Eczema is not contagious and it is not even dangerous. You don't give him a chance. I agree that sometimes he is a bit absent minded. He is highly intelligent—he might even be a genius. He is always respectful and loving towards me."

While the eczema didn't bother me, Mammy hit a nerve when she said he wasn't Catholic. Not only was he not Catholic but he was very much anti-Catholic which I hadn't mentioned to my mother.

Nevertheless, I continued going out with him. I loved being in his company. He was brilliant and there was never a shortage of subjects to discuss. He had a droll sense of humor and I loved hearing about university life; the lectures, the theater and his professors. He had funny nicknames for all his professors; "Shugee" was Dr. Sugarman and "Old Hoppy" was a professor who had a gimpy foot.

He wrote love poems to me and brought me little posies of violets or other small thoughtful gifts. We usually went out once during the week and always on Sunday afternoons.

He was thrilled when he bought an old used car. We called it "The Blue Tango" because it was blue and we loved to dance to the music of The Blue Tango. The car had no heat and no radio but it was better than standing in the cold and rain waiting for a bus. We made plans to go to a dance in The Arcadia in Bray. Harry, Hilda and Olga came with us. David was fond of Olga; he said she had a beautiful figure, which she had. Olga was fond of him too and she felt sorry for the way my mother treated him. On our way to the dance, we bought a bottle of gin and drank it between us. The old banger broke down a few times and we had to get out and push, this only added to the fun of the evening. The ballroom was packed when we arrived and the band was playing "Glow Worm". We danced every dance and David requested one of his favorite songs, "The Rose of San Antone". The vocalist Rose Tynan sang it beautifully for him. We enjoyed The Arcadia and we went there often.

◆

David bought tickets for The Commencement Ball to be held at The Shelbourne Hotel. I was sick with excitement getting ready for my first dress dance. I wanted to look beautiful for him in a new dress but I didn't have any money. My friend, Peg, at the office came to my rescue. She had a formal dress she said I could borrow. I couldn't believe my luck; it fitted me perfectly and the color was <u>blue.</u>

When David arrived, he looked very handsome. He was perfectly groomed and wore an impeccably cut black dinner suit. His plain white shirt had gold studs and matching cuff links. He wore his gold signet ring containing his family crest. His tall slim figure and his fair aristocratic looks were made for evening wear.

He was obviously pleased with the way I looked. He said I was enchanting and that blue was my color.

We had a table close to the dance floor and David introduced me to his friends; Brendan and Patricia, Harry and Jan and Ken's lady friend, Damaris. After a delicious dinner of roast beef and Yorkshire pudding, the speeches were made and we danced the night away. David told me he loved me. I was the only girl in the world for him and he wanted to marry me. I was dizzy with excitement. There was no doubt in my mind that I wanted to marry him.

When we arrived home we were sitting in the car hugging and kissing outside our front door and under the street lamp. Next there was a loud rapping at the car window. David rolled it down and there was my mother in her nightdress and fuming:

"Young man, what do you think you are doing carrying on like this at this hour of the night? Have you no respect for my daughter?"

David was shaking. He got out of the car to face her

"Mrs. Wright I can assure you I have nothing but the utmost respect for my dearest Nora. I wouldn't harm her or bring disgrace on your family for the world. Even if I'm not of your religion, I do live by a code of moral and ethical behavior."

"Go inside this minute" she said to me

For the first time in my life, I disobeyed her and I didn't budge.

When she was gone inside, I apologized to David. I was embarrassed—I felt she had ruined a perfect evening. He said to me

"I don't know why your mother dislikes me and she doesn't seem to understand you. You must not be upset with her. She has had a difficult life with too many children and not enough money. It is natural that she would be worried about your reputation. Nevertheless, I shall be eternally grateful to your mother for having reared the most perfect human being for me to love."

He walked me to the door and kissed me goodnight.

I had Peg's dress cleaned and returned it to her with a note of thanks and a small gift. The girls were interested in hearing about my romantic evening. I told them everything but I left out the bit about Mammy. I didn't want to think about it and I knew what they would say

"Weren't you very foolish to park outside your own front door and under the lamp post at that?" They would have been right.

◆

David was planning on spending Christmas with his family in England so we decided to have our first Christmas dinner together and to exchange our gifts on the evening before his departure. I had knitted him a scarf in the Trinity colors; black with stripes of red, green and white. I added generous fringe to the ends and I was delighted with the way it turned out. I brought it in to the office to show the girls and they said it was a very thoughtful present and they were sure he would love it. I wrapped it in tissue paper and put it in a box. I couldn't wait to give it to him. We celebrated at The Gresham Hotel in O'Connell Street. David ordered champagne and we had a traditional turkey and ham dinner. While we were having our coffee he lit a cigarette for me and handed me a beautifully wrapped package with a card that he had designed and made himself. Inside the package was an elegant navy blue box stamped *J. Weir & Sons, Grafton Street*. Gleaming on the satin lining was a beautiful gold bracelet. I was beside myself with happiness.

"Are you sure you like it darling"? He said modestly as he kissed me and fastened the safety clasp on my wrist.

"I adore it" I said "I never expected such an extravagant gift."

This was true. He was on a tight budget and he probably had to forego many lunches in order to buy me that bracelet.

When he opened his present he was so touched he could hardly speak

"Did you really do this for me, my love? It is so beautiful it must have taken you hours and hours. Nobody has ever done anything this nice for me in my life. You can be sure, my darling, I will treasure it for ever."

We parted sadly when the evening was over. He said he would be counting the minutes until his return and we could look forward to spending New Year's Eve together at The East Africa Dress Dance.

◆

Christmas at our house was a time of festivity. The main decorations were holly and ivy which grew abundantly in Ireland. Sprigs were placed over all the pictures and mirrors. Colored paper chains were strung crosswise from corner to corner of the ceiling. Christmas cards were displayed on the mantelpiece and over strings hanging from the corners. Cards were sent only to friends and relatives living far away.

Mass was packed to overflowing. The priest dressed in golden vestments and we joined the choir singing "Tantum ergo sacramentum". After mass we visited the famous crib at The Oblates.

Christmas dinner was the most elaborate meal of the year; roast stuffed turkey, boiled Limerick ham, roasted potatoes, Brussels sprouts, Marrowfat peas and a rare treat—lemonade. For dessert we had Christmas cake and plum pudding smothered in hot Birds' custard. Friends dropped in to have a drink and a piece of cake.

◆

David was happy to be back. He said he had a dull Christmas and he missed me terribly. The New Year's Dinner Dance was held at the popular old Metropole in O'Connell Street. The Metropole had a cinema, a ballroom, three restaurants and two bars. We went into The Long Bar where a dignified waiter in tails took our orders for gin and tonics. The smoke filled bar was crowded with beautiful women in ball gowns and handsome men in evening wear enjoying a drink before the dance. I wore a red dress belonging to Olga and a white imitation fur cape. David said I looked beautiful and very festive. We sat with Ken and Damaris and all the other nice friends I had met previously. The band played our favorite tunes and we danced every dance. At midnight there appeared an old man with a long white beard and a new born baby to signify "out with the old and in with the new." After the Auld Land Syne we went outside to listen to the pealing of the church bells. Crowds of people were dancing in the streets, hugging and kissing and welcoming in the New Year. We were carefree and gay. Little did we know the changes 1953 would bring?

16

The Interrogation

*"Advice is like snow; the softer it falls,
the longer it dwells upon,
and the deeper it sinks into the mind."*

—Coleridge

Over the years, I had kept in touch with my old friend and confidant, Sister Anne. She was interested in everything about me and I had told her of my romance with David. She said she would like to meet him. He agreed to go and see her.

The meeting didn't go well. Although he was honest with her, he didn't give her the answers she wanted to hear. He felt that, while she had my best interests at heart, she had too much influence over me. When she sent for me he was worried she might try to persuade me to give him up.

She greeted me with her warm smile and ushered me into the comfortable little parlor. There was an air of peace and tranquility in the room and she motioned to me to sit on one of the easy chairs by the side of the fire. She sat on the other.

"Nora I can see how you would be attracted to a man like David. He is cultured, highly intelligent, well educated and he has beautiful manners. He is very much in love with you and he wishes to marry you. You would be an excellent wife and helpmate for him especially as he is studying to become a doctor. Your interests have always leaned toward the medical profession. However, I see huge problems facing you. Do you realize that he is anti-Catholic and that he blames the Church for the poverty and ignorance in Ireland?"

She was making me nervous.

"Well, Sister, it is only because he has so much sympathy for Irish mothers. They have all these babies and few resources. It upsets him to know that at age 14, the children are forced to leave school, find jobs and help support their families. Even if they are brilliant, they have no hope of getting an education. He fails to see where the church helps in any way."

"Do you think your dear mother regrets having all of you?"
"She might not regret it now that we're here but she would have been happier with fewer children. She didn't consider us blessings from God. Each new pregnancy filled her with dismay. She was fortunate she was strong willed and healthy and she could cope. Many mothers couldn't."

"And what about you, Nora, would you welcome as many children as God sends you?"
"No, Sister, I wouldn't like my mother's life at all and I know I could never manage as well as she does."

Just then a frail little nun tapped on the door and brought us tea and biscuits. I was becoming exceeding uncomfortable and wished to make my escape. Sister Anne had plenty more to say to me.

"David told me he might be willing to marry you in The Catholic Church but he would not promise to raise his children in the Catholic faith. Now you know Nora this is a strict requirement in mixed marriages and if he wouldn't agree to raise his children Catholic then the church would not marry you at all.
You are young now Nora and probably you won't relate to what I have to say but, in the grand scheme of things, our earthly life is but a trivial moment which has slipped from eternity. It glows for only a very short time before it is snatched back. Think of when you will be on your death bed and the wax from the candles is dripping over your lovely rings and you know you have turned your back on your faith. Will it have been worth it? I don't think so Nora. I feel you are being tested; you are being asked to make a huge sacrifice. Don't abandon your faith; many have gladly died for it."

"Dear Sister, I can assure you that I have no intention of abandoning my faith. If there is a marriage at all it cannot be for at least three years when David graduates from college. I have plenty of time to work on him and I don't think you need worry. He is a kind and good man and I know he wouldn't do anything to cause me unhappiness."

As I left, she hugged me and said she would pray for me. I was glad to get out into the fresh air and I was sorry I had gone there at all. I was upset and confused and her words burned in my brain.

When I met David I told him the whole story and he put his arms around me and said

"Never mind, Darling, I think we are wise enough to work out our own problems without interference. In the meantime, let's go to the Palm Grove and enjoy a sinful banana split."

◆

I was devastated to notice that I was becoming quite nearsighted. I could read a book from cover to cover but anything at a distance was a blur. I was like the cartoon character, Mr.Magoo, squinting to read the numbers and the destinations on the buses. At the pictures the faces of the movie stars were foggy and when Mrs. Granby at the office was speaking to me from her desk several feet away I didn't respond because I didn't know she was looking at me. I got into trouble one day when I was walking up Bulfin Road toward Saint Michaels. Apparently Granny Wright was waiting at the bus stop on the opposite side of the street and she was killed waving at me to get my attention. She was quite hurt when I just sauntered along and ignored her. I simply didn't see her. She told Mammy about it and this upset me very much because of all people, I loved Granny Wright and I would have enjoyed a chat with her. Mammy said

"I'll tell you what to do. Go to the off-license and buy her a baby power. Bring it up to her and tell her you're sorry and that you didn't see her."

She was loving and forgiving when I explained to her about my poor eyesight.
I started getting migraine headaches which I attributed to the strain on my eyes so I made an appointment with an ophthalmologist in Henry Street. After a thorough examination, he told me I had myopia and he prescribed glasses. I picked out what I thought was a nice frame and I couldn't believe the clearness of my vision. When I tried them on to show my mother she said

"Take those things off you, you're a show. I always hated glasses."

That did it. I was so self conscious I only wore them furtively and then when it was absolutely necessary. I would put them on in the pictures to have a good look at the faces of the movie stars and then put them back in my bag.

The American magazines, Modern Screen and Photoplay were full of ads for contact lenses. I made up my mind if I ever got to America I would have myself fitted for contact lenses.

◆

By the time my 21st Birthday rolled around, my mother had lost interest in giving big birthday parties. However, she did order a fancy birthday cake for me and she put on a nice tea for my office colleagues and my old friend Polly. I wore Olga's mauve see-through blouse and a black taffeta full skirt and a "waspie". The waspie was a waist cincher made of elastic and fashionable at the time. David was not invited neither were any of Mammy and Daddy's friends. Daddy gave me a present of an elegant pearl choker from his Customs' stock. The office girls pooled their money and bought me a beautiful blouse from Madam Nora's in O'Connell Street.

The week before, David and I celebrated our joint birthdays by spending the day together at the Japanese Gardens in Kildare. It was a glorious day; the sun was splitting the trees. David was interested in horticulture and he explained to me the oriental symbolism of the gardens; the progress of man from birth to eternity and the triumphs and failures of man's existence. Not only were the gardens a delight to look at but they were religious and philosophical as well. I was constantly in awe of David's vast knowledge and he took delight in sharing it with me.

When we came back to town, he suggested we open our gifts over high tea in Mitchell's. I had saved my money for weeks to buy David a Parker fountain pen which he wanted but couldn't afford. He was surprised and most appreciative. He thanked me with a tender kiss. He then presented me with my gift; an unusual gold pin on which was perched a little owl. The owl had tiny amethysts for eyes. He said he had chosen it for me because the owl was wise and I was too. I loved it and my heart was happy.

20 Railway Avenue,
Inchicore, Dublin

My mother with my sisters Olga and Hilda.
I am on my grandmother's knee.
She cut herself out of the picture!

Rows and rows of look alike houses.
Not a tree in sight.

My grandmother, Margaret Wright.

My father (on the right) beside the wireless
detection van in County Cork.

1936. My sister, Olga's,
First Holy Communion, Saint Michael's Church, Inchicore.
Olga is in the top row on the far left.

My sister, Betty Wright
Born April 10, 1936
Died April 17, 1941

Betty, Billy, Nora
About 1937

Newspaper picture of Olga and Betty at the May processions.
The caption read "A sister to assist her."

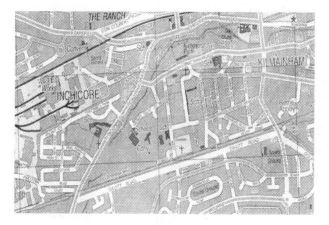

We walked to school from Railway Avenue to Tyrconnell Park,
to Emmet Road, to Spa Road,
to Thomas Davis Street and into Golden Bridge Convent.

Golden Bridge Convent School

The Wrights and The McLoughlins.
About 1947

My young sisters, Doris, Ada,
Joan outside our house on Kickham Road

My mother and her Monday washing.

The Famous Christmas Crib
at the Oblates Church, Inchicore

Auntie Molly at The Pier in Dun Laoghaire.
The mail boat is in the background.

The family
on holidays in Laytown.

The hand-carved ebony oars
Pappy Mooney brought from West Africa.
They are now in Ada's house.

Olga's 21ˢᵗ Birthday Party. April 7ᵗʰ, 1950. Left to right:
Harry McGill, Joan, Hilda, Olga, Billy, Nora and Doris in front.

Myself presiding over the picnic at Glendalough.

THE

IRISH HOSPITALS' SWEEPSTAKES

Olga, Frank, Nora—
Kickham Road

Myself with my self-styled
poodle haircut.

CITY HONORS ST. PATRICK—The wearing of the green, which all true Irishmen did Wednesday, St. Patrick's day, was given civic recognition when the Irish flag was flown on the city hall flag pole under the Stars and Stripes. Shown raising the two emblems, left to right, are Gerald Murray, president of the Grand Rapids Friendly Sons of St. Patrick; Joseph O'Brien, Miss Esther McAleer; Thomas E. Walsh, Timothy Milley, chairman of the Friendly Sons annual banquet Wednesday night; Albert Merini, an attache at the Irish consulate in Washington, and Leland Verkury, city hall cus...

My mother in America beside
Uncle Gary on the left.
Auntie Gin is on the far right.

Brother Jack in
his cowboy outfit from America.

Brother Billy, British Army,
R.E.M.E. Unit

Trinity College, Dublin.

My dad handing me the key of
the door on my 21ˢᵗ Birthday.

Myself at the Gaiety Theatre.

17

Farewell

"Like some low and mournful spell
We whisper that sad word, 'farewell'."

—P. Benjamin

A letter arrived from Uncle Gary with an urgent request. Friends of his, an Italian family, were desperate to adopt a baby. This was nearly impossible in the United States. Birth control was widely used and abortion was commonplace. There simply were no babies available. This particular family was lucky to have been able to adopt one little boy but they wanted a brother for him and, if possible, a little girl as well. Uncle Gary stressed that money was no object; they were willing to pay anything asked as well as the plane fare for whoever would accompany the babies to the United States.

My mother appreciated Gary's help to her over the years and she wasted no time making enquiries. She found out there was a home for unmarried mothers on the Navan Road which had babies available for adoption. Looking respectable in her best coat and hat, off she went on the bus to visit the sister in charge. The sister was reassuring and, provided the children were going to a good Catholic home, she saw no reason why my mother's request could not be granted. The endless paperwork began.

The next question was who would accompany these children to the United States? Olga had already visited the U.S. and while she enjoyed her holiday she felt much more at home in Ireland. Life in the U.S. held no attraction for her especially as she was now dating the staff manager of The Irish Hospitals' Trust, William Kinsella. Hilda definitely did not want to go having had a traumatic experience some years earlier and she was also dating a nice fellow named Richard Woods. My mother said she would take the babies herself unless I wanted the chance to see America.

This was something I needed to think about. I was quite happy in Ireland. I loved my job and the people I worked with and I would certainly miss my family.

David was another matter; he was still firmly anti-Catholic and Sister Anne's words about my deathbed and the wax dripping from the candles haunted me. I was also troubled by the fact that I was getting no support from my family. I knew David was devoted to me but I began to notice a dark morose side to him which confused me. He told me he had had mental breakdowns in the past. It seemed to me that the fates which brought us together were now doing their best to break us apart. Perhaps a short separation would be the deciding factor.

I also wanted to go to America to get the contact lenses I had been reading about in the movie magazines and I wanted to earn some money.

I met David for afternoon tea in Fuller's to discuss the situation. He was very much against me going. He suggested we just elope and get married. Romantic as this sounded, I knew it could never happen. In the first place we had no money and the only person in the family that I knew of who had eloped was my mother's sister, Auntie Gretta. She ran off to England with her Protestant boyfriend and the family didn't speak to her for years. David didn't like America. He was very British and class conscious too. He said Americans were loud gum chewing braggarts and that they lacked manners. He begged me not to leave. He said being with me was the only happiness he had.

We talked some more; weighing up the pros and cons. In the end he agreed it was a good opportunity for me provided I didn't stay too long and that I didn't come home with an American twang.

After our tea we headed off to The Gaiety Theatre to see the romantic ballet, "Les Sylphides". Chopin's music and the grand waltz as the finale were memorable.

It took several months to process the paperwork. A social worker had to interview the adoptive parents to make sure the children were being sent to a suitable home. They had to have a letter from their parish priest stating they were a good Catholic family and a letter from their family doctor stating that they were in good health. They also had to have statements from their bank manager and their accountant showing they were financially sound and that they were in good standing with the IRS.

I had to go to The American Embassy in Dublin and apply for my visa. I also had to have a complete medical exam and x-rays, which I had to carry with me, to show that I was free from tuberculosis or other communicable diseases. I also had to have a vaccination against smallpox. I had to take an exam to show that I could read and write the English language which was a requirement at that time to enter The United States.

During this time, David was studying hard and amassing a string of degrees after his name. His health was being challenged; his eczema and asthma attacks were becoming more frequent. He was struggling with bouts of depression. He blamed this on the intense study requirements and on my upcoming departure.

Olga said I needed a nice traveling outfit and she took me to a consignment shop in Fairview. Mrs. Russell sold only near new designer clothes. Olga had good taste and a good eye for quality. She picked out an elegant Richard Allen navy blue suit with a velvet collar. She said it was gorgeous on me and might as well have been made to measure as it fit so well. She paid for it and said it was a little going away present from her to me. Olly was always doing nice things like that.

My friends at the office were envious and excited about my trip. A chance to go to America with all expenses paid was every Irish person's dream. They took me out to The Carlton for a farewell dinner and made me promise to write and send pictures. They said they would miss the stories of my romance and all the laughs we had together. They gave me a pretty blue dressing gown as a going away gift. Mr. Boyd said he was sorry to lose me and I would always have a job there when I came back.

The last movie David and I saw together before my departure was the romantic "Waterloo Bridge". It was one of the best black and whites I have ever seen and may have been an omen of things to come. It was a tear jerking story of destroyed love and broken fates.

◆

On the morning of my departure, Daddy took Mammy and me in the car to collect the babies at the orphanage. I had already said my goodbyes to all my brothers and sisters before they left for work and school. Ada gave me a bar of Cadbury's Fruit & Nut and a "Woman's Own" to enjoy on the plane. The kindly sister at the orphanage had the children waiting in the hall all packed and ready to go. The little boy, Eric, was 2 1/2 years old. He was a solemn, sturdy little lad with rosy cheeks and sad brown eyes. He was dressed like a little gentleman in a tailored tweed coat and matching cap. The little girl, Angela, was eighteen months. She had fair curly hair and large expressive blue eyes. She was dressed in a pretty pink coat and matching bonnet. The sister gave me their papers and their satchel with their necessities for the long journey. I fought back the tears as the nun kissed them goodbye and handed them over to me. They were leaving the only home they had ever known.

As we arrived at Dublin Airport I could see the huge Pan American plane. I was nervous and excited at the prospect of my first flight. David, tired and sad, was waiting at the departure gate. He said he had had a bad night and very little sleep. We tried to make small talk and I was relieved when my flight was called. He hugged me and kissed me and said he would never love anyone but me and he would be miserable until I came back to him.

When Daddy tried to say goodbye he got a fit of asthma and he started coughing which brought tears to his eyes. He hugged me and could barely say

"Cheerio, Bernie. All the best. I'll miss you." I felt sad leaving him.

Mammy hugged me and put a brown scapular around my neck

"Wear this and never take it off. The Sacred and his Blessed Mother will protect you and look after you. And here take your coat; you'll be freezing over there."

I didn't want to take my ugly brown tweed coat, I loved Olga's navy suit I had on me, but there was no use arguing at the last minute so I took it. Mammy said

"God be with you now and have a safe journey. Mind you don't break the Waterford in your bag for Uncle Gary. We'll be dying to hear from you."

As we boarded I looked back to wave and wondered what madness had gotten into me to cause me to leave all that was near and dear to me; my beloved Dublin with its charm and beauty and the gaiety I had known there, my home, my family my friends and, most of all, my love. I was consoled by the fact that I was only going for a short while; to save some money, to get my contact lenses and then to book my ticket home.

The airline stewardesses were kind and helpful and they were most attractive; tall and tanned with dazzlingly white smiles. They wore hats, gloves and high-heeled shoes as part of their uniforms. They took the children from me and seated us at the bulk-head where there was a tiny cot set up for Angela. They strapped Eric into the window seat beside me. Up above the clouds we went and all I could see was a blanket of white below.

The children were like little angels, not a whimper out of them. I gave Angela her lunch of baby food and her bottle and changed her nappy. After that she slept in her cozy little cot. Brave little Eric, sitting silently beside me, occupied himself looking out of the window and scribbling away with crayons. A delicious lunch was served with a special plate for Eric; a hot dog and fries and a chocolate shake—his first American meal. He ate well and then he took a long nap.

18

Grand Rapids, Michigan

"Only that traveling is good which
reveals to me the value of home, and
enables me to enjoy it better."

—Thoreau

I didn't expect such a big welcome when we arrived at the airport. The adoptive parents, Mr. and Mrs. Lemucci and their three-year-old son were there. Many of their neighbors and friends had come to get a first glimpse of the children. Uncle Gary and Auntie Gin were there as well as members of the press. There were tears of utter joy as Mr.Lemucci took his little daughter in his arms for the first time. Mrs. Lemucci picked up Eric and she was overcome with emotion as she hugged her precious little boy. They had brought a doll for Angela and a cuddly stuffed dog for Eric. The children were retiring and quiet, no doubt confused by all the attention. Mr. Lemucci was a short stocky man with a heavy Italian accent. He owned a dry cleaning business. Mrs.Lemucci said I should call her Rosa. She was a kindly pretty little woman with a light olive complexion. It was bitterly cold and there was snow on the ground. I was glad my mother had insisted I take my coat. It had been arranged that I stay with the Lemucci's until I got settled. Uncle Gary and Auntie Gin said their goodbyes and told me they would come for me the following day to take me to dinner and to hear all the news of Ireland. We drove home in the Lemucci's big posh car.

Their home was warm and comfortable. There was no doubt that they were good Catholics; statues and holy pictures were much in evidence. There were loads of toys for the children to play with. The photographer followed us home to take some more pictures and when he left Rosa showed me to my room. It was a pleasant airy room with highly polished wood floors, pretty lacy curtains and a pink counterpane on my bed. There were fresh flowers on the nightstand. I had my own bathroom and Rosa showed me how to use the shower.

As I was unpacking, the delicious smells emanating from the kitchen reminded me of how hungry I was. I brought out the beautiful Irish linen tablecloth and napkins that Mammy had sent for The Lemucci's and a fire truck for their little boy, Stephen. We sat down to dinner at the kitchen table. There were two new high chairs for Angela and Eric. We had spaghetti and meatballs, a huge bowl of salad tossed with Italian dressing and garlic bread. Mr. Lemucci showed me how to twirl the spaghetti around my fork. "Mange, mange" he shouted—I think it meant "eat up, eat up". Rosa had made a special dessert called Tiramisu—Italian for "pick me up"—how could all that Marsala-laced mascsarpone and ladyfingers soaked in brandy fail to do so?

The following day, Uncle Gary, Auntie Gin and my cousins, Pat, Mike and Tommy took me out to dinner at s place called "Chicken in a Basket". That's exactly what it was; golden breaded fried chicken piled high into a basket and served with plenty of chips or, as I had to get used to calling them, French fries. There were no knives and forks, we ate with our fingers and it was indescribably delicious! I reached over and picked up a bread roll from another basket and started to bite into it when everyone at the table started to laugh. The "bread rolls" were tiny rolled up wet napkins for wiping our hands. For dessert we had something called mud pie; a rich and luscious concoction of chocolate, nuts, ice cream and whipped cream. It was sinfully delicious.

After dinner we went back to Uncle Gary's. He had a lovely big house in a nice part of town. Cousin Pat gave me the grand tour. Everything was fresh and clean and they had all the modern conveniences. They even had a television set. There was a huge basement where Auntie Gin did her laundry. She had a washing machine and a wringer. No wonder my mother said that there was no drudgery in housework for the American housewife. We sat in the beautifully furnished living room. Uncle Gary made me a gin and tonic and Auntie Gin offered me a cigarette. It all seemed so civilized. There was no smoking and no drinking at the Lemucci's. Uncle Gary couldn't hear enough about Ireland, he had so many questions for me about places in Dublin he knew and about his family still living there. Although he liked America and he was successful, I could see that a big part of his heart was still in Ireland. Late in the evening when he drove me home, I gave him the lovely Waterford bowl that Mammy had sent for him. He had brought presents for the Lemucci children and he told me if I wasn't happy there

I could always stay at his house. He gave me his phone number and told me if I needed anything to call him.

◆

Mr. Lemucci said "I hava nica job for you at my store. Would you like to start on Monday?" He said he would pay me $30.00 a week and give me free room and board. He would also do all my dry cleaning free. This was more than I ever expected; men in Ireland with families weren't earning this much.

On Monday morning, I was awake early and got myself ready; shower, full makeup, my good navy suit and my high heel shoes. When I came into the kitchen, the children were already in their high chairs having breakfast. Rosa squeezed fresh orange juice for them. They had cereal followed by two large boiled eggs apiece, toast and their vitamins. They seemed to be enjoying it all and I thought to myself how fortunate they were to have been adopted by such a loving and caring family. My breakfast was all ready for me—a feast for a king; bacon, sausages, hash browns, two fried eggs, toast and freshly brewed coffee. I ate it all but I told Rosa I couldn't eat that much in the mornings, a boiled egg and toast would be plenty. She had packed a lunch for me of ham and cheese sandwiches, homemade cookies, and a thermos of coffee.

Off I went to work in Mr.Lemucci's big warm car. I was amazed at the beautiful homes and clean tree-lined streets, not a pick of litter to be seen. The cars on the road were all big and in colors I would never associate with cars; turquoise, pink, and red.

I was to work at the reception counter.

> "Now when dey bringa da clothes, they put them on the counter. You aska the name and write it on the ticket. Then you write down alla da stuff they brought in and put the amount beside each item. Usea this price list. When you make the total you give the customer the ticket stub. You smile to the customer and say 'Hava nicea day!' Then you put everything into a bag with the ticket and take it to the back. Whena they come to pick up their order, you take the ticket and look at the number. Then you go to the carousel over there and finda the garments with the same number. You bring them over here, hang them on the bar and puta de plastic over them and take the money-capice?"

It seemed straightforward enough and it was easy for me to understand the money; all denominations of ten. It wasn't confusing like our Irish money; farthings, ha'pennies, pennies, three penny bits, sixpences, two shilling pieces, half crowns, twelve pence to the shilling and twenty shillings to the pound.

Mr. Lemucci had left before my first customer arrived. She was a heavy set blond woman. She drove to the front of the store in a big fancy car and by the way she jumped out she seemed to be in a terrible hurry. She dumped a big load of clothes on the counter and barked at me what sounded like "Krauski". I imagined that was her name.

"Could you spell that for me, please?" I asked

She rolled her eyes and strummed her fingers impatiently on the counter

"K-R-O-L-I-K-O-W-S-K-I"

"Oh yeh, I got it, sure" I said. I didn't dare ask her to pronounce it.

There was a steady stream of customers throughout the day with strange names like Niewiarowski, Hryniewicki, Van der Lan and Ver Halen. I guess there were a lot of Polish and Dutch people in the area.

I brushed the cuffs with the wire brush and checked all the pockets before I brought them to the back. There were several black men working in the back singing along to a tune on the radio "Whatever Lola Wants, Lola Gets" as they sorted, spotted, cleaned, pressed and steamed the clothes. There were a couple of middle-aged Italian women washing and starching the shirts and table linens. They also did minor repairs. They were cheerful and friendly to me.

Mr. Lemucci came back at six o'clock to close the shop. By this time my feet were killing me—I wasn't used to standing all day especially in high heels. My good navy suit was ruined from brushing all the debris out of the trouser cuffs. Before we left, I had to count all the money and make sure it balanced with the tickets. He put the money in a paper bag and said to me "You did a gooda job"!

When we got home, Rosa had another huge meal prepared for us. There were stacks of clean folded laundry all over the place. The mister played with the children, tickling them and throwing them up in the air until they choked with laughter. Before dinner Mr. Lemucci took off his work shirt and sat down to eat in his sleeveless undershirt. I found his great hairy chest and underarms at the dinner table quite objectionable. Although he was good natured, he had coarse table manners. He slurped his soup, shoveled his food and talked with his mouth full "mange, mange" he bellowed "you no eata nothing—that's why you so skinny."

After dinner, I helped Rosa put the laundry away. We then did the dishes. She was sweet and gentle and she talked very little. She was delighted with her two new babies and she was coping well with the extra workload. She had no extra help in the house. I helped her give the children their baths and we put them into their pajamas. I read a little story or sang a song for them before putting them to bed. They were three lovable children. Rosa then changed into her nightgown and housecoat.

"Why you donta get into somating comfortable?" Mr.Lemucci said to me. I couldn't see myself putting on a dressing gown at eight o'clock in the evening. In Ireland we would be getting ready to go out at that hour. We sat on the couch watching Ozzie and Harriet on the small screen black and white television. Rosa brought in a big bowl of buttered popcorn. After the show I went into my room and wrote home telling about my trip, the children, the wonderful reception at the airport, The Lemucci's, Uncle Gary, my cousins and my first job.

◆

On Saturday morning, Rosa took me downtown to do some shopping. She said I needed comfortable shoes and suitable clothes for work. I was mesmerized at the variety of shops and I couldn't believe how inexpensive the clothes were. For one week's salary, I could outfit myself from head to toe. In Dublin I had to scrimp and save for a whole year to buy a winter coat. Looking around at the shops, I noticed an optometrist's office with a sign that read

"Doctor Stanley Cohen
World beyond eyeglasses
Contact lenses in one hour"

I made a mental note that when I got the chance, I would be coming to visit Dr. Cohen.

We went into Wurzburg's famous department store. There was everything there to pamper the shopper; the air was filled with a delicious smell of perfume and soft music played in the background. The sales people were extremely pleasant and helpful. Rosa bought me several skirts and jumpers (sweaters) for work and a gorgeous turquoise knit outfit for Sundays and special occasions. She also bought me two sets of luxurious lingerie. At the shoe department she picked out a pair of ugly looking flat heeled shoes and she said they would be comfortable for standing in the shop. She paid for everything with a credit card and the sales girl smiled as she handed us our packages and said "Have a Nice Day"!

◆

The greatest pleasure for me at that time was receiving letters from home. My mother was always prompt with her replies. I could figure out to the day when to expect to hear from her. The letters took at least seven days each way. I could visualize Mammy reading my letters and immediately clearing off the end of the kitchen table and sitting down with an air letter to reply. If I had sent money, she would thank me and then systematically she would go down the whole family and tell me everything that was going on. She even brought me up to date on what was happening with the neighbors. David wrote sad and romantic letters. He said he missed me very much and he would give all he possessed and more just to be able to hold my hand. Ada wrote telling me she missed me and she sent me holy pictures. The girls from the office wrote with their news. Maureen had married and she went to live in Scotland with her new husband. Peg had become engaged but couldn't afford to get married for a couple of years. Eileen Carney was in The Mater Hospital suffering from an ulcerated leg. They complained about the rainy weather and how hard up they were. They envied the grand life I was having in America.

◆

As time went by, I was becoming restless with my daily routine. I had no mental challenge at the dry cleaning place and no one of my own age to associate with. Although The Lemucci's were good and kind I felt they had done enough for me and it was time they had their privacy with their new little family. I needed to be out on my own and working in my own field. I was also getting mighty tired of all that rich Italian food; a nice feed of fish and chips wrapped in newspaper and a good cup of tea would have suited me fine. I would miss the children but they were now well settled and happy. I noticed the Irish rosiness was fading from their cheeks. This could be expected; they had too much rich food, too many vitamins and the house was overheated. They never played outside in the fresh air.

I talked to Uncle Gary about making some changes and he said he would see what he could do for me. In a few days time he had set up an interview for me with the well known stockbrokers, Merrill, Lynch, Pierce, Fenner and Smith. Mr. Robertson, the manager had me fill out the application forms and take the inevitable tests. He was a nice looking middle aged man, perfectly groomed and well dressed. He had a kind fatherly personality. He said

"I see you're from Ireland Nora—there were no formalities, everyone was on a first name basis. My grandmother came from County Cork. I hear it rains there all the time and it is a beautiful green country. I would like to go some day and find my roots. What a cute accent you have. We sure would like to have you work here with us. We would like you to start as soon as possible. Your salary would be $211.00 a month. How does that sound?"

It sounded fine to me and I could hardly thank him I was so happy and excited. My salary wasn't quite that much by the time they deducted for F.I.C.A and something they called Employees' Profit Sharing Plan.

Uncle Gary talked to The Lemucci's and they understood. Mr. Lemucci said there wouldn't be any problem finding someone to work the counter—he had done it himself before I came. Uncle Gary suggested I come and live with them as I would be closer to my new job. I thanked him for the offer but I didn't want to impose as he was busy raising three active teenagers of his own. He understood that and helped me find a place to live. We were lucky to find a fully furnished bed sitter. It had everything I needed; a small frig and stove, a pull out sofa bed, a table and two chairs and central heat. The rent was reasonable and it was within easy access to the old Michigan Trust Building where I would be working. My landlady was a bird-like little woman. She wore a knitted hat like a child's bonnet tied under her chin. She was a lonely widow and a bit nosey although caring.

On my first day, Mr. Robertson introduced me to a girl named Pam. He said she would show me the ropes. Pam was a pretty blond lady of Irish and German descent. She was well known in Grand Rapids as she was one of the first women to become a registered member of The New York Stock Exchange. She also modeled for Wurzburg's Department Store. She told me she had been to Ireland. She loved the lively atmosphere in Dublin and she found the people there charming. She planned on going back. She introduced me to the large staff of men and women. Many of them wanted to tell me about their Irish ancestors who came over in the coffin ships.

I came to work early every morning and looked forward to my breakfast in the coffee shop in the lobby. I always ordered a pecan Danish—a delicious warm coffee cake packed with pecans and cinnamon and slathered with melting butter. With this I had a good cup of coffee. I never asked for tea because what they served didn't taste like tea at all. It was a tea bag served on the side of a cup of hot water and a slice of lemon. Nobody seemed to know how to brew a decent cup of tea and the shops only sold Lipton tea bags. I wrote home to Mammy to send me a pound of Lyons' loose tea.

There were many girls my own age in the office. Most of them were tall and attractive and had double names like Cherry Lynne, Mary Kate, and Bonnie Lee. Some of them were married—no babies yet—they had to have the right house, the right furniture and it had to be the right time before starting a family. I was thinking if only my poor mother and all the mothers in Ireland could have had that luxury. A couple of the girls were pregnant and it looked to me as if their babies were about to be born—they worked up to the very last minute. They strolled around the office visiting each other. They admired each other's clothes and hairstyles and showed pictures of their cute babies. They were always collecting for presents for somebody getting engaged, married or leaving.

The men in the office had crew cuts, big athletic shoulders, light colored suits and some even wore pink shirts. I was shocked when I learned of the affairs among the staff that were going on openly. Nobody seemed to mind as the lovers sauntered out arm in arm for their "nooners".

The girls often invited me to lunch "Wanna come to lunch with us, Irish?" There was a good variety of restaurants in the area; Chinese, Italian and American. Before the meal they would order a fancy cocktail, a Manhattan or a dry Martini. They sipped their drinks and smoked their cigarettes as they discussed the menu. I ordered a cocktail as well and enjoyed it—it gave me a powerful appetite. The lunchtime conversation mostly centered around the "noo" refrigerator, the "noo" car, or the house they had bought or were buying. I couldn't relate to this and I missed the funny lively conversations I was used to at home. I noticed the American sense of humor was different from ours. What would be an obvious joke to an Irish person, they would take literally. The explanations became tedious after a while so I was careful not to make flippant remarks. I had to get used to calling things by different names; a biscuit was now a cookie, a jumper was a sweater—a jumper in America is a gym slip—the lift was an elevator, the lavatory was the bathroom, sweets were candy, push pins were thumb tacks, the pictures were the movies and knickers were called panties. I also had to get used to new spellings—most of our words with "our" were now simply "or"; colour was now color, flavour was now flavor, jewellery was spelt jewelry and gaol was jail. Everyone laughed when I wrote cheque for check. They thought calling my mother "Mammy" was hilarious; the only Mammy they ever heard of was Scarlett's Mammy in "Gone With The Wind".

I was handling the work pretty well until one day I was asked to take over the teletype machine for a girl who was absent. The teletype had a keyboard the same as a typewriter with a roll of paper tape at the back for sending and receiving messages. I was given a pile of buy and sell orders which had to be telegraphed to New York. Hurrying through the pile, somehow I added an extra nought to an order to sell a hundred shares of a certain stock. Fortunately, someone had questioned the order before it went through; the guy didn't own a thousand shares. Mr. Robertson called me into his office to let me know how much a mistake like that could cost the company. I was hoping they wouldn't ask me to operate the teletype again.

There was a big difference in my social life between Dublin and Grand Rapids. Grand Rapids had movies and drive-ins, restaurants and a small local civic theater. There were plenty of winter and summer sports. There were no glamorous ballrooms, ballets, operas, comedy theatre or musicals.

One Friday night I agreed to go ice skating with a group from the office. I explained to them I had never even roller skated before. The Irish climate did not lend itself to such activities. We seldom had snow and if we did, it didn't stay on the ground for more than a day or two. The extent of my athleticism was rope jumping, riding my bike, and ballroom dancing. They assured me there was nothing to it, they would help me and I would find it was great fun. It was bitterly cold and the lake was terrifying—an enormous solid sheet of glass. There were hundreds of skaters racing around backward and frontward, twirling like tops, jumping in the air and doing all sorts of fancy maneuvers. Ruthann had brought a pair of skates for me belonging to her sister. We laced up and I couldn't even hold my balance. They took my hands and held me up as we started off slowly around and around. Then they took up speed, faster and faster, until they decided it was time to let go of me. I came crashing down and banged the back of my head on the ice. For a moment I saw stars. On they went and left me lying there. Skaters were jumping over me and jabbing me with their sharp blades. My so-called friends finally came back and led me off the ice. They apologized; they thought I had gotten the hang of it and that I was doing fine. They said that was the way they all learned. My head was bleeding and I was bruised everywhere. I never wanted to go ice skating again.

I declined when they asked me to go ice fishing. I couldn't see any enjoyment in bundling up and sitting beside a hole in the ice waiting for hours to catch a fish. I leaned more toward the comfort of a blazing fire, sheltered from the elements, and the pleasure of a good book or interesting conversation.

◆

The nicest thing my landlady could say to me when I came home from work was

"Nora, there are some letters here for you."

She would hand me the letters with the familiar handwriting and I would break my neck up the stairs to open them.

My mother was delighted to hear that I got out of the dry cleaners and that I had a secretarial position in a posh office. She said my apartment sounded lovely and imagine having my own frig. and stove. She was happy to hear that I liked my landlady and that she was kind to me. She thanked me for the money and wasn't America the greatest country in the world to be paying that kind of a salary to a young girl? She was glad to know that her brother, Gary, was looking out for me and helping me. She said there was talk of a doctor friend of his looking to adopt a baby from Ireland. The news from home was that Daddy had been in St. Vincent's Hospital. He had some kind of a growth on his neck that had to be operated on. The doctor was annoyed with him for not coming in sooner. He was home now and he was grand. Joan, now 14, was tall and slim and she had joined Betty Whelan's School of Modeling. She loved the clothes I had sent. Doris was doing well at her Irish dancing and she was competing at the feis in Drogheda. Ada wanted to know when I would be coming home. My friend, Polly, had gone to Canada with her boyfriend, Willy. Her sister, Mary, became friendly with Mammy and often came over to share news and photographs.

There had been a terrible tragedy on Bulfin Road. Five little children lost their lives. The mother had left them alone while she ran down to the store to buy a loaf of bread. Apparently the eldest child, a six year old, held a rolled up piece of newspaper to the fire. When it started to light he got scared and shoved it under the settee. In seconds the whole room was ablaze. The children huddled together in the small space under the stairs. They all died from smoke inhalation. I cried when I read this as I knew the family well.

Olga wrote telling me of her engagement to Billie Kinsella. She described her beautiful diamond ring and she told me about the plans for their wedding. I was sorry to have missed this special occasion.

The letters from David were heartbreaking. He wasn't impressed with anything I had told him about America. He said he was miserably lost without me. He wasn't eating and he was getting thinner and thinner. His eczema had flared up and he had to be wrapped in bandages like a mummy. He had failed obstetrics and didn't think he could get finals unless I was there with him. He pleaded with me to come home, I had been away long enough. He felt he was heading for another breakdown but would try to hang on until I returned. This upset me and I felt responsible for causing him so much misery. Neither of us had a 'phone so I couldn't talk to him. I wrote immediately to tell him I was making plans to come home.

My financial situation wasn't good. I had to buy heavy winter clothing and boots. I also had to buy bed linens and towels for the apartment. But then I got carried away buying all sorts of frivolous things because they were so lovely and so inexpensive. I also bought myself a radio and a record player. Now I knew I would have to tighten my belt and start saving in earnest. There would be no more Martini lunches with the office staff. I needed to save every penny for my fare and hopefully arrive home with some money.

I made an appointment with Dr. Stanley Cohen for my contact lenses—after all that was one of my reasons for coming to America.

Dr. Cohen was a pleasant elderly gentleman of slight build. He had a good head of white hair and he wore glasses. He examined my eyes and said no problem; he would have my lenses ready for fitting in a couple of weeks.

The next Sunday I went to Mass with Uncle Gary, Auntie Gin and my cousins. It seemed odd to me to see couples kissing, rubbing each other's backs and mauling their children at Mass. In Dublin, they didn't do that sort of thing even in the privacy of their own homes. Uncle Gary introduced me to the parish priest named Fr. McKee and he invited him to join us for breakfast. Fr. McKee was a hearty overweight Irish American with pale skin and pale eyes. He had been to Ireland many times and he planned on going again within the next few weeks. He asked me for my mother's address and said he would go and visit her. He asked me if I knew many Irish people and I told him I didn't know any except my Uncle Gary. He said he wanted to introduce to me a nice Irish gal who was over here working as a maid and she was lonely.

19

Maggie

"Friendship improves happiness, and abates misery…"

—Addison

I hadn't realized I was so homesick until I met Maggie. There was an instant bonding that could only happen between people of the same background. She was a great talker and she had a natural wit. She had a Waterford accent which The Americans loved. She was the stereotypical Irish colleen and she knew how to use this to her advantage.

"Is it true that the pigs sleep in the kitchen in Ireland?
"Ah only when *'tis* cold—we let them sit in front of the fire. They're great pets really, very clean, they're just like dogs"

Maggie was attractive—"black Irish"—dark hair, brown eyes and a light olive complexion. She was of medium height and very slim.

She told me she was engaged to a fellow from Cork. They didn't have money to get married so she answered an ad in the newspaper to come to America and hopefully earn some money. The people she worked for were wealthy furniture manufacturers. Grand Rapids was one of the chief furniture producers in the U.S. They were an elderly couple and they lived in a magnificent big home overlooking a lake. Maggie had her own suite of rooms; a living room with a television set, a bedroom and her own bathroom. There was a full time maid and a cook. Martha, the cook, was a fanatical Jehovah's Witness. Her bible was always open alongside her cookbook on the counter. She seemed to be in a trance as she sang the praises of Jehovah. We avoided her as much as possible because if she ever got our attention she felt it her duty to convert us. Apart from this, she was an excellent cook. Maggie's job was to answer the door and the 'phone and to serve dinner in the evenings. The Bristol's entertained lavishly. Maggie was supplied with a wardrobe of differ-

ent colored uniforms and she was required to wear the uniform that comple-
mented the theme for the evening's festivities. The Bristol's were very fond of
her and they treated her well.

Maggie had Sundays and Thursdays off. On Thursdays she would meet
me after work and we would go to a restaurant called Brahms. Maggie loved a
Dubonnet and I had become accustomed to my Manhattans. As we sipped
our drinks the waiter brought a complimentary relish tray. There were
assorted raw vegetables, cottage cheese and the most delicious little red crabapples which we had never tasted before.

When Mr. and Mrs. Bristol were out of town I would spend the weekend
with Maggie. We watched The Arthur Godfrey Show and "I Love Lucy" on
her television. We played records; I will never hear "Cherry Pink and Apple
Blossom White" or "Mack the Knife" without thinking fondly of Maggie,
these were her favorite songs. We tried on all Mrs. Bristol's prissy old-lady
hats

"Imagine" Maggie said "she pays $50.00 for these hats and has them sent
all the way from New York." At that time you could get a nice hat for $2.98
and nobody went to Mass without a hat. On Sunday mornings Maggie would
laughingly bring my breakfast on a tray complete with the morning newspaper and a fresh rose "Now you can pretend you're 'Ma' Bristol," she'd say.

She introduced me to two Irish friends of hers, Nancy and Peggy. They were
also working for wealthy families in Grand Rapids. We often went out together
and had some good laughs.

◆

Dr. Stanley Cohen sent me a card to say my contacts were ready. He told
me it would take a while to get used to them and I was to persevere and
wear them for longer periods every day. He tried them on me and they
didn't feel too bad. It was a gift to be able to see so clearly in the distance
without glasses. I wore them home but in no time at all my eyes became
bloodshot and teary and I had to take them out. I tried them again over the
next few days and found them most uncomfortable. I think I was one of the
first in Grand Rapids to get contacts. They were the hard lenses and the
procedure hadn't been perfected. There wasn't much call for them either; it
seemed to me every other person wore glasses without giving them a second
thought. Dr. Stanley was patient with me and he adjusted them several
times. I was conscientious about trying to get used to them. In the end I

gave up. I was sorry they didn't work and regretted all the money I had spent on them.

◆

In Mammy's next letter, she told me Father McKee had come to visit her. "Such a big fat man—I invited him in and he took up the full width of Daddy's chair. We talked for a while. He was full of praise for you. He said you were a lovely girl and very well liked by the Americans. After about an hour I made him a cup of tea and a plate of salad sandwiches. He ate every one and I'm sure he could have gone for another plateful. I wasn't having any of that. By this time I was spun out of conversation and getting bored with him. There wasn't a sign of him leaving. He had no cop on at all; he didn't seem to realize he was overstaying his welcome. All the children came home from school and he still stayed to chat with them. Eventually at about five o'clock he stood up to go and told me he had had a lovely visit. Now for God's sake Nora, don't be giving out my address to your American friends in the future."

In the next part of her letter she said that Hilda was coming out to join me. There was another baby ready for adoption and she could travel free if she brought the baby over. She wanted to give America another try. She was older now and more mature and the fact that I was settled with my own apartment would make all the difference. She had broken off her romance with Richard. Joan planned on leaving school to take Hilda's job in Daddy's shop.

◆

Naturally, I was delighted to hear that Hilda was coming but it meant that I had to delay my plans to come home. I knew David wouldn't be happy with this news.

He didn't reply for a while and I was devastated by what he had to say. He said I was being completely selfish by breaking my promise to him and putting Hilda's arrival before our plans. He should never have agreed to let me go in the first place, he knew something like this would happen. He would never love anyone but me but he wasn't waiting for me any longer. He was now dating a student from Trinity. She was a lovely girl; an aristocrat and a Protestant. Her family liked him and made him welcome in their beautiful home in Foxrock. He had given up on ever seeing me again.

I was so upset I couldn't bring myself to write to him. I talked it over with Maggie. She said

"He might be only saying that to trap you into hurrying home. If he's meant for you, you'll have him. Anyway you can't do anything about it at the moment."

Eventually I answered his letter saying how sorry I was with the way things had turned out and, even though my heart was breaking, I said I was happy for him that he had found a suitable girlfriend. It was a long time before I heard from him again.

I was upset with everybody and everything; myself for being so stupid, my mother, Sr. Anne, the babies, America, the contact lenses, and the Catholic Church. When I calmed down I looked at the situation more realistically. I tried to convince myself that he would be better off with a Protestant lady friend. A Protestant wouldn't mind going to bed with him before marriage and when the time came he could marry her in his own church without being forced to sign anything regarding the religion of his children.

◆

There was a college across the street from my apartment and I often looked out my window envying those students with their armloads of books going to and from classes. What a privileged life they had; listening to their professors, studying in the library and earning their degrees. One day I plucked up courage and walked up the steps to the admissions office. I was amazed to find out that I could sign up for classes then and there—it was almost as if they were delighted to have me. What a great country this was where a university education was available to everyone. In Ireland, a country with such a great reverence for learning, a college education was out of the question for children of the working classes.

◆

A few days before Hilda was due, I gave my little apartment a good spring cleaning. My landlady was worried that it would be too small for two people—little did she know how eleven of us were crammed into that tiny house on Railway Avenue. I assured her we would manage fine. I bought some extra towels and the groceries I thought we would need. I bought fresh flowers for the table and a package of banana cream cookies not dreaming that Hilda would go wild over these.

I was sick with excitement when she arrived; she was just what I needed to perk me up. She was slim now and she looked really well. We had so much to say we didn't give each other a chance to finish a sentence. She brought me loads of presents from home; a letter and a sweep ticket from Daddy, a pound of Lyons' loose tea, an Arklow teapot and an Irish cottage tea cozy from Mammy, pink satin pajamas from Olga, a box of Black Magic from Joan and Doris, my usual treat from Ada—a big bar of Cadbury's Fruit and nut and a Woman's Own—and a box of Jacob's afternoon tea from Hilda herself. She brought the duty free booze and cigarettes for Uncle Gary.

I made a pot of good strong Irish tea—the first I had had since I left home. We drank our tea, ate our goodies, smoked our cigarettes and sat up all night talking.

In no time at all, Hilda landed herself a job at The Bell Telephone Company as a trainee. She learned quickly. She was conscientious and soon became an operator. She was popular with the staff—they were captivated by her Dublin accent. Her base salary was good and she didn't miss an opportunity to work Sundays or Holidays when she was paid time-and-a-half or double time.

Hilda was happy to be back in America. We shopped together and she couldn't get over the selection of gorgeous clothes at a fraction of what we would pay at home. We could even return the clothes if we didn't like them. They just gave us our money back with no questions asked. In Ireland if you returned anything, the assistant would look at you suspiciously "Did you wear this?" she'd say. She would then proceed to examine the garment carefully and even smell under the arms. If you were lucky you got a store credit but never your money back.

It amused us to see American children shopping with their mothers. The children had the run of the store and could choose anything they wanted. The doting mother would say "Are you sure this is what you want, honey?" They didn't only buy one outfit; they ended up with an armload. This was a far cry from the way we shopped in Ireland. Mammy decided what we would wear and we had no say-so in the matter. We were lucky to have anything new at all.

I introduced Hilda to Maggie and they took to each other right away. She enjoyed our Thursday dinners, the little red crabapples and the Dubonnet at Brahms. We both spent weekends at Maggie's when "Ma" Bristol was out of town. We seldom argued and doubled our wardrobes by swapping clothes with each other.

◆

My office friend Pam invited Hilda, Maggie and me to a party at her house. She said there was somebody she would like me to meet and that it was a

B.Y.O.B party. I was clueless as to what that meant and I had to ask her. She laughed when she told me that it meant to "bring you own bottle".

We were excited at the prospect of our first American party. We dolled ourselves up to the nines and decided to bring gin and tonics between us. When we arrived at 7:00 p.m. there was a big crowd already there—most of them I knew from the office. They were all casually dressed which made us feel a little foolish in our high heels and party dresses. There was a table set with a bucket of ice, plastic glasses, plates of finger foods and crackers and cheese. Everyone stood around talking shop. They talked about *Scatty's* visit to the *dactor*. We thought it funny the way they pronounced their o's like a's and the way they said *the noos* for the news. I introduced Hilda and Maggie to the people near us. They said they loved our Irish brogues and it seemed they all had ancestors who came from Ireland. Pam then introduced me to Tom McGovern. Tom was a short serious fellow and he wore glasses. He wasn't my type but, not to hurt Pam's feelings, I made a date with him. We were still waiting for the party to begin when at about 9:00 p.m. people started looking at their watches and saying they'd better be off. We couldn't believe that this was the end of the party; no piano, no singing, no dancing, no funny stories and home to bed early—very different from the lively nights we were used to in Dublin. We said goodnight to Pam and thanked her for the lovely party. She told us to be sure and pick up our bottle. We couldn't wait to get outside and have a good laugh.

◆

A good friend of Uncle Gary's had died and Gary picked up Hilda and me to take us to the funeral home for the rosary. This was the first time we had seen a dead person in the States. The man didn't look dead at all. He was dressed in a blue business suit complete with shirt and tie. His head rested on a white pillow and his face was all made up; he even had his glasses on. The casket—they didn't use the word coffin—was a beautiful heavy oak with golden handles and lined with white velvet. There were huge arrangements of flowers on tall stands and shaped into crosses and hearts. Soft music played in the background.

In Ireland, there were no funeral parlors at that time and people were laid out in a bedroom in the home. They looked dead; waxy white skin and a rosary entwined around icy fingers. They were dressed in a simple religious habit of blue or sometimes brown. Lighted candles surrounded the bedside and the mourners knelt and recited the rosary. The coffin was generally a simple pine box.

◆

Hilda and I were becoming a bit cramped in our tiny apartment and as we were both earning good money we decided to look around for something bigger. We were lucky to find a three room apartment on the ground floor of a lovely house on Ransom Ave. The owner, Mrs.MacNamee, had been widowed recently and she decided to convert her large home into apartments. There was a long entrance hall and a door to the right where Mrs.M lived. A newlywed couple rented the upstairs. At the end of the hall directly facing the front door was our apartment. We had a living room, dining area, kitchen, bedroom and bathroom. It was furnished in comfortable solid maple. Best of all was the thermostat on the wall where we could magically turn on the central heating. No more chopping sticks or going up to the shed in the freezing cold to fill the coal bucket for the fire. We had the use of a washing machine, a mangle and a clothesline in the basement. We couldn't believe our luck finding such a perfect place. Mrs. M was kind and protective toward us. She was a pretty lady in her sixties. She wore pastel dresses and fancy costume jewelry. Like all Americans, she was perfectly groomed; beautifully manicured nails and well coiffed hair. She often invited us in to her apartment for a cup of coffee or to watch "I Love Lucy" with her on her TV. She adopted us as her daughters as she didn't have any family of her own.

Although we weren't good cooks we enjoyed having friends from work over for dinner. Maggie came too when she had time off. They seemed to enjoy the simple Irish fare—corned beef and cabbage or a stew. The Americans were generous—they never came without a bottle of wine or a pie from the bakery.

◆

One night we got a bit of a scare in the apartment. It had been snowing steadily all day; mountains and mountains of beautiful white powder, something we had never seen in Ireland. The snow ploughs were clearing the streets and Mrs.M had hired a young lad to clear her driveway. The power went out early in the evening and since we had no electricity we decided to have an early night. We piled coats and blankets on our beds to keep warm. We locked our bedroom door as we had heard stories of strange things happening in America. We even had weapons beside our beds—I had a broken chair leg and Hilda had a stout branch of a tree which looked like a shillelagh.

I was in a deep sleep when I heard it—someone was jiggling a key in our bedroom door. Hilda was sitting bolt upright in her bed with a look of terror on her face. She had heard it too. We heard it again. My heart was thumping wildly. We were sure someone was trying to come in to murder us. The sound seemed to be coming from the living room. We grabbed our weapons, tiptoed to the bedroom door and opened it cautiously. We crept into the dark living room and although the power was back on we dared not turn on a light. We heard the jiggling of keys again. We crouched behind the big armchair scarcely daring to breathe. No more noise, they must have left. We waited a while longer before venturing into the hallway. We woke up Mrs.M and told her what had happened. She said she hadn't heard a thing and the front door was locked and double bolted. She put on her coat and boots and took a flashlight to check outside. All around the house we went—no sign of anyone and no footprints in the fresh snow. Could it have been our imagination? Mrs.M came into our apartment with us and we all heard the sound again. I seemed to be coming from outside our window. Out we went again and there it was—the telephone wire had broken with the weight of the snow and when the wind blew, it brushed the loose ends against our window. What a relief. Mrs.M assured us that in her thirty years living there, there had never been a break in.

◆

Hilda was dating a good looking fellow named Raul and I was going out with Tom. We usually went to the movies. Marilyn Monroe was a big hit in "Gentlemen Prefer Blondes". Since we had no TV, I enjoyed the newsreels before the main feature especially the European news and the pictures of Britain's new young Queen Elizabeth 11.

Tom was polite, generous, and boring. He talked about the stress of his job that was causing his stomach ulcers—he was manager of a hardware company. He was proud of his Irish roots. When he invited me to meet his family I knew he was getting serious. In order to break it off gently, I told him I had a boyfriend in Ireland.

My office colleagues were constantly setting me up with dates. I was taken to hockey games, ball games and bowling. I was never any good at sports and I didn't even understand them. My problem was I was experiencing a severe case of homesickness. I missed the interesting conversations with David. I missed my family and friends and I missed the gaiety of Dublin. America was big and bright and beautiful and rich but I felt I simply did not fit in.

◆

My old friend, Polly, wrote from Canada. She had found a job in an insurance office at $33.00 a week. She had made some new friends but she said they were just not the same as the old ones; their sense of humor was different and they thought she was loony when she laughed at things they didn't think funny at all. Her boyfriend was working at Canadian Broadcasting. He got the job through a friend of his who made up all kinds of lies about his education and experience to get him in. Polly thought the Toronto men were good looking but she would have nothing to do with them because they only had one thing on their minds and she wasn't having any of that. She said the Canadian women had a much harder life than the Irish women; their men expected them to hold down jobs—to stop working would be a sign of laziness. She said she missed us and the good times we had in Dublin. However, she said she didn't think she could ever go back to that life of poverty.

◆

While Hilda was working nights, I continued to enjoy my college classes in English Literature and Journalism. My professor, Dr.James Thornboro, was a tall, gray haired man. He expressed his thoughts clearly and he was supportive of our efforts. We were required to read the classics and textbooks on writing. We had to research and submit articles on current events. He advised us to join a writers' club and attend writers' conferences which I never did. His motto was:

"And, above all else, get understanding"

I liked that.

I admired the self confidence of the students and the way they interacted with the professor. They called him by his first name, sat on his desk and laughed and joked with him as though he were an equal. To respect their superiors would have made no sense to them.

◆

Maggie's contract with The Bristol's was coming to a close and she did not want to renew as she said she couldn't stand another winter in Grand Rapids. She wanted to visit New York before heading home for good. She asked Hilda and me if we would go with her. We didn't need persuading. We knew New York was a sophisticated city with theaters, art galleries, ballrooms and exclusive shops and we were ready to explore.

While we were making our plans we spent many a happy Sunday on Lake Michigan's sandy beaches. It was a relief to replace our woolen leggings, scarves and snow boots with bathing suits, shorts and sandals. Our favorite beach was Grand Haven. We would take sandwiches, a flask of tea and Maggie's portable radio and spend the long sunny days facing the sun in a futile attempt to get a tan. We had never even heard of sun block. We slathered ourselves with cocoa butter; this was supposed to promote a great tan. At the end of the day we were as red as lobsters but we didn't mind as we expected it would turn brown. It didn't. It blistered and peeled and in no time at all we were back to our fair Irish complexions.. We were envious of Maggie—her olive skin tanned beautifully.

When I told my boss of our plans, he said he didn't blame us—there wasn't too much excitement for young people in Grand Rapids. He said he would write to the manager in the Madison Ave. Branch and arrange a transfer for me. Hilda could also get a transfer to The Telephone Company in New York.

Before our departure we said goodbye to all the people who had been so kind to us. We went to visit The Lemucci's. They were extremely grateful to Mammy and to me for being instrumental in completing their family. They were a happy little group and the children were thriving; they were deprived of nothing. They had their own rooms filled with toys and books and clothes. Most of all they were very much wanted and loved. They wished us good luck and gave us money to treat ourselves to a dinner in New York.

The office staff threw a party for me and gave me a present of a gold pin shaped like a leaf and a card with messages of good wishes from everybody. We promised to write to each other.

20

New York, New York

"It's a wonderful place to visit, but I'd hate to live there."

—a common quote about New York

Uncle Gary arranged for us to stay at a hostel for Christian Women in Manhattan. He said New York could be a dangerous place for young single girls, it was full of Puerto Ricans and they were well-known gangsters. The hostel would be the safest place for us until we got our bearings. He drove us to the airport in Chicago and told us to keep our passports, money and valuables with us at all times. This proved to be good advice. He wasn't happy that his only relatives were leaving Grand Rapids but he wished us God speed and every success in "The Big Apple".

We took a cab from the airport to the hostel, paid the cabbie and gave him a tip. He put our luggage out on the sidewalk and took off. We were craning our necks admiring the tall skyscrapers and not paying attention to our business when we realized our leather train case was missing. We went over to a burly policeman who was standing at the corner and we told him what had happened. It turned out he was from Ireland like most of the New York policemen. He told us where the police station was and advised us to go there and report our loss. We never found our case and, fortunately for us, there wasn't anything of value in it only junk jewelry and make-up. It was a cheap lesson to remind us to be more cautious in the future.

We were as excited as children as we looked forward to our new adventure. Hilda and I had our jobs and the first order of importance was to find a job for Maggie. The matron of the hostel said that The Biltmore Hotel was always in need of waitresses. Maggie wasted no time and the next day she went there. After exaggerating her past experience and using her unfailing Irish charm, she was hired on the spot.

161

We now needed to find a place to live. Here again the matron came to our aid. She gave us an address on East 58th Street which she thought might be suitable. The Sutton Place Hotel was old and a bit rundown. They offered us a large room with three single beds and the use of a kitchen and bathroom. Between the three of us, the rent was affordable. Our room was fully furnished. It had a wall to wall closet, a desk, bedside tables with lamps and even a small black and white TV. We had daily maid service—something we were not used to. It embarrassed me later to think of the shambles we left our room in as we rushed out to work early in the mornings; beds rumpled and clothes scattered everywhere. When we returned in the evenings our beds were neatly made, our clothes were hanging, ashtrays were emptied and washed and our room was vacuumed and dusted. There was a clerk in the lobby that operated the switchboard and handled our mail and messages. We didn't realize it at the time, but our location was the most enviable to be found anywhere in New York.

We got to know the other residents in our building. It seemed everyone came to New York with a dream of finding fame and fortune. The city was full of talented and lonely people. There was the beautiful little dancer from Peru. She showed us the photo album she was taking around to the various agents in the hopes of getting into a Broadway show. To us she already looked like a movie star with her dark good looks and obvious talent.

Then there was an elderly writer named Hank Betancourt. He was working on The Great American Novel and sustaining himself by writing articles for magazines and newspapers. He often came in to visit us. He said he liked the company of the Irish; he thought we were witty and light hearted. He was familiar with New York and proved to be a great guide in directing us to places of interest. He also knew where we could find the best bargains in town. It was easy enough to find our way around because most of the streets had numbers instead of names.

Our other neighbor, Marguerite, was an artiste from the Midwest. She had run away from an abusive husband and she loved the anonymity of New York. She was short, chubby and pretty. She discovered a way to save money by doing her own dry cleaning. Any time we went to her place her clothes were spread out to dry all over the floor. We had to tiptoe between the sweaters to reach a chair. She highly recommended this method of cleaning to us but we weren't sold on the idea.

We had all settled in nicely at our jobs. My office was located on prestigious Madison Avenue—the advertising capital of the world. It was only a short walk from our hotel. The offices of Merrill, Lynch were on the seventh floor of a sleek modern skyscraper. Across the street were equally tall buildings. Our office had a large staff of men and women. Most of them commuted from Queens, Brooklyn or Jackson Heights. There were executives, stockbrokers, managers, secretaries, a typing pool, teletype operators and mail room people. I was to work as secretary to Mr. Nichols. He was a kind little man who smiled all the time despite his ill-fitting false teeth. My work was easy and Mr. Nichols was always appreciative. He complimented me on my outfits, something a boss in Dublin would never do. Once he brought me a box of chocolates because of a letter I had written that resulted in getting his beloved daughter admitted to a prestigious New York school.

I was introduced to a girl from Drogheda named Clair. She had big sad eyes. She was married to an American and she hated him and she hated New York. She was just waiting for a chance to make her escape back home. She counted herself lucky that she didn't have any children.

Hilda loved her job at the telephone company. There were plenty of Irish and Scottish girls there who made her feel right at home. She was earning great money because of the overtime that she never refused.

Maggie said working at The Biltmore was like going to a posh party every day. Everyone who was anyone rendezvoused there. They met for lunch, for afternoon tea, for cocktails or for dinner. She met celebrities, heirs to fortunes and movie stars. Cary Grant was even better looking in real life than he was in the movies. She raved about his height, his elegant style, his deep tan and his magnificent speaking voice. She couldn't stop gawking at Elizabeth Taylor; no living creature had a right to be that beautiful. The guests kidded her about her Irish accent and left her generous tips. Maggie had a knack of making her stories sound even funnier than they were and we enjoyed hearing about the rich and famous.

The Biltmore was hosting a huge convention and they were short of waitresses. They asked the staff if they knew anyone who could help out for one evening. Maggie asked me if I would come along and give it a try. She said the pay was excellent and she would be there to help me out. She knew I had no experience but she said there was nothing to it. With some reservation, I agreed to go. The required uniform was a black dress and a white apron. I had a black dress and Maggie ironed a man's white handkerchief into pleats which was to do for my apron. She had a spare frilly headpiece which she loaned me.

Off we went on the appointed evening. The dining room was huge and formidable with sparkling chandeliers, immaculately set tables and fresh flowers everywhere. It was abuzz with hundreds of important-looking businessmen. There were numerous doors leading to the kitchens. The kitchens were in a state of confusion as many temporary staffers tried to load up trays of chicken dinners for so many guests. Maggie pointed to a door and said

> "When the red light goes on, you go through that door. Your table is right beside it, number 31. You carry your tray like this (she demonstrated how to hoist the tray on my left arm leaving my right hand free to serve the dinners) and that's all there is to it until dessert, then you just repeat the same thing."

I picked up my tray; I didn't think it would be so heavy. The red light went on. Which door did she say? All the doors had red lights. Everyone scrambled through in a mad rush and I followed out the nearest one. With my short sight and my hopeless sense of direction, I couldn't find Table 31. I fumbled around peering at table numbers and avoiding the eyes of the businessmen who seemed to be highly amused at my predicament. I thought I saw Maggie waving at me from the far side of the room. She was pointing to a table which was number 31. By this time, all the other diners had been served. The men at my table looked without compassion at my scarlet face. I set a plate down in front of the gentleman nearest me and then there was unmerciful crash—the whole tray slid off my arm and chicken dinners scattered everywhere. Maggie rushed to the kitchen, picked up another tray and served my table with expert efficiency. In the meantime, two busboys cleaned up the mess. I was a nervous wreck and Maggie came to my rescue again by serving my desserts. I didn't think I deserved to be paid but Maggie insisted I join her on the payroll line. They thanked me profusely as they handed me my pay and said they hoped I would be available to help out again.

◆

World-renowned Fifth Avenue was only a stone's throw from our apartment and it provided us with a wealth of sightseeing and entertainment. It was there you could see the most elegantly dressed men and women in New York as they stepped out of their air-conditioned limousines to do their shopping. There were exquisite high-quality stores; Saks, Bergdoff Goodman, Chanel, Gucci, Brooks Brothers, Tiffany's, Cartier's and dozens of specialty shops. One of our favorite pastimes was to window shop on Fifth Avenue. The window displays were extravagant. We couldn't afford to buy anything but it was nice to admire the latest styles and then look for cheaper versions in the bargain basements.

Other places of interest we visited on Fifth Avenue were Saint Patrick's Cathedral, The Empire State Building, Rockefeller Center, The New York Public Library, the museums and, of course, Central Park. The route for the Saint

Patrick's Day Parade was down Fifth Avenue. Apart from the fact that there was a huge Irish population in New York, the Chinese, Ukrainians, Polish, Puerto Ricans and every other ethnic group came out to march on Saint Patrick's Day.

We found the heat and humidity oppressive. The streets were claustrophobic because of heavy traffic, overcrowding and the skyscrapers rising to the sky from both sides. We didn't have air conditioning in our apartment and the fan we bought wasn't much help. The make-up ran down our faces and we had to sew dress shields under the arms in our clothes because frequent showers and the use of deodorants were not enough. To add to our discomfort, we wore dresses, high heels and nylons as most office girls did at that time. How I would have welcomed a downpour of soft Irish rain. I would have gone outside barefooted and danced in it.

◆

One day I came home from the office tired and cranky from the heat. I was delighted to find a thick letter from mammy and lo and behold a letter in David's familiar handwriting. I hesitated to open it because I was sure it contained his wedding announcement and plans for his future. I opened Mammy's first. There were beautiful photographs and all the news of Olga's wedding. She had married her sweetheart, William O. Kinsella, (Billie). They had a traditional Catholic wedding in Saint Michael's Church. Olga was a beautiful bride and I was sorry to have missed her wedding. Joan was Maid of Honor and she looked lovely in a turquoise dress and hat that we had sent her from America. After their honeymoon in Amsterdam, Olga and Billie moved into their brand new house in Terenure.

David's letter was eight pages long in his tiny cramped style of writing. He said he had chucked his Protestant girl friend—she had proven to be mean, cruel, domineering and untrustworthy and he could never imagine spending the rest of his life with her. He said I was the only one in the world for him and he must have been mad to think that any one could ever take my place in his heart. He apologized profusely and said he would be the happiest man on earth if I would write back to say I had forgiven him and that I would take him back.

I showed his letter to Hilda. She was a surprised as I was.

> "Well, he certainly loves you and he seems to be very sincere. You had no interest in anyone else you dated. It wouldn't hurt to at least write back to him and see where it takes you."

Of course Hilda was right. I had dated a few fellows from the office. They took me to expensive restaurants and to Broadway shows—places I could never have afforded myself. The extent of my dining out was the blue plate special at Woolworth's lunch counter or a toasted English muffin at one of the fancy coffee houses. My office colleagues were clean cut nice young men but they all had baggage; some were divorced and paying child support and alimony, others admitted to being married. There wasn't a Catholic among them. Once I agreed to go to see "The King and I" with a broker from the office. I wore my new black dress and took great pains getting myself ready. When he picked me up at the apartment he complimented me and said I looked ravishing. We had only gone about a block in his car when he looked at me and said

"I'm going to have you tonight."

I thought to myself

"That's what you think."

We stopped at a red light and out I jumped in the middle of traffic. I ran the whole way home. When I told Hilda what happened she said

"The cheek of him—you did the right thing. Lucky you hadn't gone too far before he made his intentions known—they're all after the same thing—that could have been very dangerous."

I was sorry to have missed "The King and I", everyone said it was the best show on Broadway.

I answered David's letter. This was the beginning of a stream of correspondence filled with romance and remembrances of the times we enjoyed together in Dublin. He wrote the most glorious love letters, the kind of letters any woman would long to get. I read and reread them. His envelopes were sealed with red sealing wax and his family crest imprinted with his ring. He told me how wonderful I was and how much he loved me. He told me about his studies—his exams were becoming more difficult. He missed having me there to encourage him. He wrote about his family and his loneliness without me. He was depressed most of the time and the persistent rainy weather only added to his misery.

He was interested in hearing about all the wonders I was seeing in New York. I told him of our visit to Saint Patrick's Cathedral and how impressed we were by the beauty of the stained-glass windows. I sent photographs of the flags of the world around Rockefeller Plaza—headquarters of The United Nations. I also sent him photographs of Broadway and Times Square. He didn't pressure me into hurrying home but he said he would be waiting for me when I was ready and then he would spend his whole life making me happy.

◆

To escape the congestion and the heat of the city, we often spent our Sundays relaxing in nearby Central Park. It was very much like Stephen's Green only much larger. We walked along the cool tree-shaded pathways and people-watched by the tranquil lakes. Americans fascinated us; they all looked so clean, so tan, so rich and so confident—that's because they were never told to shut up and stop asking so many stupid questions. We took the popular tour in a horse-drawn carriage. We often stayed until evening to enjoy the free band concerts. It was cooler then when the breeze came up and rustled the trees. Even though it was overlooked by vast skyscrapers, Central Park was a peaceful retreat away from the bustle of the city.

Coney Island in Brooklyn was another place we liked to visit to escape the heat. It was a seaside resort and only a short subway ride from the city. It reminded me of Bray. People flocked there by the thousands to cool off in the ocean or to just stroll along the boardwalk eating their hot dogs or ice cream cones. There was a penny arcade and an amusement park offering roller coaster rides for the fearless. I couldn't even look at them without remembering the terror I felt as a child when I got violently ill on the top of one of those things. They had to abort the ride to get me down. I vomited all over the grass. They gave me a drink of water and told me to put my head down between my knees. I felt better after a while but that finished me with roller coaster rides. We always stayed late at Coney Island as we couldn't bear to go back to the stifling heat of our apartment.

◆

I was on my way out of the lobby one Saturday morning when our mailman, Bill, approached me with a package. He was smiling

"Looks like a special day for you, Nora; I need your John Hancock here."

I signed for the package which was registered and insured and went back upstairs to open it. Hilda examined the label

"Look at this—'diamond engagement ring—value £2,000.00'—oh my God, hurry up and open it."

My fingers were shaking as I cut through the tape. Inside a larger box padded with tissue was a smaller blue box from J.Weir & Sons, Dublin. Perched on dark blue velvet was a sparkling solitaire diamond engagement ring set in platinum. I put it on the third finger of my left hand. It was a perfect fit. I admired it in the mirror because I had heard somewhere that that is the right way to look at a diamond. Hilda and Maggie tried it on and they were excited for me. I read the enclosed letter from David. He said he hoped I would accept his ring and if I did it would mean that we were now officially engaged. He would be anxiously waiting for my reply.

This all happened so suddenly, I didn't know what to say. I wrote back to tell him I was in a state of shock and overcome with happiness. I hoped I wouldn't wake up to find that this had only been a pleasant dream. Of course I accepted his proposal. My ring was exquisite—it was hard for me to believe it belonged to me. I asked him what his plans were and if he expected me to come home immediately.

His answer was that he was the happiest man on earth that I had accepted him as my future husband. He did not expect me to rush home, even though he would have liked me to be there for his graduation which was now only weeks away. He said as soon as I came home he would take me to England to meet his family. We would then get married and he would do his internship in an English Hospital.

These arrangements suited me fine. I needed to save money for my fare home. I also wanted to see more of New York because I knew that once I left I would never ever go back again.

I wrote to tell my mother the good news. She wasn't a bit impressed

"I'm telling you this is all wrong for you. You come from two different worlds. You won't be happy in his world any more than he wouldn't be happy in yours. He is a delicate man. Of course you are flattered by his attention, any girl would be. Send him back his ring and keep your good job in New York. Now that you have been away from him for so long it will be easy to forget him."

In a way, I knew my mother was right, but I knew in my heart I had to go back to him.

While I was saving and making my plans, I made sure to see as much of New York as possible. We saw an extravagant show featuring the famous Rockettes at Radio City Music Hall. We wanted to see some Broadway shows but the tickets were too expensive for us. We took the elevator to the 102nd Floor of the Empire State Building and we visited The Hayden Planetarium.

It was too early to tell my boss of my plans and I didn't wear my engagement ring to the office.

I was writing often to David telling him of the lovely presents Hilda and Maggie had bought me for my trousseau and of all the grand places I had been seeing in New York.

He answered that he was happy I was making good use of my time and he was counting the days until we would be together again. He said I should book my passage home so that he would have a definite date to look forward to.

When I had booked my passage aboard the luxurious liner The S.S. America which was to sail from New York in two months time I wrote to tell David. He said it was the best news he had ever had in his life. He was the luckiest man on earth and he would be waiting for me at Cobh.

A month before my departure date, I wore my engagement ring to the office and gave my boss a month's notice. He was happy for me and he announced my engagement to the staff. They crowded round me to admire my ring and wanted to know all about my romance. Before I left they gave me an engagement party. They brought wine and a fancy cake with our names on it. They brought beautifully wrapped gifts; negligees, scented soap and candles, a lace trimmed slip, photo albums and a generous check from my boss, Mr. Nichols. They wished me the best of luck and made me promise to send the wedding photos.

I had a love/hate relationship with New York. I knew I would miss the great bargains at Kline's on 34th Street. I stocked up on everything I thought I would need for my trousseau and I invested in a beautiful blue suit for my arrival. I bought gifts for all the family, a large box of chocolates for my old friends at R.H. Boyds and a good-looking leather writing case for David with his initials engraved in gold. I would miss the variety in the stores; anything that could be bought in any city in the world could be found in New York and usually at a better price. I would miss the cleanliness of the streets, parks and all public places. Nobody threw away a candy wrapper—there were trash receptacles everywhere. I would miss my job, the good salary I was earning and my kind boss, Mr. Nichols. I would miss going to Horn and Hardarts Automat with Hilda and Maggie. We got a big kick out of eating there. The prepared food was displayed behind glass windows. You made your selection, put your coin in the slot, and presto, out popped a lovely hot dinner.

On the other hand, the city scared me. There was too much confusion, congestion and heat. There was not enough air and not enough light. People rushed about looking tense and irritable. The normal frustrations of everyday living seemed to be magnified in New York. Traffic was snarled and taxis, if you could find one, drove with desperation. Apart from the black headlines in the daily newspapers; murder, rape, child molestation and gang warfare, I was terrified that one day a low-flying plane would crash into one of those skyscrapers and kill hundreds of innocent people.

21

The S.S.America

"Far out in the ocean the water is as blue as the petals of the
loveliest cornflower, and as clear as the purest glass.
But it is very deep too...."

—Hans Christian Anderson

Hilda, Maggie and our dry cleaning neighbor, Marguerite, came to the pier to see me off. I was filled with excitement as this was my first ocean voyage. I was told it was great fun—just like staying at a luxurious hotel for a week except that this hotel would be floating. There were huge crowds, great fanfare and confusion on the pier as luggage and cargo were loaded and the tugs were being readied to push the enormous ship into the Atlantic. There was a band playing and people threw colored streamers into the air. They hugged and kissed and laughed and cried as they said their last goodbyes. As Hilda hugged me she said she would be seeing me soon as she was almost ready to leave New York. Maggie planned on leaving also as her fiancé now had a good job in London and he was ready to get married. Horns blasted, whistles blew and orders were shouted as the ship inched its way from the pier. With tears in my eyes, I waved at Hilda, Maggie and Marguerite until they were just three little dots in the distance. As we steamed eastward we passed The Statue of Liberty and Ellis Island. I thought about the thousands of unfortunate Irish arriving there after The Famine and scared to death for fear they might be sent back because of TB or some other disease. Many were.

We were greeted on board by the officers and crew all looking handsome in their immaculate white uniforms. Waiters hurried around delivering enormous baskets of flowers, fruits, chocolates and champagne to First Class Passengers. I was shown to my cabin which I was to share with a girl from Scotland. It had two single beds and a private bathroom. There was a reading light over each bed. The steward had folded the towels into amusing animal shapes and placed them on our beds. As soon as we were unpacked, we were called to the deck for life boat drill. As I looked into the deep churning ocean around me I was thinking of The Titanic and praying that nothing like that would happen to us.

The S.S. America was the epitome of luxury. It was spacious, comfortable and beautifully decorated. I would have needed more than a week to take advantage of all the entertainment the ship had to offer. There was deck tennis, shuffle-board, a swimming pool, a sauna, an exercise room, a library, a cinema, shops with merchandise from around the world and even a chapel where Mass was said every morning. The ship's bulletin was slipped under our door listing the movies that would be shown and the special activities for each day. There were bridge tournaments, talent competitions, raffles for extravagant prizes, ice sculpture demonstrations and dancing every evening to the romantic music of John Davies and his orchestra.

My cabin mate, Rose, was a big cheerful fresh-faced girl. I liked the way she said my name *Nurra*. She married in Scotland and they came to Chicago imme-diately afterwards. She was a nurse and her husband was an electrician. They were earning good money and looking forward to the day when they could return to Scotland. They had two small boys and they didn't want to raise them in The States. She said the American children were spoiled—they had an abundance of everything but not enough discipline. She said the school day was too short and started too early. It saddened her to see sleepy little children with their lunch pails waiting for the bus at 6:30 or 7:00 a.m. on freezing cold mornings. She deplored the twelve weeks summer vacation—it was a burden on the parents and it was detrimental to the continuity of the children's education. She thought the extra-curricular activities placed unnecessary stress on the children. She thought tenure for teachers was a bad idea—they couldn't be fired even if they were not doing a good job. She felt the American children were being cheated and she preferred the commonsense approach to education in Scotland for her two boys.

Rose and I were seated together for meals. There were eight at our table—two talkative English girls, a young married couple and two tall, handsome students who were on their way to Baden-Baden, Germany. The dining room had a delightful ambiance; glittering chandeliers, unique arrangements of fresh flowers and beautifully dressed passengers. The table setting for dinner was always for-mal; five glasses, four for wines and one for water, six pieces of silverware and expertly folded monogrammed napkins at each place. The meals were superb, we had different menus every day and the staff took great pains to ensure that our slightest need was met. There was lots of fun and laughter at our table—everyone was in a lively holiday mood. There were two formal evenings—The Captain's Dinner and The Officers' Cocktail Party. I had packed two new evening dresses;

a gorgeous green and an elegant black and I was delighted to have the opportunity to wear them. All the ladies looked lovely and the officers were extremely handsome in their dress whites.

Apart from the meals served in the dining room, bouillon was served on deck every morning at 11:00 and afternoon tea was served at 4:00 p.m. Cocktails were served in the lounge at 5:00 p.m. and at midnight an elaborate smorgasbord feast was set up in the ballroom. Tea, coffee and sandwiches were always available.

Rose was a great swimmer and while she went to the pool I explored the ten decks of the magnificent S.S.America. Sometimes I sat in a comfortable deck chair enjoying the sun and other times I browsed around the shops. There was an exclusive smoke shop and as Daddy enjoyed the occasional cigar, I bought him a box of good ones on the recommendation of the assistant who seemed to know about these things.

Every evening we went to the ballroom. The orchestra was excellent and they played traditional romantic dance music. Rock & Roll was barely surfacing and Elvis was just beginning to gain popularity from his appearance on The Ed Sullivan Show. We usually sat with our dinner companions and the young students were good dancers. As we were sipping our drinks and enjoying ourselves Rose whispered to me

"That gorgeous looking fellow in the orchestra keeps staring at you."

"Which fellow" I said squinting and looking over in the general direction of the orchestra

"The tanned, blond first violinist" she said

Sure enough when I located him, he was bowing and smiling at me. I smiled back at him. At intermission he came over to our table and introduced himself. His name was Werner and he came from The Black Forest Region in Germany. He bought us drinks and asked if there was any particular music we would like the orchestra to play. Rose requested her favorite, The Blue Danube Waltz, and I asked for Somewhere Along The Way. The music was divine. After that he sat with us when he could. He always sat beside me. I noticed him looking at my engagement ring but he didn't comment on it and neither did I.

All too soon our journey was nearing an end. We exchanged addresses and promised to keep in touch. The horns blared and the passengers rushed to the deck to get their first glimpse of Ireland. Unfortunately, there was little to be seen as it was dark, cloudy and lashing rain.

22

Home Sweet Home

"The proper means of increasing the love we bear to our native country is to reside some time in a foreign one."

—Shenstone

Dressed in my new blue suit and with my hair freshly done, I felt healthy and relaxed. As I walked down the gangplank I saw David waving at me through the crowds. He presented me with a perfect red rose. He kissed and embraced me so passionately he nearly took my breath away.

"Let me look at you. You are even more beautiful than you were when you left. I will never ever let you out of my sight again."

He teased me about my American accent and said I would have to lose that before meeting his Mama. I didn't like this and hoped he wasn't serious.

Maybe it was because I had become accustomed to seeing the well-built tanned Americans bursting with good health that I found him so frail and haggard. It didn't help that the weather was miserable and he was chilled to the bone from hanging about for hours waiting for me. Aboard the train for Dublin, we drank tea and talked non-stop. The train was filthy; crisp wrappers and sweet papers strewn about and cigarette butts stubbed out on the floor—not a trash can in sight. On the seat opposite us a little girl was reading. Her mother said

"Mary, will you put down that *boook.* I'm telling yeh, you'll ruin your eyes."

The mother looked at me for help

"That wan always has her nose stuck in a book—she'll be blind before she's eighteen—I'm sick of talking to her."

This struck me as funny when The Americans were spending fortunes on tutors trying to encourage their children to read.

Although David disliked everything American, he was interested in hearing about my work and my life in Michigan and in New York. He asked me about Hilda and Maggie and about the voyage home. He was now a doctor and his plans were that he would take me to England to meet his family and we would then make arrangements to get married in England. I didn't care for these arrangements—I wanted to get married in my own parish in Ireland and I wanted my dad to walk me down the aisle. I didn't say anything for fear of upsetting him in my first couple of hours home.

Somehow the magic I had anticipated at our reunion wasn't there. I knew David still loved me. I also knew he could never forgive me for leaving him. I felt guilty too especially as my reasons for leaving hadn't materialized; I hadn't saved much money and I didn't get my contact lenses. It didn't seem to bother David that I was near sighted; he needed me with him and it was selfish of me to go. On top of that I had unwittingly become somewhat Americanized. From being on my own, I had gained maturity and a new self assurance. This did not please him—he was used to me looking up to him and complying with his every wish. A shadow was cast on our relationship and I was confused.

I was delighted to see Mammy, Daddy and Ada as we pulled into Heuston Station. Mammy was all smiles as she hugged me. She was wearing a smart black and white dress and a lovely hat. Daddy took a fit of coughing as he kissed me and said

"You're looking very well Bernie. I'm glad you're home."

His asthma always acted up when he became emotional. Ada flung her arms around me and in her soft loving way she said

"I thought I would never see you again."

Ada was now nearly as tall as myself. She was a picture in a fresh summer dress and her hair was plaited around her head with a stiff white bow on top. As always, she was warm and affectionate.

After David helped Daddy put my luggage in the boot of the car, he kissed me, said goodbye to everyone and told me he would see me in a couple of days.

"I'm glad he didn't decide to come back to the house with us" said Mammy "I wasn't in the mood for him today."

I sat in the back seat of the car with Ada. She had brought a "party" to share; a box of smarties, a bag of dolly mixtures and aniseed balls. She kept her arm around me the whole way home. I asked her about her school and about her friends and she wanted to know if America was the same as it was in the pictures.

Before we got home, the rain had stopped and the sun was shining. The gardens we were passing were alive with bright summer flowers and the lawns were a dazzling green. This was something I missed in New York—roof top gardens just couldn't compare.

Olga was at the gate as we pulled up to the house. There were tears in her eyes as she hugged me and said

"I can't believe you're home Nody. You're looking marvelous. I'm sure you're hungry and tired after such a long journey. Come on in and I'll make you a nice cup of tea."

Before going in, I stopped to admire Mammy's roses. She was proud of her garden and I had never seen it look better. The purple clematis around the door was in full bloom and the hollyhocks, sweet pea, busy lizzies and London Pride were a pleasing picture. After the rain everything took on a fragrant freshness. For my coming home, Mammy had painted the front gate and the railings a bright spring green. The frilly curtains we had sent her from America looked lovely on the windows.

Daddy poured us a whiskey and water in our seldom-used Waterford glasses. He said a drink always tasted better in a proper glass. After the toasts were made we sat in the dining room to enjoy the welcome home feast; back rashers, fried eggs, Donnelly's pork sausages, black and white pudding, fresh brown bread and a pot of good strong tea.

After tea, we sat in the lounge getting caught up on the news. Daddy was finally able to sell his share of the bicycle shop. Through an ad in the newspaper and with Joan's enthusiasm, he bought a tobacconist shop on Emmet Road. It was a great location opposite Saint Michael's Church. Joan practically ran the shop and thanks to her common sense and ingenuity it was turning into a little gold mine.

Olga had to go home to make Billie's dinner. She said she was dying for me to see her new house. Arrangements were made to bring David to tea the following day. Before she left I gave her her present—a "welcome" mat for outside her front door.

As Olga left, Joan and Doris came home from the shop. They gave me a huge welcome. Daddy smiled as Joan handed him a thick envelope—the cash takings for the day. She talked animatedly about the shop and said she couldn't wait to take me there and show me everything. Doris, the beauty of the family, was prettier than ever. At the merest hint of sunshine, she took a glorious tan which was enviable in Dublin. She was studying for her Inter. They were delighted with the presents I brought them from America.

My young brother Jack came home later—he was red and sweaty from playing football with the lads on the road. He was a good-looking boy with fine blue eyes and lashes so long they should have belonged to a girl. When he was a baby Olga used to trim his eyelashes—she said that would make them long and thick. She was right. At about this time Jack was developing a good ear and a great interest in music.

At this time brother Billy was still in the army. Frank was working for Irish Shipping and traveling the world on board "The Irish Ash". Both of the brothers continued to send most of their pay home.

Mammy was delighted with the beaded cardigan I brought for her and as Daddy puffed away he said that was the best cigar he had ever smoked.

◆

The next day a neighbor knocked at our door with a batch of hot scones fresh from her oven. I invited her in and Mammy gave me a dagger's look and put her tight mouth on her the way she did when she got annoyed.

Mammy had no time for this lady. She said she was just an idle gossiper with too much time on her hands. This wasn't true; she was a sincere good woman and helpful to anyone in need. I thought it was lovely of her to come for a chat and bring the scones—I missed that sort of thing in America. I asked her if she would like a cup of tea and I got the dagger's look again. My mother followed me into the kitchen

"I'll kill you so I will. You don't know her, she'll never leave now."

I brought in the tea and butter and raspberry jam for the scones—they were scrumptious.

Mammy was right—the neighbor talked and talked and didn't want to budge. She had been in America visiting her relatives in Chicago. She said she couldn't live in America, the people weren't neighborly. In the end I had to excuse myself to get ready to meet David. She finally left and Mammy warned me

"Don't you ever ask her to come in again. She just wants to look around to see what I have. She's a nosey person and I have no time for her."

◆

When I met David in O'Connell Street, he was carrying a bouquet of beautiful yellow roses

"These are for Olga" he said "I know they are her favorite flowers."

Olga and David got along well. He thought she was beautiful and he was relaxed in her company just as everybody was.

We boarded the bus for Terenure and took our seats upstairs. David was in a cheerful mood and he looked much better than he had the previous day. We chatted easily and he told me he had booked our flight to England for the following week. I was looking forward to meeting his family but I would have liked more time in Dublin to revisit our favorite haunts and perhaps rekindle our romance.

We had no trouble finding Olga's house. It was a brand new development in various stages of completion. Olly was at her hall door and she gave us a big warm welcome. She thanked David for the roses and while she was arranging them in a vase, I asked her if we might look around the house. All the rooms were bright and airy and tastefully furnished. To the left of the entry hall were the lounge and the dining room. At the end of the hall was a well-equipped modern kitchen. There was a new stove, a new refrigerator and finely crafted wood cabinets. The large kitchen window looked out on to a beautifully landscaped back garden. Tall fir trees covered the back wall and an abundance of bright flowers surrounded the manicured lawn. An ornamental wishing well and a lighthouse added to the charm of the garden. David was very impressed. Olga placed the vase of roses on the hall table and joined us upstairs. There were three spacious bedrooms. Olga showed us swatches of the material for the bedspreads and draperies she had on order. The bathroom was luxurious; deep burgundy and gray tiles on the walls and a burgundy bathtub, toilet and wash hand basin. I loved everything about Olga's house and hoped that some day soon I would have a house like that myself.

We sat in the comfortable lounge and Olga brought in a tray of Irish coffees and a plate of piping hot bite sized sausage rolls. We chatted about the house and some of the problems with contractors and decorators. Olga showed us the sketches for her new fireplace—a lovely design in Connemara marble. She also showed us a picture of the Waterford crystal wall lights she was getting for either side of the fireplace. We talked about America and David's appointment as an intern at a hospital in Kent.

The Mercedes pulled into the driveway and Olga's husband, Billie, came in to join us. He admired the yellow roses and greeted us warmly. I was delighted to see Billie. He was always generous with me and we got along well. He talked about The Sweep and the new policy that guaranteed certain positions to be made available for the handicapped, the retired and the underprivileged. He said the place was beginning to look like a nursing home between the cotton heads, the wheel chairs and the crutches. Nevertheless, he had genuine sympathy for these people and he was happy to give them employment. He talked about a problem they were having with American agents—apparently they were selling the sweep tickets but not sending the stubs or the money back to Ireland.

Although Billie was anti British (he could never forgive England for their atrocities against Ireland) he was polite to David and congratulated him on becoming an M.D. Billie loved Ireland. He had served in the Irish army and although he had traveled a good deal he said he preferred a holiday in any part of Ireland to other places in the world.

Our tea was ready and we moved into the dining room. The table was invitingly set with a Celtic design Irish linen table cloth, "Old Country Roses" fine bone china, gleaming silverware and Waterford crystal glasses—all wedding presents and mostly from the staff of The Irish Hospitals' Sweepstakes office. The centerpiece was a rose bowl filled with multi colored short-stemmed roses. The meal was a feast for the eyes as well as the palate. We had fresh poached salmon served on an oval platter and garnished with thin slices of cucumber. There was a bowl of steaming new potatoes tossed in butter and sprinkled with chopped parsley. There was a mixed green salad and a bread basket filled with fresh brown bread, soda bread and scones. Olga was the essence of hospitality—she spared no expense and no detail was overlooked. We were all in high good humor and there was plenty of chat and laughter at the table. David was doing justice to the feast and I was happy to see him eating so well. When we were nearly finished, Olga disappeared into the kitchen and came back with a crystal bowl of plump ripe strawberries and a jug of clotted cream. She told us to help ourselves as she cleared the plates and set out fancy dessert dishes. The strawberries I had tasted in America weren't anything like the luscious sweetness of the Irish strawberries. When we had demolished the last delicious morsel, Billie poured out the tea and lit a cigarette. David lit one for me and offered one to Olga. Olga refused; she had never smoked. This was one of the most enjoyable meals I had ever had.

As the summer evenings in Ireland were long and bright, after tea we took a stroll around the neighborhood. I missed twilight in America; it went from daylight to darkness in no time at all. It was lovely to see people out cleaning their windows, digging in their gardens or pushing their rosy-cheeked babies in their Silver Cross prams at ten o'clock in the evening. Everyone stopped to chat and I felt right at home. These were my people and they were wonderful. Their voices were so expressive and they were loaded with personality. They shared their gardening tips and invited us in to see their homes.

◆

The following day, I went with Joan to see the shop. As we walked along Bulfin Road we admired the neatly kept houses and the well-tended flower-filled gardens. I remembered most of the people who lived in these houses. A girl I had gone to school with, Frances Keely, was opening her gate as we passed. She was an attractive girl and she was allowed to keep all of her salary and spend it on beautiful clothes. She was an only child and indulged by her parents.. She had her passage booked for America and she wanted to know all about it. Had I been telling her the truth, I would have told her not to go—she had America at home. I wanted to tell her you get all mixed up when you go to America—when you're there you are homesick for Ireland and when you are in Ireland you miss all the good things about America.

Joan filled me in on all she was doing in the shop. It had been run down and neglected and Daddy bargained to get the already low price reduced even further. Joan could see the potential and she got busy cleaning, painting, redecorating and buying stock. She was a natural born organizer and salesperson. Thanks to her, it was now a lovely bright clean shop. They sold newspapers, magazines, paperbacks, cigarettes, pipe tobacco, boxes of chocolates, sweets of all kinds, ice cream, lemonade, fizzy drinks, greeting cards and wrapping paper. Anything a customer asked for that they didn't have, Joan made sure to order it. She hired Jack Collins to make new racks to display the greeting cards and she ordered huge supplies. There was great profit in greeting cards. Daddy was afraid Joan was overbuying but she assured him that everything would sell. She was right. Mammy worked in the shop nearly every day. Doris came after school and Daddy helped when he could. They hired extra staff for their busiest times—Sundays after the Masses and before and after the football matches.

I stayed for a few hours but I wasn't much help as I wasn't familiar with the merchandise and I didn't know the prices. I was hopeless at that sort of thing anyway. When a poor raggedy child came in with only a penny, I filled up a bag of sweets for him. Joan said I couldn't do that as pretty soon I would have the whole neighborhood in looking for the same good measure.

In the afternoon Mammy arrived and I left to visit my old friends at R.H. Boyds. I enjoyed the walk to Islandbridge. Happy memories came flooding back as I passed the familiar shops; the chemist, Pay an' Take (where we bought the cracked eggs and broken biscuits), The Monument Creamery, Dowling's, Kay's

Sweet Shop and Dr. Roche's office. On the opposite corner was Mrs.Molyneaux's filthy little huckster shop. The big black cat was still sleeping in the window amongst the shriveled vegetables. For fun, I went in to say hello to her. She was well known for her gloomy and negative outlook.

"Hello Mrs. Molyneaux—lovely day isn't it? I said
"Ah yes but the radio said it will rain again tomorrow. Shure you'd be fed up wouldn't ya?

When things went wrong at home we would laugh and repeat Mrs. Molyneaux's miserable refrain—'Shure you'd be fed up, wouldn't ya?'

Things had changed in my office since I left. There were a few fresh new faces and some of my old pals were gone. Peg had left to get married. Anne had gone to live with an aunt in Boston and as far as they knew she was getting along well. Eileen had retired. At the tea break, Mrs. Granby opened the box of American chocolates and passed them around. I didn't notice anyone worried about cholesterol or calories. They were interested in hearing all about America and about my plans to get married in England. They oohed and ahed over my engagement ring. I went into the executive office to visit Mr. Boyd. Being an English man himself, he said he was sure I would love living in England and he wished me the best of luck. I felt sad saying goodbye—I liked working there—my life at that time was carefree and uncomplicated.

That evening I met David for dinner at The Metropole. He thanked me profusely for his initialed writing case and said I shouldn't be spending my money so extravagantly. I told him about my day at the shop and at my old office. He had spoken to his mama and she was looking forward to meeting me and she invited me to stay at their house. David said a couple of days would be more than enough and then he would make other arrangements for me. I asked him what kind of a gift I should bring for his mother and he told me everything in the house was antique and he doubted if I could find anything suitable.

23

Hants, England

"The stately homes of England!
How beautiful they stand.
Amidst their tall ancestral trees,
O'er all the pleasant land!"

—Felicia Dorothea Hemans

We flew from Dublin Airport to London and on the way David talked about his family. His mama was a titled lady and he loved her. Papa was a retired colonel and David didn't care for him. He said he was mean and cruel to Mama. He remembered one time when he was a small boy, they were on a boat and Mama was pregnant. Papa gave her a belt that sent her reeling on the slippery deck. He didn't even help her up. David could never forgive him for that. He said I should address Papa as Sir and Mama as Ma'am. If I was offered a drink, I should only take a little sherry—it wasn't considered proper for young ladies to drink anything stronger.

There was no one at the airport to greet us and we took a train southwest from London to a small town near Christchurch Bay. His young sister, Mary, was at the station to meet us. David embraced her warmly and it was obvious they were fond of each other. Mary was a cheerful country girl. She was of medium height and build with rosy cheeks and unkempt brown curly hair to her shoulders. She was dressed in a thick tweed skirt, woolen jumper, heavy stockings and sensible walking shoes. David introduced us and I liked her right away. She said she was happy to meet her future sister-in-law and she hoped we would become good friends.

The short drive to the family home was diverse and pleasant. The inland forests gave way to wide open fields that looked like green water. David said much of the land we were passing through was designated as National or Local Nature

Reserves. The aim was to protect the landscape, the wildlife and places of histori-
cal significance.

The gate was open as we approached the gravel driveway. The house was an
old Georgian style set in its own vast grounds. It looked somewhat forbidding.
Faded rose colored velvet drapes hung against the windows. His mother greeted
us at the door. Her welcome was warm and friendly and I was immediately at
ease with her. Her voice was gentle and motherly. She was tall, straight backed
and aristocratic. She had kind blue eyes and a generous mouth. Her natural gray
hair was arranged in a flattering style to suit her face. She was dressed very much
like her daughter in the style of a country woman. She said Mary would show me
to my room where I could unpack, wash and rest before tea time. They had no
servants except a gardener/handyman. Mama and Mary took care of the housekeeping.

My room was spacious and comfortable. I was glad of the step stool beside the
high four poster bed. The bedspread was hand crocheted, yellowed with age and
no doubt a family heirloom. The furniture was antique, heavy, cumbersome and
priceless. Mary opened the bottom compartment of the commode and laughed as
she showed me the chamber pot "In case you need to go during the night" she
said. I wouldn't dare use it knowing there were no servants to empty it. From my
open window I marveled at the breathtaking views of the Hampshire countryside; gentle rolling hills, picturesque valleys, and lush green fields sprinkled with
daisies and buttercups. There were no other homes in sight.

Mary sat on my bed as I was hanging up my clothes. She admired the modern
American styles without a hint of envy. I gave her a cosmetic bag filled with sam-
ples of lipsticks, perfumes and make up. She was as happy as a child as she started
experimenting with them. I asked her opinion on the present I had brought for
her mother. It was an old fashioned Royal Doulton figurine in royal blue and
cream. I had thought about bringing Irish Dresden but I decided English porcelain would be safer. Mary said she would love it.

Tea was being served in the drawing room. Mama opened her present slowly
being careful not to break the ribbon or tear the beautiful paper. They would be
used again. She admired the delicate figurine from all angles and thanked me profusely. She placed it on the mantelpiece and David said I had made an excellent
choice.

The drawing room was furnished with antiques, oil paintings and a baby
grand piano. The beautifully spaced windows stretched from the high ceilings
almost to the floor. The drapes and the faded rose silk wall covering had seen better days and the dull flowered carpeting was threadbare in spots. The overstuffed

armchairs at either side of the fireplace looked decidedly uncomfortable. Ancient glass fronted book cabinets housed volumes so old that it was difficult to read the titles. I could barely make out Goethe, Burke and Aristotle's *Ethics*. The only lively additions to the room were the fresh flowers and the silver-framed family photographs displayed on the mantel and on the piano.

David introduced me to his father. He was the opposite of David in appearance; short and stocky with a paunch and bald head. He took a good look at me over the top of his glasses. "Pretty little thing", he muttered under his breath to David. He sat at the head of the table with his Pug sitting on the floor beside him. I couldn't help thinking how alike man and dog were in appearance. I was seated to his right and David and Mary sat opposite me. Mama presided at the other end of the table. She had changed into a pretty blue flowered frock and she wore pearls. While Mama poured the tea from the antique silver service Papa barked questions at me. He wanted to know all about America and particularly the Stock Exchange. Although David was looking at him with loathing, I was getting along all right with him. Just then as I was chatting away and eating a piece of seed cake, a crumb got into my windpipe and I started coughing and spluttering. The more I tried to suppress the cough the worse it became. Tears were rolling down my cheeks. David came to my rescue and took me into the bathroom. He patted my back and said the only thing for it was to have a good cough and wait for it to dislodge. I was dreadfully embarrassed and my face was a mess. David brought me my handbag and I made some hasty repairs to my makeup. When I came back I apologized. Mama was kind and she said not to give it a second thought.

After tea the old man left. David said he was gone into town to dally with his tart, a cheap little actress, and he probably wouldn't be back for a few days. The household was much more relaxed when he was gone. Mama didn't cook any more meals. David said the budget was tight and proper meals were served only when Papa was home. We ate a lot of bread and milk.

David took me on a tour of the house. The entrance hall was larger than most living rooms. There was a fireplace on the south wall and well worn black and white tiles on the floor. Oil paintings of stern-looking ancestors adorned the walls. David patiently explained to me who they were and how they were related. Among them were Dukes and Earls and important military men. To the right of the entry was the drawing room. The drawing room led into the formal dining room. In the center was a great antique table and high backed chairs. An overly ornate china cabinet was overflowing with ancestral silver, china and crystal. The kitchen was plain, old fashioned and serviceable. The green paint on the walls and on the cupboards was peeling. There was a large well-scrubbed deal table in the center and the counters had broken and chipped tiles.

Many of the rooms in the house were closed up because the family couldn't afford to keep them heated. Much of the furniture had to be sold to pay taxes.

◆

Mary was excited that we were going to the Hunt Ball the following evening. She was being escorted by Father Bogg, a Presbyterian Minister. She confided to me she was deeply in love with him. Both families were in agreement that this would be a suitable match.

Mama said she was making an appointment at the hairdressers for Mary and should she make one for me as well. Having had a few bad experiences with hairdressers, I thanked her and said I would prefer to do my own. Mammy always said I could do my own hair better than any hairdresser.

The next morning David and I went rambling around the quiet and serene countryside. It was misting and the air smelt fresh and sweet. We sat by a gentle stream and as he held my hand he told me how much he loved me and how happy he was that I was here in England with him. He said Mama approved of me and Mary adored me. I don't think he cared what Papa thought. He said we should make arrangements to marry as soon as possible. I thought he was rushing things and I wasn't sure if I wanted to live in England.

In the afternoon I shampooed my hair and took a leisurely lavender scented bath. Mama suggested Mary and I take an afternoon nap.

After tea, we went upstairs to get ready for the ball. I had brought only one semi-formal dress with me. It was a ballerina length pale blue organza with a full skirt and a tight fitting bodice. The bodice had tiny covered buttons down the front. I had a pair of satin shoes dyed to march. I wore a simple strand of pearls and small pearl earrings. When I was ready I came down stairs to the drawing room. David looked elegant in his black evening suit and he kissed me and complimented me. Mama said I looked charming. The doorbell rang—Mary's escort had arrived.

Father Septimus Bogg was tall, stooped and bald. He was quite a bit older than Mary. As the introductions were being made, Mary appeared on the staircase. Were my eyes deceiving me? Was that really Mary? She was magnificent in a floor length sea green beaded dress and matching shoes. Her hair was dressed in a smooth twist at the back of her head and her face was professionally made up. At her throat were the family heirloom emeralds and she wore long matching earrings. It was clear to see that Father Bogg was utterly captivated. I complimented

Mary and she told me later that Mama had taken her to a famous couturier in Dublin to have her dress specially made for this important occasion. Now I felt like the country cousin. Compared to Mary's creation, my off-the-rack American dress looked cheap and badly made. When I was alone with David, I expressed concern that I was not appropriately dressed for The Hunt Ball.

"Nonsense" he said "Mama pulled out all the stops to ensure that Father Bogg would see Mary at her best. You *have* me and you look perfectly lovely. I would have been upset had you wasted the hundreds of pounds that Mama spent on Mary. Believe me you will be more beautiful than ninety percent of the ladies at The Ball."

I could always depend on David to soothe my fears and make me feel better. We drank our sherry and off we went to The Ball in Father Bogg's car.

We had a wonderful evening. David ordered gin and tonics for us and the orchestra played our favorite tunes. We danced every dance. Mary was the belle of the ball and David was right—there were lots of frumpy girls there. Father Bogg was extremely good company. He was beautifully spoken and he had a great sense of humor. He was also a good dancer. The best part of the evening was that he proposed to Mary. She was ecstatic and I was very happy for her.

I learned one thing about these high-class people—they didn't waste time, effort or money unless the situation demanded it. In this case Mama's efforts were justly rewarded.

Mama was waiting up for us and there were tears and hugs as Mary told her the good news. To make the engagement official, Father Bogg had to go through the formality of asking Papa for her hand in marriage.

The next day David suggested I help Mama in the sewing room. Mary was already there ironing with a heavy black old-fashioned iron that had to be heated on the stove. She spat on it from time to time and when it fizzled, it was hot enough. Mama was bent over a large tablecloth doing exquisitely neat repairs. There were baskets of assorted clothes; collars to be turned, new elastic to be put in old underwear, buttons and patches to be sewn and gloves and socks to be darned. I was happy she asked me to do the darning—I knew I was good at it. I was also happy to see she had an assortment of matching yarns.

While we were working Mama said

"My dear, I understand you would like to be married in The Roman Catholic Church. It would please me greatly if you would reconsider. Our church is very much like yours, our theologies are very close and your marriage would be stronger if you and David were of the same religion."

I thought about this for a minute but I knew their church wasn't remotely like the Catholic Church. Some of the differences I knew for a fact were that they didn't believe in Transubstantiation, The Immaculate Conception or the Assumption. They didn't recognize the pope. Their priests could marry and women could be ordained. I didn't want to get into an argument with this lovely lady so I said

"Yes, I agree with you. David and I have discussed this issue many times. As long as I have known him he has never attended church or chapel. He told me he is an agnostic—he believes in God but not in organized religion. Since I am sincere in my beliefs and I have always practiced my religion, we have decided to marry in The Roman Catholic Church."

I knew this didn't please Mama and I was relieved that she didn't pursue the matter further.

In the afternoon, she packed a picnic basket and treated all of us to an outdoor performance of The Russian Cossacks. The weather was warm and sunny. The bandstand was set up in the center of a delightful public park. There were trees and flower beds and picnic tables. Mama chose a table near the stage and she spread out a red checkered tablecloth. Everyone helped set out the brightly-colored Bakelite dishes and the parcels of egg and onion and cucumber and watercress sandwiches. We had tea scones, oatcakes, black grapes, oranges and a pitcher of refreshing lemonade. The show was wonderfully exciting. There were folk singers and exceptional Russian and Ukrainian dancers. There were gypsy bands and the Russian balalaika. The costumes were marvelously colorful. Father Bogg was loving and attentive toward Mary. She sparkled with happiness and Mama did too.

♦

David told me he thought I had had enough of Mama and her darning and her talk of religion and that he had found me a nice room in a small respectable hotel in the village. He had also made an appointment for us to see the local parish priest to talk about our wedding.

My room at the New Barton was plain, cozy and clean. It smelled of wax and soap. The single bed was covered with bright print chintz and there were matching curtains at the window. There was a washstand, a wardrobe and a bedside table and lamp. From my window I could look out on the square. Children laughed and played around the water fountain. A full breakfast, served in the dining room every morning until 11:00 a.m., was included in the price of the room. Lunch, afternoon tea or dinner could be ordered at nominal cost.

David and I explored the quaint little village. We went into the yarn shop. Skeins of gaily colored yarns and wools were on display in cubicles around the walls. There were knitting needles, sewing boxes and patterns of every description. Around a table in the center of the shop respectable old ladies chatted as they worked on baby matinee coats and bonnets. They were pleased when we complimented them on their beautiful work.

The home made jam shop had a colorful display of jars of jam, marmalade, jelly, lemon curd, honey, fruits, tomatoes, and homemade pickles. The caps of the jars were covered with perky blue and white checkered material. Blue ribbons were proudly displayed on the items that had won first prize at the country fair.

We had our tea in a charming little book shop. Bookcases lined the walls and patrons sat at the small tables writing or reading while enjoying their tea in this friendly atmosphere. After tea we went for our appointment with the local parish priest.

24

Nearly Mrs.

*"Everything that happens in the world is part of a great plan
of God running through all time."*

—H.W. Beecher

Father Pinkman ushered us into his office at the rectory. His handshake was cold and limp. He was small and thin and he had a pink bald head. He had beady little eyes, a beaky nose and a lipless mouth. He had an unattractive shrill, nasally, speaking voice. He almost disappeared behind the huge mahogany desk and his little pink hands were folded in front of him. We sat opposite him on leather chairs.

"I see here", he said "you wish to marry in my church as soon as possible. Is there a reason why you wish to rush this wedding"?

David laughed

"Oh no, nothing like that Father, I must take up my residency in Kent in a couple of months and there won't be much time after that."
"Very well. I understand the young lady is Catholic and you are not. Of course you know our Church frowns on mixed marriages. There can be no music, no lights on the altar, no flowers. Have you thought about converting to Catholicism? I could arrange instruction for you immediately. You could then have a proper wedding. Statistics show that when both partners are of the same faith their marriage has a better chance of success."

David began to squirm

"I believe you are right in what you are saying Father but it is out of the question. My family would disown me if I became a Catholic. They detest

Papists. One of my ancestors gained a Dukedom for conspiring to replace the Catholic James11 with William of Orange."

The little priest was obviously shaken and I could see he was ready to throw us out.

"Very well" he said "if you wish to go through with this all I can offer you is a quiet service in the sacristy of the church. You are aware, sir, that you will be obliged to sign an agreement that any children of this union must be raised Roman Catholic. My advice to you is to go home and think it over. Remember love is not enough for a lifetime commitment. I will pray that you make the right decision."

This meeting upset both of us.

"What an unsympathetic little man" David said "he has no right to tell me how I should raise my children. Perhaps we should try another parish."
"I think it will be the same wherever we go. Even if we were to find a kinder priest, the rules of the church are unbendable."
"Never mind, darling, we'll work it out" David said.

There was a cold feeling in the back of my mind that this was all wrong. I had a sleepless night as I thought about my dreams of a beautiful wedding. I had envisioned myself as a happy and radiant bride dressed in a traditional white gown and veil walking down the aisle on the arm of my dad. I could hear the organ playing Wagner's triumphant Wedding March. I imagined the church ablaze with lights and fragrant with flowers. I could see Mammy there in her new hat and the church packed with family and friends.

None of this was to happen. The prospect of a lonely little wedding in a bare chilly sacristy filled me with sadness. David understood but he said there was nothing we could do about it since we were getting no support from our families. He accepted the arrangements and said he didn't care if he had to marry me in a barn. He said patients and staff had more respect for a married doctor and he wanted to go through with it—he had waited for me long enough. We had no money for a honeymoon. After the ceremony we were to go straight to Kent to set up housekeeping in a 500-year-old wood beam cottage.

It was raining when we drove to Kent—The Garden of England. The dripping trees on either side of the roadway formed a romantic bower as we drove through rolling hills, wooded valleys, orchards and vineyards. I loved traveling with David. He outlined for me the history of the towns, the moated castles and stately homes we were passing. We stopped at a country pub to have a ham sand-wich and a cup of tea before visiting our cottage.

We passed the hospital where David would be working and the cottage was about a twenty minute drive from there. It was all by itself in the middle of a wooded field and almost hidden behind overgrown brambles and weeds. The door was unlocked and it creaked as we pushed it in. The front room was dark and musty and cobwebs hung from the wooden beams. There was no heat except for an antiquated fireplace. There was a tiny kitchen with an old cooker and a rust-stained sink. There were no curtains on the grimy windows. The whole place was spooky and depressing. I couldn't help thinking of Olga's fresh new house with everything in it sparkling clean and her friendly young neighbors walking their babies in their new high prams. I thought about the family coming to visit her and all enjoying their tea together. I told David I didn't think I would be happy here all alone while he was at work.

"Nonsense darling", he said "we'll get a dog and you will be so busy getting our little home in order, you won't have time to be lonely. Mama will show you how to organize everything."

The prospect of my marriage and my first home filled me with despair and uncertainty. Did I love David enough to go through with it?

Mammy's letter didn't help. She said something to this effect—

"Nora, that's not the way we do things in our family. Nobody from Dublin will be at your wedding. David is all wrong for you—he will never under-stand your religion. He will control and dominate you. I only want what's best for you and there is no shame in admitting you made a mistake. Any pain you suffer now will be nothing compared to the lifetime of misery ahead of you. Forget this madness and come home."

I showed the letter to David but he refused to read it.

"I know what your mother thinks of me and even after we are married she will still try to break us up."

He was morose and depressed. He looked ill and tired—his eczema was raging and his asthma had flared up. He knew I was unhappy about the wedding arrangements, the cottage and my mother's letter. Then the fateful telegram arrived

BERNIE STOP YOUR MOTHER IS GRAVELY ILL STOP PLEASE COME HOME IMMEDIATELY STOP DAD

We were having dinner in the hotel and I read it to him.

"Don't go" he said "It is just another ploy to get you away from me."

"I have to go David. Come with me and if everything is alright, then we will come right back and get married."

"No, I refuse to go with you and if you go we are finished—it is *over*. You broke my heart and caused me to have a nervous breakdown when you left me to go to America. You will not put me through that pain again. I love you with all my heart and I will do everything to make you happy but if that's not enough for you, you should go. If you do, we will never ever see each other again."

"You can't be serious David," I said. "What if something should happen to my mother—we would never forgive ourselves."

"I am very serious and I guarantee nothing will happen to your mother. My health cannot take any more uncertainty. This is our last chance to commit to each other. If you go you needn't come back to me. I will not make any more arrangements and I will never try to see you again."

I was stunned by his callousness; I had never seen this side of him before. I knew he definitely meant what he said. In a misguided moment, I almost felt I had to stay and go ahead with our plans. Wasn't love enough? Could Sister Anne, Father Pinkman and my family all have been wrong? If they were wrong, why was I so afraid and unhappy? Were the heartless fates busy again pulling us in different directions? Was my soul asking more from me? I didn't have the answers; I only knew I had to get away. Our relationship had become an impossible burden and we both knew it. What we had had in Dublin was lost and could not be recaptured. I asked him if he would write to me. He said

"No, once you go, that will be the end. It will be easier for both of us if we make a clean break. Let's think of our love as something never to be fulfilled but always existing. It may have perished in fulfillment. I will never love anyone but you."

I took off my ring and placed it on the table in front of him. He said

"I want you to keep it darling; you never know when you might need a *carrot*." When I left for Dublin, I knew with certainty it was over. We never saw each other again. Shortly afterwards he married a nurse from the hospital. I hoped he had found true happiness.

◆

I cried the whole way home and I felt mean, ungrateful and ashamed. At the same time I felt strangely relieved as though a great burden had been removed from my shoulders.

When I arrived in Dublin, Mammy met me at the gate, all smiles, and as hale and hearty as ever

"Thanks be to God you're home, my prayers have been answered. We were all so worried about you. You will realize in time that marriage to that man would have been a disaster."

For months I was sad and confused. I realized that this was all part of God's plan for me. David was meant to come into my life but marriage to him would have been doomed to failure. I spent a lot time at Olga's—she was sympathetic and comforting. She knew about the pain of endings as she had suffered through her own broken dreams. I could tell her how I felt and she would listen. She said

"It's all for the best, Nody—there is something else in store for you. Don't cry because it's over, be happy it happened." She was right of course.

◆

I took a secretarial job in an office on The Long Mile Road. My boss, Mr. Murphy, was a humorless slave driver. He called me into his office early in the morning and gave me enough dictation to keep me busy for the entire day. Oh, for my American days when my boss was killed thanking me for typing one letter! Mr. Murphy didn't allow smoking in the office and periodically during the day he would go into the ladies' restroom and look over the top of the toilet doors to see if any of the girls were smoking in there. At a meeting he said

"I know some of youse girls are sneaking into the lavatory to have a cigarette. If I catch you, you won't work here any more."

The girls just laughed at him, they said he was like a silly old woman.

Two friendly girls from the office invited me to go with them to a dance at The Metropole. I hesitated. I was in no mood for music or romance especially at The Metropole as it held too many memories for me. Mammy said I should buck up and go; I needed to get out more. I wore a lovely green taffeta dress and off we went. We met up with a group of good looking fellows from The North of Ireland. They were starting up a washing machine business in Dublin. They had plenty of money and they were generous with it. They took us to dances, theaters, dinners and to Belfast for a day's shopping. They were great company and it was all good fun. One of the fellows, Desi, was tall, dark and handsome and he was interested in me. When I found out he was a Protestant, I kept my distance.

25

London

"When a man is tired of London, he is tired of life;
for there is in London all that life can afford."

—Samuel Johnson

My friend Maggie wrote from London to say she was getting married and would I consider coming over to be her bridesmaid. I didn't need persuading. This was a good excuse for me to leave Dublin; it was too nostalgic for me. I found it difficult living at home; Olga, Hilda, Billy and Frank were gone and the other siblings were busy with their own lives and too young for companionship with me. I didn't care for my job. I wrote back immediately accepting the invitation and I was excited at the prospect of a new beginning.

Maggie was as lively and as full of fun as ever. She loved London. I stayed at her apartment in Kensal Rise and helped her with the preparations for her wedding. After the Church ceremony she was having a reception for seventy invited guests in the church hall. She was doing all the cooking herself. We had the use of the hall kitchen including dishes, glassware, tablecloths, napkins and cutlery. For days before the wedding, I helped her pound and bread chicken breasts, peel mountains of potatoes and shell pounds of peas. She had ordered a traditional Irish wedding cake; fruit filled and decorated with royal icing. She had hired an Irish band. The day before the wedding we decorated the hall with green, white and orange balloons and streamers and set the tables with candles and little vases of fresh flowers. We scattered ornamental shamrocks around the tables.

It was a lovely wedding and Maggie was a radiantly happy bride. The music was wonderful and I danced several dances with a fellow from Dublin named Conor. He asked if I would see him on Sunday and he would show me some of the sights of London.

Maggie and her new husband were moving into a house and she said I could take over her apartment if I wanted to stay in London for a while. This suited me fine—apartments were hard to find and I didn't want to go home. The apartment had one large high-ceilinged room sparsely furnished with a single bed, a pull out sofa bed, a breakfast table and two chairs. Down three steps were the kitchen and the bathroom. It was neither cozy nor pretty but it suited my needs and the rent was reasonable.

Kensal Rise was a pleasant area of Northwest London. It was located near Notting Hill and Portobello Market. The streets reminded me of Dublin with their neat little red-bricked houses and flower-filled gardens. There was a variety of shops within easy walking distance of my apartment where I could buy anything from clothing to groceries, to used books or antiques. Just like Dublin, public transportation was excellent and buses or the underground provided easy access to all parts London.

Posted on a glass-enclosed bulletin board on a wall outside a local shop were ads for everything; articles for sale and articles wanted, flats and houses for rent, lost and found dogs and cats, and situations vacant and situations wanted. I wrote down the phone number of a firm of stock brokers who were looking for a secretary. The man I spoke to was polite and pleasant and he gave me an appointment for an interview. The offices were located on Great Winchester Street in The City—London's Business and Finance Center.

I wore my good black suit and black court shoes and arrived in plenty of time for the interview. Once I had located the address, I took a walking tour of the City, located on the banks of The Thames, and also known as the "Square Mile". The area was dominated by the dome of Saint Paul's Cathedral where most of The Royals were married. I walked through a narrow alley which led me to the Bank of England and The Stock Exchange. The City had a small residential population but a huge daytime working population. There were many shiny modern office blocks amongst the old Roman and medieval buildings. The names of the streets fascinated me: Throgmorton Street, Threadneedle Street, Wormwood Street and Ironmonger Lane. Serious-looking business men, hurrying to their offices, wore black bowler hats, dark suits and they carried tightly rolled umbrellas. The office girls were dressed in smart suits and high heeled shoes.

My interview with the manager, Mr. Mummery, went well. He was a tall, white haired, elegant man in his mid sixties. He looked over my application and asked me questions about my past experience and about the New York Stock Exchange. Since I had never been on the floor of the Exchange nor did I have any money to invest, I had no curiosity about it. Now I wished I had learned about the workings of the market while I had the opportunity. I answered his questions as intelligently as I could and hoped I wasn't making a fool of myself. He gave me a shorthand and typing test and said he would contact me within a few days.

On Sunday Conor called for me and said he was taking me on a bus tour of London. As we climbed the stairs of the red double decker, the driver shouted

"Oi 'old the rail luv and mind yer 'ead"

Our tour guide introduced himself as Fred. He was witty and enthusiastic and he had in depth knowledge of his city. As we passed the Byzantine-style Westminster Cathedral he said it was the most important Roman Catholic Church in England. We passed the Gothic structures of the Houses of Parliament, 10 Downing Street, and the well known Big Ben. Fred said the light shining above the face of the clock meant that parliament was in session. We stopped at Westminster Abbey—the venue for the coronation of Queen Elizabeth II. It was magnificent with its crystal chandeliers and stained glass windows. We could hear the famous boys' choir as they practiced behind a partition. Fred said the Abbey was once a Benedictine Monastery.

We stopped at a crowded smoky pub for lunch and ordered bangers and mash and a shandy. The walls of the pub were lined with portraits of England's Prime Ministers going as far back as Salisbury. The nice thing about the tour bus was that we could hop off anywhere we liked, stay as long as we liked and then rejoin the tour when we were ready. There were taped commentaries in different languages.

Conor was a typical Dubliner with a ready wit and the gift of the gab. He came from a large Catholic family. He had a likeable personality and he was generous and sincere. He had a too ruddy complexion, shiny ears and bandy legs. He worked in construction. He lived in a rooming house in Kilburn with a group of Dublin lads. He said one by one they were leaving for Canada and all seemed to be doing well. Canada offered better pay and more opportunities than London and he was planning on going there himself in the near future.

After lunch, we continued on our way to Buckingham Palace. The palace was disappointingly plain and it was not open to the public. We enjoyed watching the pomp and pageantry of the Changing of the Guard—the colorful uniforms, the fur hats and the music of the Royal band.

We passed the Tower of London which housed the Crown Jewels, and where three queens were executed and numerous prisoners tortured.

Our last stop of the day was Trafalgar Square where we sat by a fountain and enjoyed watching the children as they played and chased away the pigeons.

I thanked Conor for the wonderful day and he asked me if I would go out with him again—there were so many exciting places in London he wanted to show me. I said I would.

♦

I was happy to hear I got the job and I took extra pains getting ready for my first day. I wore a lovely rust color suit I had bought in New York. I traveled on the underground or, as the Londoners called it, "the tube" which took me to within walking distance of my office. Mr. Mummery greeted me warmly and showed me into a large bright high-ceilinged office where he introduced me to the staff of executives and stock brokers. They were seated at big impressive desks which were widely spaced about the room. Some of the men were introduced as Sir This or That and others had double-barreled names. They rose, shook hands with me and welcomed me to the firm. They were posh and polite. Then Mr. Mummery said "This is the gentleman you will be working for, Miss Wright, his name is Mr. Francis (*Frawncis*) Arthur Ellicott." Mr. Ellicott's handshake was limp and clammy and he spoke with an exaggerated tony accent as if he had a mouthful of marbles. He was in his mid thirties and not much taller than myself. He was fat and pasty with pale eyes and lashes and mousy fair hair.

Mr. Mummery then took me down the hall to where I would be working. The office was small and grimy and the desks were packed closely together. There were photographs, postcards and bits of notes stuck untidily to the walls. My desk was the last one close to the door. Mr. Mummery introduced me to the other secretaries—Jackie, Doris, Katie and a gray haired lady who worked as a temporary helper. They greeted me pleasantly and said they hoped I would be happy working with them.

Over the next few weeks I became familiar with the routine and got to know the staff. Katie and I became good friends. She had worked there for a couple of years and she helped me find my way around. She had Irish Catholic parents and she lived in Woolwich. She was my own age. She had a lovely figure, a pale complexion, pretty brown hair and a serene aura about her. In the afternoons she would spray cologne on her wrists

"Just to cheer myself up" she would say smiling.

Jackie had the corner desk. She was a middle-aged spinster living with and supporting her aged mother. She was dumpy, dowdy, ungraceful and bitter. She had heavy features and she wore her dyed black hair parted to the side and showing a good bit of regrowth in shades of orange and gray. When she wasn't complaining or muttering to herself, she was expounding on politics or some other boring subject.

I had typed a pile of letters for Mr. Ellicott and Doris brought them to him for signatures. In a few minutes he stormed into our office and stood by my desk

"Miss Wright" he said "I *never* split infinitives. Please do this over."

I reread the letter carefully and found the mistake. Then I examined my notes. I had transcribed them exactly as he dictated them. Should I point this out to him or should I just correct it and let it go? I asked the girls. They were of the opinion that I would be making life difficult for myself if I told him *he* had made the mistake. They said I had been assigned the most disagreeable broker—he was peevish, picky and a dreadful snob. He lost no chance to boast of the fact that he was educated at Eton. I retyped the letter with the correction and sent it back to him. After that I was careful to watch out for his mistakes and to correct them myself.

Doris was the junior clerk in the office. She ran the copy machine and fetched and carried for everyone. She was a typical English rose; long legged, fair and pretty. She was desperate to go to America and she wanted to know all about it.

"There's nothing in this 'ell 'ole for anyone. I don't know 'ow you could leave America to come 'ere."

One of the brokers was mad about her and begged her to go out with him.

"Wat would oi be doing going out with a stuck up chappie loike 'im" she said
"soon as oi save me fare I'm off to America." Doris was cheerful, funny and well liked.

The executives and brokers had lunch every day in the firm's dining room. Maisy, their cook, was a jolly, full-figured, middle-aged widow. She had a florid complexion and the strangest burgundy colored hair. Occasionally she invited the office staff to her home in Muswell Hill for lunch. She had a modest comfortable home and a lovely English garden. She told us she had been an entertainer in the music halls. She served us large gin and tonics—mostly gin with a splash of tonic. She set a fine table and her beef steak and kidney pies and Yorkshire puddings were outstanding. After lunch she played the piano and sang some of the songs she used to sing on the stage. Then we would have a sing along—"Down by the Old Bull and Bush", "I've got a loverly bunch o' Cocoanuts", "The Lambeth Walk", and "Knees up Mother Brown". She tried to shock us with her risqué jokes. Maisy was hospitable and warm hearted and she enjoyed these visits as much as we did.

◆

Maggie said I must go to Petticoat Lane while I was in London, so when Conor asked me what I would like to do on Sunday I didn't hesitate. Maggie and her husband joined us. The name Petticoat Lane came from its long association with the clothing trade known locally as the "rag trade". There were hundreds of stalls offering great bargains and crowds of people there enjoying themselves. I was amazed at the variety of goods for sale; clothing—new and vintage, jewelry, music, souvenirs, bric-a-brac, glass and kitchen ware, antiques, toys, fruits and vegetables, talking parrots in cages, hamsters, and goldfish. The lanes were alive with music and entertainment by dancers, clowns and mime artists. There were bakeries, ice cream carts, cafes and pubs. The whole atmosphere was thrilling. I got a great buy on a beautiful leather handbag and Maggie found a Claddagh clock for her kitchen. We sat in a pub to rest our feet and we ate bagels with cream cheese and smoked salmon. At the end of the day Conor insisted on buying me a bright yellow parrot in a cage—he said it would keep me company. The stall owner said he could talk if I trained him. Hard as I tried, I could only get an irritating squawk out of him. He was good company though—I gave him the freedom of the flat and I enjoyed watching his antics as he flew around the place trying to hide from me. I put a cover over his cage at night so that he wouldn't disturb me. I named him Ko-Ko.

◆

I looked forward to the weekends when Katie would come and stay with me. She was good company and we were never short of conversation. We gossiped about the people in the office, talked about fashion, the movies we had seen and the books we had read. She was interested in hearing about my family in Ireland and about my time in America. She loved to cook and we had good fun planning our meals and shopping for the ingredients. She taught me how to make Toad-in-the Hole, Welsh rarebit, pasties and apple fritters. She knew her way around London and after Mass on Sundays she decided on how we should spend the day. One of our favorite places was Hyde Park. Hyde Park got its name from the land which has an area of one hide (anything between 60 and 120 acres.) Speakers' Corner was always entertaining.

Anyone could turn up and talk about any subject. It was funny to see them being harassed by the hecklers. Apart from the ordinary speakers—Karl Marx, Lenin, George Orwell and William Morris used Speakers' Corner as their platform. When we had had enough of the debates and the protests, we would sit by the Serpentine Lake, watch the rowboats drifting by and try to identify the vast range of water fowl. Katie had much more knowledge of that sort of thing than I had. We would then take a stroll through the elegant and romantic Kensington Gardens with their shimmering fountains bedecked with flowers. This was a fashionable venue for promenades. There were nannies pushing expensive baby carriages, well-behaved children in their Sunday best, lovers strolling hand-in-hand and lots of dogs. I enjoyed these times relaxing in London parks.

Occasionally I spent a weekend with Katie's family. Katie was the only girl and the eldest. She had four young brothers. They were warmhearted people and always made me feel welcome.

◆

I had a letter from my mother telling me that my brother Billy had finished his five years in The British Army. He was now living at home and working for Thomas Thompson Engineers. He was seriously dating a beautiful young Dublin girl named Marie Murphy.

Brother Frank was now sailing the high seas aboard "The Irish Ash". He worked in the engine room and although the work was strenuous, he enjoyed life at sea and visiting faraway places such as Africa, India and Australia. He continued to send most of his pay check home.

Joan had had a row with Daddy and she left the shop to find another job. Mammy was now working full time as they were extremely busy. She went to 8:00 o'clock Mass every morning in St.Michael's and from there she opened the shop and stayed all day until Daddy came to relieve her when he finished his day's work at the Post Office. She loved the work and meeting the people but she hoped Joan would change her mind and come back.

In Mammy's letter she enclosed a letter for me which had come from Germany. It was from Werner, my violinist friend from the S.S.America. I had forgotten all about him. He said he was coming to Dublin and, if I agreed, he would like to visit me. He sent photographs of all of us having a merry old time on board the ship.

I answered his letter telling him I was happy to hear from him and I thanked him for the pictures. I said I was sorry I would miss him in Dublin as I was now living in London.

◆

Katie loved to travel and she was brilliant at finding interesting tours at bargain prices. She brought an advertisement into the office which offered a three day two night stay in Lourdes at an unbelievably low price. I had a great interest in Lourdes not only because I was named after Saint Bernadette and familiar with her story but also because of the replica of the grotto close to our home at The Oblates Church in Inchicore. The grotto in Inchicore was built with voluntary labor by local men. The women donated their precious jewelry and even their wedding rings to be melted down and made into a crown for the statue of Our Lady at the entrance to the grotto. The nuns in school often reminded us of Our Lady's words to Saint Bernadette

"I do not promise to make you happy in this world but in the next."

Irish people had great faith in Our Lady of Lourdes and special devotion to The Rosary. Many made pilgrimages to Lourdes to pray for healing and we were told of the miracles that occurred there. The movie, "The Song of Bernadette" starring Jennifer Jones as Bernadette Soubirous played to packed houses in Dublin.

We stayed in a comfortable pensione located in the heart of the city and within easy walking distance to the many places of interest. The owner of the inn greeted us with "Bien venue" and introduced herself as Madame Jolie—the name suited her perfectly. She was a warm friendly country woman not more than five feet tall and about the same width. She showed us to our room. It was clean, bright and airy with two single beds and decorated in the colors of the Mediterranean. From our window we had a panoramic view of the city—the beautiful Pyrenees Mountains, the Castle of Lourdes and the magnificent Basilica. When we had washed and unpacked we came downstairs to the dining room. The house was filled with the fragrance of Madame's home cooking. Continental breakfast and dinner were included in the price of our package.

The round dining room tables were set with blue checkered tablecloths, pretty blue and white china and dark blue napkins. Each table had a small vase of wild flowers, a bottle of Burgundy and wine glasses. Madame said "Bon appetite" as she guided us to the sideboard where the meal was set out buffet style. There were glass mugs of steaming clear consommé, a huge orange colored dish of hearty cassoulet, pickled red cabbage slaw and a basket of fresh crusty French bread. For dessert we had luscious black grapes and excellent cheese. There were eight other guests and we were seated with a cheerful young couple from Australia. We did justice to our meal—it was absolutely delicious. We drank our wine and talked and laughed late into the evening.

Next morning we were awakened by the sun streaming through our window and the tantalizing aroma of baking bread. When we were bathed and dressed we came down to breakfast. On the sideboard were glasses of assorted juices, a carafe of hot café au lait, crusty bread rolls baked that morning by Madame Jolie, sliced date nut bread, a variety of muffins, a crock of sweet country butter and a selection of homemade jams.

After breakfast, we joined our tour group for 9:00a.m. Mass at the Basilica. We were dazzled by the beauty of the church; the mosaics, sculptures and paintings were awe inspiring. Our guide then took us to the rock of Massabielle grotto which is the cave where The Blessed Mother appeared to Saint Bernadette. It amazed me that our Inchicore grotto was such a perfect reproduction of the grotto I was now standing in front of in Southern France. It was humbling to be in the presence of The Immaculate Conception exactly where she appeared. The walls of the cave were worn smooth from the millions of pilgrims touching them.

There were crowds of people there, many in wheelchairs, some on crutches and others on hospital beds. Most were praying the rosary. We met worried, troubled, sick and healthy people who came to the grotto to find peace or perhaps even a miracle. The first apparition was on February 11, 1858—seventeen others were to follow. We lit candles and prayed for the sick and deceased members of our families and for the friends who had asked us to pray for them. We climbed the winding steps to the top of the Cathedral and were rewarded for our efforts with the magnificent views, the sparkling blue skies and the invigoratingly crisp air.

That evening, after another delicious meal, we went back to the Grotto to walk in the torchlight procession. Hundreds of people were there praying the rosary and singing the same familiar hymns we sang in the Inchicore processions—"The Bells of the Angelus", "Immaculate Mary" and "Hail Queen of Heaven". It was calm and peaceful and a wonderfully moving experience. Masses of flowers surrounded the Grotto left there by grateful pilgrims.

Next morning, after Mass, we visited the Sanctuaries Notre Dame De Lourdes. This was a complex built around the Cave. At the tap water wall we filled bottles of holy water to bring back to family and friends. The waters are from the miraculous spring and are said to have healing properties. We went to the bathing pools and got in line to be immersed in the sacred waters.

On our third and last day we explored the quaint old villages and drank in the essence of this holy place. We browsed in the little shops which sold religious articles and we bought miraculous medals, rosaries, pictures of Saint Bernadette and Our Lady of Lourdes and booklets on Bernadette's life to bring home as souvenirs. We admired the cheerful little cottages with their white lace curtains and flower-filled window boxes. We visited the small museum at Chateau Fort and strolled in the beautiful park. We enjoyed delicious French pastries and coffee at a tiny bohemian café.

The experience of my visit to Lourdes is indescribable. It renewed my devotion to my patron saint—a poor, simple fourteen year old girl who was chosen to gaze into the eyes of the Mother of God and who taught the world the merits of prayer, penance, poverty and church.

I would be forever grateful to my friend Katie for organizing the trip. I had told her about the replica of the Lourdes Grotto at the Oblates in Inchicore and invited her to come to Dublin sometime to see it for herself. I felt fortunate that I could visit there anytime and recapture the memories of the real Lourdes.

◆

As was my usual ritual on Saturday mornings, after a light breakfast of tea and toast, I shampooed my hair and put it up in curlers. I then smothered my face with nourishing cream, donned my old working clothes, found some good music on the radio and prepared to tackle the cleaning of my apartment. I stripped the sheets off my bed and off the pull-out couch, washed them and hung them on the clothesline to dry. I was on my knees scrubbing the linoleum on the kitchen floor and singing along with Vera Lynn

"We'll Meet Again" when I heard a knock on the door
"Feck it" I said "that's somebody trying to sell me something or the Jehovah's Witnesses trying to convert me."

I didn't bother getting up and continued my scrubbing. There was another knock—louder this time. I wished they would go away and let me get on with my work. I was really irritated when they knocked again. I had no peephole to see who was there so I thought I had better go and see.

Standing in front of me, smiling his dazzling white smile, and carrying a bouquet of red roses was Werner, my handsome friend, the violinist from the S.S.America. He was gorgeous—tanned and elegant in a well-cut navy blue blazer and an immaculate blue shirt. I was speechless, I wished the ground could have opened and swallowed me up. I could only think of how dreadful I looked; my hair in curlers, my tattered old work clothes, my arms red from the hot water and the scrubbing brush still in my hand.

"Oh, Werner" I blubbered "How lovely to see you, come in. I'm afraid you have caught me at an awkward time; you see I'm in the middle of my house cleaning. I thought you were going to Dublin. I never expected to see you in London."

He was smiling

"No I won't come in to disturb you unless I can help you with anything. The only reason I was going to Dublin was to see you again. When you wrote to tell me you were in London I came here instead. I just had to see you again before settling down in Germany. When may I call back?"

"Give me about an hour" I said "and I will meet you at the little tea shop down the street." This pleased him—he bowed and smiled as he left.

I put the beautiful roses into a vase of water and left things as they were while I concentrated on getting myself ready. I put my makeup on, brushed out my hair and wore my best suit and high heels.

He was reading the newspaper when I came into the teashop. He greeted me with a hug and a kiss. I apologized for the state I was in when he came and he said

"My dear, you looked positively charming in your working clothes and I loved the idea of you taking care of your household chores."

Werner was staying in a hotel in Mayfair and he had rented a car. He was familiar with London as he had been there many times performing with the London Philharmonic. He suggested we spend the afternoon at Kew Gardens. We had a wonderful day. He held my hand as we strolled around the delightful pathways admiring the magnificent display of flowers, the stream with the aquatic birds, the rock gardens and the greenhouses filled with exotic tropical plants. He told me of his travels around the world and said he had now taken a job with a German orchestra and he was ready to take a wife and settle down in Germany.

That evening, we came back to his hotel where we had cocktails and dinner. He showed me photographs of his family. He was obviously fond of his mother. He said she was a wonderful cook and housekeeper. (Maybe that was why he liked seeing me busy doing my housework). In the photographs she looked like a typical German housefrau—a large-boned serious looking woman with plaits wound tightly around her head and wearing an embroidered apron.

He surprised me with a beautifully wrapped package. It was an exquisite black-faced watch—something I had never seen before. He fastened it on my wrist and seemed pleased that I liked it so much. In Ireland, the wrist watch was generally the precursor to the engagement ring. I had no way of knowing if this was the custom in Germany. He said he wanted to spend as much time as possible with me while he was in London.

He took me to the theater and the ballet and we went dancing to the music of the big bands. He said he loved me from the first moment he saw me on the ship and he wanted me to come back to Germany with him to meet his family.

I liked and admired Werner and who wouldn't—he was good looking, charming, well educated and gloriously talented. However, I had no desire to settle in Germany. I didn't care for the language and from my limited knowledge of their culture, I envisioned the German hausfrau as being a compulsive housekeeper, taking great pride in a spotless home and delighting in cooking fabulous meals for her family. The Herr was lord and master of the household. Even though Werner was gentle and artistic, I couldn't see myself fitting into his culture. Besides this, Werner was a strict Lutheran and I did not want to become involved with a non Catholic again.

We were both sad when we parted and he said he hoped I would change my mind and come to Germany. I never did.

◆

I had two letters from Dublin—one was from my young sister, Joan, and the other one was from my dad.

Joan thanked me for the evening dress I had sent her to wear to The Betty Whelan Fashion Show. She was delighted with it.

She said she had left Daddy's shop after a row with him over her buying too much stock. She took a job with O'Dwyer's, the wholesalers. She really wanted to work in one of Dublin's exclusive department stores—Switzers, Arnott's or Brown Thomas. She had sent in her applications and she was hoping to hear of an opening. She said all the girls in the agency had good jobs in the bank or in high-end department stores.

She told me she was dating a nice fellow named Ross (Russell). She said he was very good to her—he would do anything to please her—unlike the Irish fellows she had gone out with. She was really fond of him. Russell was born in Ireland. When he was six years old, his mother died and his dad took him and his sister, Wendy, to live in California. After graduating from High School, Russell returned to Dublin to study medicine at Trinity College. He met Joan in The Mocha Coffee Shop where she helped out occasionally.

In my dad's letter, he told me the general election had returned Fianna Fáil to power with a large majority.

He said my brother Jack had gone to live in America. He explained that Uncle Gary's friends, Mr. and Mrs. Muldoon, were visiting our family in Dublin and when they met Jack they were so captivated by him they offered to take him back with them to The States provided he wanted to go. Although only 14, Jack wasn't enjoying life in Dublin at the time and he jumped at the opportunity. The Muldoons were well off—they owned a bakery in Michigan and promised to send Jack to a good school. Daddy had misgivings on account of Jack's his age but the people assured him that he could come home anytime he wished. When the letters started coming saying that Jack was settling down well, enjoying his new school and life in America, Dad felt much better about his decision.

In the next part of my dad's letter he said he didn't like the idea of me living alone in London. He said there were plenty of good jobs available in Dublin and I should consider coming home.

◆

By this time I was becoming disenchanted with London. Winter was setting in. It was bitterly cold and pitch darkness fell early in the evenings. I was terrified of the London fog. I had heard of "pea soup" fog but never imagined it could be so threatening. When I was walking home from the tube in the evenings I could hardly find my way to my apartment. I couldn't see my hand in front of my face and as I clutched on to the railings to guide me I had an eerie feeling that "Jack the Ripper" was lurking in the darkness ready to grab me. My apartment was cold and lifeless since nobody was in the building in the evenings except me. I didn't even have my little parrot any more. One morning I took his cover off to feed him and give him his water and there he was lying on his back with his little yellow feet in the air, dead as a doornail. I'm sure he died from hypothermia. Since he had given me a lot of pleasure I thought it fitting to give him a decent burial. I wrapped him in cotton wool, put him in a little box and buried him in the back yard. I marked his grave with a cross made from two tongue depressors.

I liked my job well enough but my salary barely covered my expenses. I lived from paycheck to paycheck without a penny over to save for emergencies. I was crushed when my friend Katie told me she was leaving as she would be moving with her family to Devon. I would miss her droll humor, our lunches in the pubs, our shopping excursions to Harrods and most of all her companionship on the lonely weekends.

Conor was also leaving me to join his buddies in Canada. He said he hoped I would follow him there eventually.

◆

During this time, Hilda had had enough of New York and she came home to Dublin for a while. She was now settled in Toronto, Canada. She loved Toronto. She said it was a clean, safe, beautiful city. She felt more at home there than she had in The States. There were Irish clubs for dances, Irish pubs galore, and you could buy all Irish foodstuffs in the regular grocery store. Brother Billy and his new bride Marie were living there, also our friends Harry, Polly and Mary. Hilda said jobs were plentiful and salaries were quite good. She was once again working for the telephone company. She said she didn't know what I was doing living on my own in a place like London—I should pack it in and come over and stay with her.

I was ready. The question of money, or rather the lack of it, reared its ugly head again. Where would I get my fare to Canada? The only valuable possession I had was my engagement ring. It was now time to let it go. I went to a local jeweler to have it appraised and I was disappointed in the amount he was prepared to give me. He said the ring was old and the diamond had many flaws. I thought he was trying to hoodwink me so I got a second opinion. This fellow said much the same thing and he offered me only slightly more. It was barely enough to pay my passage to Canada. I booked my ticket aboard "The Ivernia" sailing from Cobh to Quebec in a few weeks giving myself enough time to hand in my notice at the office and to spend a short while in Dublin before departure.

Mr. Mummery said he was sorry to lose me but he appreciated the fact that I had given him enough time to find a new secretary. He said Canada was a beautiful country and there were many opportunities for young people. He thought it was a great advantage for me to have family already there. He gave me a good reference saying I was efficient, trustworthy and cheerful and that I showed a lot of initiative.

Maisy threw a jolly farewell party for me and Katie. Everyone was sad that we were leaving. We promised to write to each other and Katie said one day she would like to come and visit me in Canada. I hoped she would—she was a good friend and I already missed her.

Maggie invited me to her house for a last supper together. I would miss her too. She had been a big part of my life in Michigan and New York. I could always rely on her wit and common sense to get me out of the doldrums. She was sorry I was leaving but she thought I was doing the right thing. She said if she had the chance she would go herself but she and her husband had extensive families in Ireland and the short trip from London made it convenient for their frequent visits.

Another chapter of my life was coming to a close. While I enjoyed my London experience, I had no desire to live there permanently. A new world of adventure awaited me in Canada.

26

Canada

"You have a great country up here.
And a great people too."

—William Jennings Bryan

I was looking forward to going to Canada. As much as I loved Dublin, changes had occurred gradually while I was away and I was not a part of them. The economy had improved thanks to the generosity of sons and daughters who had emigrated. New families had moved into our neighborhood and most of my old friends had emigrated or married and moved away. Joan and Doris were dating seriously. I met Joan's boyfriend, Russell. He was quiet and reserved and he had the dark good looks of Gregory Peck. It was obvious he was very much in love. Olga and Billie had started a family with their new baby girl, Bernice.

On the morning of my departure I went to Daddy's bedroom and said a tearful goodbye to him. He was happy I was joining Hilda and Brother Billy in Canada. He was ill and weak and could barely whisper

"Goodbye Bernie and good luck. Mind yourself and write as soon as you can."

I kissed him and tried to hide my tears as I ran down the stairs.

Mammy, Joan, Doris and Ada came to Heuston Station to see me off on the train to Cobh. I had given Ada a few shillings for herself but in her typical way she spent it on buying me my favorite things. Ada couldn't do enough for me and she hated to see me leave. With heavy hearts, we said our last goodbyes as the whistle blew and the train pulled out from the station. I looked out the window; Mammy and Doris were waving and Mammy had her arm around Ada. Joan had disappeared—partings upset her terribly—she couldn't bear to say goodbye.

Although I was heartsick and lonely on the train, I was naturally optimistic and I was looking forward to seeing family and friends now settled in Toronto.

When we arrived in Cobh we waited in The Commodore Hotel to get on the tender to ferry us to The Ivernia. Huge crowds were milling about and there was mass confusion as cargo and luggage were being loaded. I felt very much alone and couldn't help thinking of the joy I had felt boarding the S.S.America and the anticipation of the exciting future I thought lay ahead of me.

The Ivernia was a smaller ship and not nearly as luxurious as the S.S.America. It had been built as a cargo/passenger ship and there were few amenities. I don't remember too much about the voyage except that the ocean was choppy and I was miserably seasick.

My roommate was pregnant and she vomited and cried all the time.

I was happy when it was announced that we had entered The Saint Lawrence Seaway and only had a thousand more miles to go to reach Montreal.

The day before our arrival I felt much better and ate a hearty breakfast in the dining room. Most of the other passengers looked seedy—they hadn't fared any better than I had. I wrote some postcards home and spent the rest of the day packing. I was excited at the prospect of planting my feet on terra firma again.

◆

I was delighted and surprised to see that Hilda, Billy and Harry had traveled all the way from Toronto to Montreal to meet me. Hilda looked lovely—slim and tanned and beautifully dressed. The enthusiastic hugs and kisses of welcome made me feel wonderful. We were all in high good humor and talked over each other excitedly on the drive to Toronto. We stopped at an Irish pub to have a drink and a meal. There were no complaints about Canada—each had found a good job and they liked the lifestyle.

The house where Hilda lived was an old comfortable three-story on a shady tree-lined street called Marion Avenue. Harry and another couple of Irish lads rented rooms there also. Hilda shared her room with me and we stayed up half of the night drinking, and talking. We had the use of the large kitchen and since Hilda was the first home from work in the afternoons, she did most of the cooking for the lads in the house. She had saved a big box of clothes for me saying she thought they would come in handy until I got established. They were beautiful. I tried them on right away and they fit perfectly.

The next day I wrote letters home and my old friends Polly and Mary came over to visit. It was great seeing them again. We got caught up on each other's news and made arrangements to go dancing at The El Mocombo at the weekend. They missed the good times we had in Dublin but they were doing well and making the most of their Canadian experience.

I called to make enquiries on several ads in the newspaper for secretaries and I got an appointment for an interview with a company called Massey Ferguson on

King Street. They were manufacturers of farm equipment—tractors, bulldozers and harvesters. Harry said it was a good company and he offered to drive me there for my interview.

The interview went well and after filling out the questionnaire and taking the tests, I was hired as executive secretary to a Mr. Hall at $260.00 a month.

Hilda's good friend Betty came to visit and she was all excited about the beautiful new apartments on Jameson Avenue. She couldn't afford to rent one herself but she said if the three of us went in together we could manage the payments. We went to look at the apartments and, right enough, they were gorgeous. It was a brand new building. The apartments had two bedrooms, polished wood floors throughout, a modern kitchen with refrigerator and stove, a large living room and dining area and a bathroom. We did some calculating, decided we could afford it and paid our deposit. It was decided that Betty would have one bedroom and Hilda and I would share the other. We shopped at Eatons and bought all new Danish furniture on credit—a dining room suite, a white couch, coffee table, end tables and lamps. We bought bedroom furniture and big green potted plants. We were thrilled with the results.

We had a great life in that apartment. Betty was an attractive girl from Australia. She had a trim figure and a great flair for style. She was a gourmet cook and we lost no opportunity to invite friends in for parties and elaborate dinners.

We went dancing during the week and on weekends we took trips to Lake Simco, Port Credit or Niagara Falls. Sometimes Harry, Billy and Marie came with us.

I liked Toronto. It was a clean, safe and ethnically diverse city. There was Chinatown, Greek town, Old town, Cabbage town, Korea town, Little Italy, Little India, Little Poland and many others. I didn't find any Irishtown but we had enough Irish pubs, clubs and shops to satisfy our needs. Toronto had good theater, a great variety of restaurants, beautiful ballrooms and efficient public transportation.

Everything was going well at work. I had my own modern office and my boss was agreeable and generous with his compliments. I became friends with a lovely girl named Helen. She looked like a model; tall, thin and elegant. She was engaged to be married and she introduced me to her ex boyfriend, Dick. She was hoping we would get along well and he would stop carrying the torch for her. To please Helen, I went out with him but I wasn't at all attracted to him. He was tall and pasty. He had no conversation and no sense of humor. He had a most peculiar laugh which sounded like a honk. He didn't drink or smoke and if I lit a cigarette he said "There goes another nail in your coffin"! I went out with him a couple of times. He was generous and he took me to nice places—dinner and a dancing at The Embassy Ballroom and The Seaway Hotel. After that I made some lame excuses as to why I couldn't see him.

27

Frank

"How often events by chance, and unexpectedly, come to pass,
which you had not dared even to hope for!"

—Terence

Hilda, Betty and I were excited when we got an invitation to a party at The German Club. We had heard that this was one of the best places in Toronto—the music was great, the food delicious and a lot of handsome Europeans went there. Having tried on several outfits I decided on a flattering green dress with a vee neckline and a fitted waist of satin ribbon. The décor of the club was old German style; pictures depicting German street scenes, taverns and the snowy Alps. There were decorated plates and steins on shelves around the walls. There was a big dance floor and tables set around the perimeter. The band was excellent—they played traditional ballroom and many polkas. Hilda and Betty were dancing and I was sitting alone at our table sipping my drink. Sitting opposite me, smoking a cigarette and blowing smoke in my direction was an extraordinarily handsome man dressed in a brown suit, starched white shirt and brown tie. He continued smoking and blowing smoke in my direction. He put out his cigarette and smiled at me. I smiled and he stood and came over to my table. He asked politely if I minded if he sat with me. How could I refuse! He told me his name was Frank Szechy and he came from Hungary. He had a pleasant speaking voice and a delightful accent. He told me he blew the smoke at me because in Hungary they say

"The smoke blows to the prettiest one!"

Just then the band played "The Blue Danube Waltz" and he asked me if I would care to dance. I could have danced with him all night—he was a magnificent dancer. After each dance he thanked me and I melted when he kissed my hand. I had danced before with what I thought were good dancers but Frank danced like a professional. He led me so expertly; I felt I was a good dancer too. Back at our table I made the introductions. Frank went to the bar to get us drinks and Hilda said,

"He's only drop-dead gorgeous, the image of Rex Harrison, where on earth did you find him?"

He sat with us for the rest of the evening and he danced with Hilda and Betty. As we said our goodnights, he asked me if he could see me on the following Saturday. He told me later he was nervous about asking me out because, in typical European fashion, he was embarrassed that his English wasn't good and he didn't think I would want to go out with a manual laborer. By coincidence, he was also working at Massey Ferguson as a spot welder.

We dated steadily after that. He was generous with his compliments, always polite and affectionate and very romantic. I liked everything about him and couldn't believe my luck when he told me he was Catholic and he had never been married. He called me "Szivi" which is the Hungarian word for darling. Hilda and Betty were very fond of him and invited him to our apartment for dinner. He was a good cook himself and he introduced us to the delights of the Hungarian kitchen. Many times he brought the ingredients and made goulash, stuffed cabbage, chicken paprika and delicious apple pastry. Hilda was dating a good looking Italian at the time and he often joined us for dinner. To balance things out Betty cooked her specialties—veal parmigiana and spaghetti Bolognese.

Frank was also very obliging at helping us with small repairs in our apartment. He could fix anything—a leaky faucet or a stopped up drain. He could open a window that was stuck or make a jammed drawer run smoothly. Betty said he was so gifted he should be bottled and sold!

He was living with a Hungarian couple, Roby and Eva. They were interesting and fun and they considered him part of their family. Frank surprised me at how well he played their piano. He appreciated good music and he was familiar with the classics. I admired his well-shaped artistic hands. Roby was a brilliant writer of poetry and fiction. Eva enjoyed cooking and she invited me to dinner many times. These evenings were enjoyable and their precocious little girl, Aniko, provided us with entertainment.

Frank and I had much in common—both of us came from large Catholic families. We loved to dance and spent many enjoyable evenings at the romantic Casa Loma mansion and at The Royal York ballroom. Frank cut a dashing figure on the dance floor with his good carriage, broad shoulders and trim waist. We enjoyed good music—Frank could identify the composer after hearing just a few bars of any piece. We liked the same movies and on Sundays we toured around the wonderful sights of Toronto in Frank's turquoise Chevy Bel Air. We visited museums, art galleries and strolled hand in hand through the magnificent parks. In the evenings when I helped with his homework for his English classes he was most appreciative. We shared letters and photographs and became familiar with each other's family.

Over late night espressos at The Candlelight Restaurant, the tragic stories of Frank's life in Hungary and his escape to Canada were unfolding.

When Frank was one and a half years old and his mother was expecting her eighth child, his father was drenched in a storm and died of pneumonia within two weeks. Without a husband, there was no income and at that time there was no welfare or Social Security. His mother eked out a living for her brood by planting vegetables and fruits and raising livestock. She baked her own bread and made the children's clothes. They had no running water and no electricity. The kerosene lamps had to be used sparingly as the fuel cost money.

During World War11 Hungary was bombed day and night—there was total devastation. Russian foot soldiers came by the thousands and stole everything in sight. Frank's mother had to dig a hole under the floor boards to hide anything they had of value. After the war Stalin got most of the Eastern and Middle European countries and implemented Communism. People changed—they became suspicious of each other. If they were suspected of trying to overthrow the regime, they were sent to the gallows.

Frank's schooling in Hungary was just as strict as mine was in Dublin—they were caned for the slightest infraction. He was drafted into the army when he was 21 years old.

In 1956 political oppression became unbearable and on October 23 students demonstrated against Communism and the Russian language. The Russians retaliated by sending a thousand tanks to surround Budapest and bomb a sleeping city. Hundreds of Hungarians were executed; thousands imprisoned and 200,000 fled the country. There were tanks and machine guns at every street corner. Frank's little apartment was ransacked. The soldiers broke down the door, threw all of his clothes on the floor and mashed butter into them with their boots.

Frank made up his mind to leave. On November 27, 1956, he packed his things and headed for Austria, the nearest free country. On his way to the railway station he met a lady, named Fini, who had two brothers living in Vienna. She said her brothers could help them once they got to Austria. Crossing the border was dangerous—there were patrol towers every 300 yards and mine fields thirty feet wide. They were captured by Russian soldiers who mercifully let them go after they gave them their money and a bottle of Palinka. Under cover of night they finally reached the canal where they crossed to safety in waist deep freezing water. At daybreak they saw the red, white and red flag of Austria and they knew they were free. An Austrian patrolman took them to a hall where they were given warm dry clothes, a meal and registered as refugees. Fini's brother helped Frank get his registration and traveling papers to Canada. He stayed with his sister in Montreal and got a job in a steel factory at $1.00 per hour. Later he moved to Ontario and worked on a tobacco farm. The work was back breaking but the money was good. He saved enough money to buy a three-ton truck with a contract from the Toronto Brick Company. He was unloading up to 12,000 bricks per day by hand. Later on he sold the truck and got a job as a spot welder. It was at this time we met and started dating.

Frank was devastated to be laid off work at Massey Ferguson's. He said he didn't like working for a company when they could let you go any time they liked. He wanted to go into business for himself. He planned on going back to Montreal and buying a taxi. He knew there was good money to be made. He liked driving and he had a good sense of direction. He said as soon as he got settled he would like me to come. We talked about marriage and he said if I agreed we would become engaged before he left.

The night before his departure we went out to dinner. He brought me a bouquet of red roses, a framed photograph of himself and an engagement ring with a small diamond. I hated to see him leave but I knew it was the right thing for him.

We telephoned and wrote to each other frequently. He liked Montreal. He was living with his sister and his taxi business was going well. He had found a small apartment for me and he was waiting for me.

The best was yet to come.

Maggie, Hilda, Nora,
Grand Rapids, Michigan.

Myself at Grand Haven, Michigan.

Myself in Central Park, New York.

~ S.S. AMERICA ~
UNITED STATES LINE
1946 - Nov 1964

My mother, Ada, myself, Jack
Kickham Road.

My dad's shop, Emmet Road, Inchicore.

Myself at Lourdes, France.

Myself in Canada

Frank

The photograph Frank gave me.

Our engagement

Frank's family. Frank is on the far right.

978-0-595-39178-3
0-595-39178-8

Printed in the United States
61740LVS00006B/77